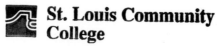

St. Louis Community College

Forest Park
Florissant Valley
Meramec

Instructional Resources
St. Louis, Missouri

Freudian Analysts/Feminist Issues

Freudian
Analysts/
Feminist
Issues

Judith M. Hughes

Yale University Press

New Haven and London

Portions of chapter 1 are adapted from Mark S. Micale and Robert Dietle, eds., *Enlightenment, Passion, and Modernity: Historical Essays in European Culture and Thought.* Quoted with permission from Stanford University Press.

Printed in the United States of America.

Library of Congress Cataloging-in-Publication Data
Hughes, Judith M.
Freudian analysts / feminist issues / Judith M. Hughes.
p.   cm.
Includes bibliographical references and index.
ISBN 0-300-07524-3 (alk. paper)
1. Psychoanalysis and feminism.   I. Title.
BF175.4.F45H84   1999
150.19′5′082—dc21   98-30486

A catalogue record for this book is available from the British Library.

The paper in this book meets the guidelines for permanence and durability of the Committee on Production Guidelines for Book Longevity of the Council on Library Resources.

10 9 8 7 6 5 4 3 2 1

For Reva Pollack Greenburg and Amy Kovner White

Contents

Acknowledgments

In June 1990 I was invited, along with Phyllis Tyson, to comment on a paper Elisabeth Young-Bruehl was presenting to the San Diego Psychoanalytic Society and Institute. In preparing my remarks, it dawned on me that for quite some time I had been chewing over, not fully consciously, questions about psychoanalysis and feminism and that I would like to write a book on the subject. A year later I began psychoanalytic training at the San Diego Institute, and that training and this book have proceeded in tandem. Among the faculty I would like to thank in particular Ada Burris and James Beatrice. They taught a course on gender that was helpful in providing a guide to current psychoanalytic thinking. Beyond that, they were admirably patient with my doubts, disagreements, and historical digressions. I have also profited from, and very much enjoyed, the Psychoanalytic Interdisciplinary Seminar. For a dozen years it was sponsored by the Department of Psychiatry at the University of California, San Diego, and run by Robert A. Nemiroff. I twice presented work, or rather thoughts, in progress that fed directly into this book. I am grateful to him and to my fellow seminar members. More recently Robert Nemiroff joined Nancy Chodorow and Peter Loewenberg in initiating the University of California Interdisciplinary Psychoanalytic Consortium, and at its annual conferences, I have tried out lines of argument and received valuable feedback. Additionally, I would like to thank Peter Loewenberg for acting as an informant about the Los Angeles psychoanalytic scene and for introducing me to Sybil Stoller, who kindly filled me in with background details about her late husband, Robert J. Stoller.

Once I had a draft, actually a second draft, on paper, I asked Reva Pollack Greenburg and Allan D. Rosenblatt to go over it for me. They proved to be ideal readers: conscientous, careful, and critical. I have made many of the changes they suggested, but not all. Before the manuscript was finished I also showed it to Gladys Topkis at Yale University Press, and I much appreciated her encouragement.

And finally I want to thank my husband, Stuart. As with past writing projects, so too with this one, he has listened to me as I struggled aloud to formulate my ideas and to decide how best to present them; he has been called upon to give editorial advice, and he has given it graciously. More than that: for over three decades the issues addressed in this book have been part of our marriage—not always consciously—and I have invariably been able to count on his tolerance and good will.

Introduction

"The sexual life of adult women," Freud wrote in 1926, "is a 'dark continent' for psychology."[1] How did Freud and psychoanalysts after him explore that continent? What bits and pieces of theory did they pack in their baggage? What maps did they devise along the way? And how after their return did they fashion their tales? These questions are not new. Over the past twenty years, psychoanalytic accounts of women, of their bodies, their gender identity, and their sexuality have been appropriated also in bits and pieces by feminist theorists. The connections, however, among the items packed in psychoanalysts' baggage and/or appropriated by feminists have not been established. It is these connections that I want to elucidate. In so doing, I hope to provide a guide to the psychoanalytic representation of a continent that is no longer perceived as utterly dark.

To fashion my own tale, I am exploiting the notion of science as a selection process.[2] To what precepts have I thus committed myself? First, selection in nature does not operate on a species as a whole but rather on biologically unique individuals, and conceptual systems may be thought of as similarly particularized. Second, conceptual histories can be written by tracing lineages, by tracking the appearance of ideas in Freud's corpus and their reappearance in the work of later theorists who can be reckoned his direct descendants. At this point my commitment to a selection model helps me choose my cast of characters or, rather, does the job for me. Among early psychoanalysts Helene Deutsch, Karen Horney, and Melanie Klein obviously demand inclusion. They were working with Freudian concepts and little besides.[3] Among those born around 1900 Erik H. Erikson deserves attention, and in a younger generation Robert J. Stoller stands out. For the most part both were loyal to Freud, but both were writing in cultural milieus far different from his.

This brings me to a third commitment: selection is a social process. The "social" that interests me is the "social" of scientific communities, in particular the psychoanalytic community, and along with it the struggle to bring concepts to bear on the empirical world. Deutsch, Horney, and Klein all started work within an identifiable community and were addressing issues raised by members of that community. The first round of psychoanalytic debate about women, the discussions of the 1920s and 1930s, then, can be thought of as largely endogenous. In contrast, the second round, which dates from the 1960s, was largely exogenous. And when psychoanalysts began to respond to feminism's "second wave," they turned to the protagonists I have already mentioned. Over the past decade and a half they have turned to Carol Gilligan and Nancy Chodorow as well. Neither of them was (at the time) an analyst; yet both are lineal descendants of this study's protagonists. Hence they are included in my roster.

A fourth and final commitment. If science is a selection process, transmission is necessary, and transmission involves attention to writing. The ability of psychoanalysts to get their colleagues and/or a wider audience to take their notions seriously depends not only on empirical findings and conceptual clarity but also on their capacity to persuade readers to trust them as participant observers. How my protagonists went about building their texts and establishing their credibility within them is crucial to the evolutionary tale I am constructing.

"Evolution" figures in my tale in two ways. The first, already apparent, derives from my choosing a selection model of conceptual change. The second, and more novel, derives from my characterization of the particular lineages I am tracing. They are five in number, and in each case I have discerned an evolutionary narrative. Helene Deutsch told a story of retrogression and called it such; Erik H. Erikson named his own epigenesis, and Carol Gilligan has continued in that vein; Karen Horney's discussion made me think of sexual selection; Robert J. Stoller's account brought artificial selection to mind, and so too did Nancy Chodorow's; finally in Melanie Klein's work I perceived a story of natural selection. Five chapters, then, treat Freud's descendants—arranged not chronologically but in terms of lineages and the evolutionary narratives they tell.

What about Freud himself? Two strategies for handling the common ancestor suggest themselves. The first is to summarize key Freudian concepts that constitute the legacy eventually bequeathed. The second is to refer to him piecemeal—that is, to take up his ideas at the point where his heirs sorted out their inheritance. The first approach founders on the objection that Freud does not admit of ready summary. Hence I have opted for the second.

A final word of introduction—about myself. I too am a descendant of Freud and a feminist and in that guise figure as a participant in my tale. At the end of the fifth chapter, I advance an argument of my own. It fits with the narrative fashioned by Klein—hence its inclusion in the chapter entitled "Natural Selection"—and adds a missing element to that narrative.

My study thus occupies two places at once: it falls under the rubric "history of psychoanalysis," and it joins the debate about psychoanalysis and feminism. By couching a contribution to the second in terms of a contribution to the first, I am trying to induce my readers—analysts and non-analysts alike—to participate in the ongoing selection process of conceptual change.

Chapter 1 Retrogression: Helene Deutsch

"Retrogression"—a backward or reversed movement, a return to a less advanced state, a reversal of development—conjures up the world of late nineteenth-century biology, the world of Charles Darwin and Ernst Haeckel. It was a world of permeable disciplinary boundaries, a world in which biological categories or terms might serve a variety of theoretical functions in the social or human sciences—homology, analogy, and metaphor among them.[1] Freud himself did not hesitate to borrow from biology or even to engage in biological speculation—though biological determinism was not a feature of his thought. (Given his Lamarckianism, how could it have been?) Retrogression, then, like its first cousin, regression, was a concept that would have been familiar to the psychoanalytic community in general and to Helene Deutsch in particular.

By the mid-1920s Deutsch could be reckoned a pillar of that community; by then she figured as a member of the Viennese old guard.[2] She had arrived in the Austrian capital in 1907, just as she was turning twenty-three. Born in Przemyśl, a fortress town near the Carpathian Mountains, she was the youngest child of a lawyer, a Jew who had assimilated to the intelligentsia and had prospered. (There were two older sisters and an unpromising older brother in the family as well.) At the age of fourteen, having finished the official schooling available to her, Helene launched a campaign to acquire the *Abitur* and with it the possibility of university training. Over the next decade she earned her medical degree—six other women entered Vienna's School of Medicine along with her, only two of whom finished—and then pursued a specialty in psychiatry. Doing so entailed a brief stint in Munich working under Emil Kraepelin and the better part of six years in Vienna under Julius Wagner-Jauregg at the university's Clinic for Psychiatry and Nervous Diseases. Thanks to the war and the shortage of male physicians, she rose to the position of assistant in charge of the women's division, a post to which, as a woman, she was not legally entitled. She had engaged in experimental work in Munich and again at the beginning of her association with Wagner-Jauregg, but each time her enthusiasm soon dwindled. By war's end she had had ample hands-on psychiatric experience; intellectually, she was still lacking a purpose.

In the course of her education Deutsch encountered Freud's writings and attended meetings of the Vienna Psychoanalytic Society, which, during the war, convened on an irregular basis. In early 1918 she was elected to membership. Was she in the process of becoming a psychoanalyst, and if so, what did that process entail? Of formal instruction and supervision, there was none; in fact, no prescribed program existed in Vienna until 1924, when Deutsch herself was appointed the first director of the Training Institute, a position she held until she emigrated to the United States in 1935. Of personal analyses, which, though not yet a requirement, were becoming common; she had two, the first with Freud, the second in Berlin with Karl Abraham.

Deutsch was not forthcoming about her double experience as analysand. It is safe to assume, however, that in both instances conflicts about motherhood, marriage, and professional ambitions brought her to treatment. By the time she began analysis with Freud—it went on for less than a year, in late 1918 and early 1919—she had been married to Felix Deutsch for six years, and they had a nineteen-month old son. (To provide milk for their child, Felix had brought two goats to Vienna. During her analysis Helene shared the goats' milk with Freud's wife.) According to her account, she managed to "avoid mentioning conflicts" involving her "motherhood";[3] according to her biographer, "details about her small child and her difficulties with her nursemaid" bored her analyst.[4] As for her marriage, she was frequently restless in it, and whether or not to divorce was a crucial issue in her seeking Abraham's help in 1923–1924. This time treatment lasted a little more than a year. Shortly after she began it, Freud wrote his disciple in Berlin, telling him that the Deutsches' marriage should not be disrupted by Helene's analysis. Abraham showed the letter to his patient: the marriage remained intact. Whatever inadequacies she felt as a mother, whatever doubts she entertained about her marriage, she would have to handle on her own.

Her professional activities were another matter. Here Freud offered encouragement. He expressed no discomfort with what Deutsch thought of as masculine strivings and thus provided a model of tolerance. (In this connection she recalled a dream in which she had a double set of genitals. Apparently Freud did not pursue its interpretation.)[5] He considered her marked identification with her father—in her childhood Helene had adored her father and hated her mother—a source of strength to be reinforced. She viewed it as the source of a never-resolved transference as well.[6] Throughout her subsequent career, she imagined Freud as her audience; she felt that in him she had found "the center" of her "intellectual sphere."[7]

Still, Freud or better "Freud" was not a fixed center or starting point. From his conceptual largesse Deutsch's were not the only items that could have been selected; hers was not the only evolutionary tale that could have been told. Choosing to emphasize libidinal development and along with it regression and fixation, she naturally fell into suggesting parallels between psychological and biological processes. In the 1920s and early 1930s, the biologically inflected idiom she employed was common to her audience, to Freud, and to other analysts as well. In the mid-1940s, trying to reach a general American readership, Deutsch felt obliged to steer between the sociological and the biological. Her new sensitivity to disciplinary boundaries had the curious effect of depriving her tale of both its narrative structure and its piquancy.

IN THE SERVICE OF FEMININITY

In conformity with its peculiar nature, psycho-analysis does not try to describe what a woman is—that would be a task it could scarcely perform—but sets about enquiring how she comes into being, how a woman develops out of a child with a bisexual disposition. In recent times we have begun to learn a little about this, thanks to the circumstance that several of our excellent women colleagues in analysis have begun to work at the question. . . . The ladies, whenever some comparison seemed to turn out unfavourable to their sex, were able to utter the suspicion that we, the male analysts, had been unable to overcome certain deeply-rooted prejudices against what was feminine, and that this was being paid for in the partiality of our researches. We, on the other hand, standing on the ground of bisexuality, had no difficulty in avoiding impoliteness. We had only to say: "This doesn't apply to *you*. You're the exception; on this point you're more masculine than feminine."[8]

Herewith Freud offered an olive branch to his female disciples. Given his admission that bisexuality "remained surrounded by many obscurities" and given his inability to find a place for it in his instinct theory, his remarks should not be construed as suggesting an approach to a vexing question.[9] Rather, he was suggesting a rhetorical strategy that those disciples might adopt in order to address a largely male audience on matters of female psychology. It was a suggestion that Deutsch had already shown herself willing to accept.

What in her texts brings to mind a "bisexual" (that is, masculine as well as feminine) stance? The persona of the narrator. In *Psychoanalysis of the Sexual Functions of Women* (1925), Deutsch's first book, the narrator seemed distant and detached. Most of the time, she avoided the first-person pronoun altogether. For example:

> Psychological findings, insofar as they are based on the psychology of the conscious, will not be referred to here, for it is the purpose of this book to explain what was bound to remain mysterious to the psychology of the conscious.

It was the purpose of the book, Deutsch further elaborated, to explain what had, likewise, up until now remained mysterious to the psychology of the unconscious:

> The hidden contents of the male mind have obviously been more accessible to the male because of the closer kinship. . . . Understanding of mental processes in women has lagged behind. . . . In particular, little analytic attention has been paid to the generative processes, though these form the centre point of the mental life of the sexually mature woman. Kant's saying that woman does not betray her secret still applies.

Those hidden contents of the male mind had presumably been accessible to the narrator. That was not all. Now the female mind—more specifically "woman's psychological relations to the physiological processes of sexual life"—was in the course of betraying its secret.[10] Male and female alike were within the grasp of the narrator, who thus implicitly claimed kinship with both.

At the same time Deutsch claimed membership in the psychoanalytic community and addressed the text to her fellow members. The narrator assumed that the reader had "a thorough knowledge of psychoanalysis" and of the method that allowed it to reach unconscious mental contents.[11] Her task, then, was to persuade her audience that hers was an account of female development in a distinctly psychoanalytic idiom.[12]

· · · · ·

Two texts foreshadowed Deutsch's *Psychoanalysis of the Sexual Functions of Women:* Freud's paper "The Infantile Genital Organization" (1923) and Abraham's "A Short Study of the Development of the Libido, Viewed in the Light of Mental Disorders" (1924). Freud's piece, subtitled "An Interpolation into the Theory of Sexuality," reflected his continuing effort to enlarge and modify his *Three Essays on the Theory of Sexuality.* (The first edition appeared in 1905, and the last, the sixth, in 1925.) Not until 1915, with the publication of the third edition, did he interpolate a section on pregenital organizations of the libido—that is, "preliminary stages" that constituted a "sexual regime of a sort."[13] In the 1923 paper he expanded on the role the genitals themselves came to play in the sexual life of children. What distinguished the infantile stage of genital organization from the adult variety was the fact that "for both sexes, only one genital, namely the male one," mattered.[14] The phallus had now gained primacy.

Abraham's study represented a further interpolation, a fleshing out of the oral and the anal. At the same time, as its subtitle suggested, it represented a contribution to a long-standing (and never solved) psychoanalytic problem: the choice of neurosis. From the beginning of his career Freud had tried to explain why one rather than another neurotic outcome had resulted. Why, for example, did a patient develop hysteria rather than an obsessional neurosis? He had initially linked the age at which a traumatic sexual seduction had occurred to a specific neurosis. Although he came to replace childhood sexual trauma with infantile sexuality, he did not abandon his efforts to provide an etiological account. In piecemeal fashion he undertook the task of connecting sexual development to mental disorders. It was this unfinished business that Abraham was taking up.

For Abraham's purpose Freud's two pregenital stages were inadequately elaborated. Abraham readily concurred with his mentor that obsessional neurosis and melancholia had similar features and that they shared "a common relation to the anal . . . organization of the libido"—that is, he agreed that in both instances the anal acted as a fixation point, "formed in the course of development," to which the libido retreated at the onset of the neurotic illness. These two illnesses had dissimilar features as well; and if, Abraham argued, they nonetheless took "their inception" from the same level of libidinal organization, it followed that the stage in question contained heterogeneous elements that had not yet been sorted out. The work of sorting led Abraham to postulate two anal stages, an earlier one of expelling the object (of the libidinal aim) and destroying it, and a later one of retaining and controlling the object. Further investigation into melancholia produced an additional differentiation, this time of the oral stage. The earlier, or sucking, oral stage Abraham considered pre-ambivalent; in the later, or cannibalistic, oral stage, ambivalence toward the object entered the scene. With these refinements at his disposal, Abraham was confident of locating "a more definite connection between certain kinds of illness and certain levels of the libido" than had previously been feasible.[15] But, as he was quick to acknowledge, gaps remained. The theory of libidinal development remained very much a work in progress.

Meanwhile—that is, until psychoanalysts should "have collected a greater number of thorough analyses to confirm and amplify the theoretic assumptions" he had made—Abraham thought it might "not be superfluous to consider the *prima facie* arguments" in their favor. Here he pointed to "a striking parallel between the organic and the psychosexual development of the individual." In the embryos of certain animals, for example, the "orginal mouth-opening" (the blastopore) closed up at the "anterior end" and became "enlarged at the posterior end." This "direct derivation of the anus from the blastopore," he concluded, stood as the "biological prototype" of the progress from the oral to the anal that occurred in the second year of extrauterine existence.[16] Abraham used such embryological analogies as a crutch—and nothing more.

• • • • •

"It was only the discovery of the phallic level or organization," Deutsch wrote, "that enabled us completely to explain the origin and significance of the 'masculinity complex.'"[17] The phallic level may have been Freud's concept; its significance as "progress" it owed to Deutsch.

Her little girl, even more than Freud's, started out as a little man. Deutsch pictured her as the proud possessor of an "organ of absolutely sterling value"—the clitoris—to which large quantities of pleasure were attached.[18] She also equipped her with a primary paternal identification equivalent to the one Freud, in other texts, ascribed to the boy.[19] The two went together. For the little girl the clitoris had the significance of a penis and served as the vehicle for this identification. It also served as a vehicle for activity. Thanks to the clitoris, the little girl was richly endowed with masculine attributes.

What happened to little girls when they discovered the anatomical distinction between the sexes? In Freud's account, on catching sight of the boys' genitals, girls immediately noticed "the difference . . . and its significance too."[20] They made their judgment and decision "in a flash." They had "seen it," knew that they were "without it," and wanted "to have it."[21] They fell "victim to 'envy for the penis.'"[22] Deutsch elaborated: Some girls regarded "the castration . . . as a punishment," and in them it produced "inferiority feelings." Some "felt it to be an injustice suffered," and in them it produced "intensive tendencies to exact revenge." And then there were those who, like Freud's little boys, responded with denial: they energetically maintained that everyone had a penis. Such a girl clung to "the assumption of real possession" of it, did not "accept the sexual difference," and continued to see herself as like father. As a consequence, for her the clitoris retained "its fully satisfying sexual role," and the vagina remained permanently without sensation.[23] Here was the masculinity complex in its purest form.

But it was the impure variety that Deutsch never failed to encounter in clinical practice. "Psychoanalytic experience," she wrote, forced her and her colleagues—her rhetorical "us"—"more and more to the conclusion that the 'masculinity complex' in women" was "a permanent component of their psychical structure." Permanent—and non-pathological—for "only under definite conditions," which Deutsch left unclear, did its presence lead to "neurotic phenomena." Its permanence could be explained by invoking a "residue of a past state of development"—that is, the phallic phase. Seen in this light, the masculinity complex served as a memorial to "a biogenetically conditioned masculine phase," which, Deutsch added, "must be regarded as . . . progressive."[24]

• • • • •

In a girl "the final phase of infantile organization," Deutsch explained, "represented progress towards the 'female attitude,'" but was "nevertheless a regression from the point of view of libido development."[25] Upon abandoning the clitoris, the little girl—or her libido—took up components of the anal phase; she took up again an interest in fecal matter. In the meantime, feces had acquired symbolic meaning: they had come to stand for baby. Here Deutsch was being faithful to Freud. She parted company from her mentor, however, in embedding this wish for an "anal child" in a tale of "retrogression."[26]

She continued her story: clitoral sexuality and father were linked—hence "giving up the clitoris" entailed giving up the thought of possessing what father possessed (never completely accomplished);[27] anal child and mother were linked—hence wishing for a fecal baby entailed identifying with mother. Note that the maternal identification—in contrast to the paternal—did not rest on anatomy: the little girl did not move from clitoris to vagina; the vagina itself remained undiscovered. The identification derived from an understanding of coitus; that is, the understanding that to have a child—anal or otherwise—the little girl had to assume the mother's position in intercourse. And that position in turn entailed passivity and masochism.

What happened when the wish for a fecal baby was disappointed, when the little girl was obliged to give up hope a second time? At this point Deutsch interpolated reflections on superego formation. It took place, she argued, in two phases. The first, following the "renunciation of the clitoris," elevated the identification with father to the "higher plane" of the superego. The second, following the abandonment of the wish for a fecal baby, elevated the identification with mother to that same higher plane. Father and mother identifications both found their way into the superego, and with complementary functions: "father" was responsible for the ban on incest; "mother" was responsible for "idealized maternity and a definite sexual morality and sexual inhibition characteristic of the moral woman."[28] The little girl was in the course of adopting a "female attitude," and along the way she had accepted a plethora of sexual inhibitions.

Deutsch had concentrated her attention on the aim—active or passive, sadistic or masochistic—of the libido; she had said little about its objects. Where in Freud's account of superego formation, the superego was the precipitate of abandoned object-choices and could be read as a history of those choices, in her account the superego vouchsafed no such history.[29] Sexual object-choice would have to be fitted into a narrative framework that had already been set.

• • • • •

In a footnote subsequently added to her paper "Homosexuality in Women" (1932), Deutsch explained what had prompted her to publish her material. She had been analyzing female homosexuals—"more or less thoroughly"—for over a decade;[30] she had collected data on eleven such cases and had planned to report her findings to the International Psycho-Analytical Congress in 1931, but the world economic crisis led to its postponement. That same year Freud had produced his essay "Female Sexuality," in which he specifically addressed the question of how, when, and why the little girl detached herself from her mother—that is, the question of object-choice. Deutsch had thus missed two opportunities to have her work recognized as crucial to understanding that question.[31] It was high time to publish.

In his essay Freud had struck a diffident pose. Everything about the girl's earliest attachment to her mother, he wrote, had been difficult for him to grasp—"so grey with age and shadowy and almost impossible to revivify that it was as if it had succumbed to an especially inexorable repression." Perhaps, he added, women in analysis with him clung to their "attachment to . . . father"—an attachment that, after their turning from mother, had been a refuge for them—and hence his impression of inexorable repression. By the same token, women analysts, thanks to the maternal transference they elicited from their female patients, were well placed to correct his impression. Deutsch took care to accept Freud's implicit invitation: she took care to portray herself in her clinical role as a "suitable mother-substitute"[32]—so much so that at one point in the text she failed to distinguish between the real mother and the analyst as maternal figure.[33] (Note that there are two personae, not one, in this text. There is the persona of the narrator and the persona of the practicing psychoanalyst.) The practitioner, in contrast to the narrator, had nothing "bisexual" about her.

That practitioner was most clearly in evidence in Deutsch's first case. The patient had come to her under dramatic circumstances. "For years she had suffered from fits of depression." They "had become more and more frequent" and more and more severe. "On quite a number of occasions the patient had made unsuccessful attempts to commit suicide; the last of these had brought her to death's door"—and to Deutsch's as well, thanks to a referral from the attending physician. During treatment the patient recalled a scene just after the last attempt (by poisoning): "She woke up out of deep unconsciousness, still strapped to a stretcher, and saw the physician bending over her with a kindly smile. She was conscious that he had saved her life (as was actually the case), and she thought: 'Yes, this time: but all the same you cannot really help me.'"[34]

When the analysis began, the patient was married. She had never been hostile to men; "she had many men friends and did not object to being admired and courted" by them. Still "she had never really fallen in love with a man"—not even her husband.[35] She had been disappointed in his lack of sexual passion and masculine activity; she had been most disappointed when she had been in an anxious state about her household staff, and he failed to protect and support her with sufficient vigor. Marriage notwithstanding, Deutsch regarded her patient as homosexual.

When the patient started treatment, Deutsch wrote, she appeared to be a case of inversion—"manifest, but not actively practiced." She was "perfectly aware that her capacity for love and her sexual fantasies were confined to her own sex" and that she "experienced quite unmistakable sexual excitations when embracing and kissing certain women with whom she was in love." That love, however, went no further. "She could not explain why her homosexuality did not take a more active and urgent form; she knew only that her inhibitions were too strong, and rationalized them on grounds of social timidity, her duty to her family, and her dread of 'bondage.'" About a year after leaving treatment, the patient saw her analyst again. With evident pleasure she reported an "uninhibited sexual relation with another woman."[36]

During the analysis itself, during the periods of depression the patient experienced, she reported dreams containing "nearly all the known symbolism relating to the mother's body: there were dreams of dark holes and openings into which the patient crept, dreams of cosy dark places which seemed to her known and familiar and where she lingered with a sense of rest and deliverance. . . . Again and again, one particular dream picture appeared: the patient saw herself wrapped up like a baby in swaddling clothes." The dream led to a memory of a dangerous operation her mother had undergone and to her "having seen her mother wrapped up . . . and carried on a stretcher to the operating theater." The memory, in turn, led to a revival of "murderous hatred for her mother," which "now became the focal point of the analysis."[37]

Another dream about eight months further along in the treatment led to another memory. In the dream the patient "saw herself sitting behind the bars in a police station, having been accused of some sort of sexual misconduct. Apparently she had been brought in from the street under suspicion of being a prostitute. The police inspector, a kindly man, stood on the other side of the bars without helping her." The childhood memory went back to roughly the patient's fifth year, to the time when her masturbatory practices had drawn her mother's attention and disapproval:

> What happened, according to the patient, was that her mother, not knowing what else to do, resorted to the following plan: she tied the child's hands and feet, strapped her to the cot, stood beside it and said: "*Now* go on with your games!" This produced a twofold reaction in the little girl. On the one hand it evoked a feeling of furious anger with her mother. . . . On the other hand it gave rise to a violent sexual excitement, which, in spite of her mother's presence or perhaps in defiance of her, she tried to gratify by rubbing her buttocks against the mattress.
>
> To the child's mind the most terrible thing about this scene was that her father, whom her mother summoned, remained a passive witness of it and did not try to help his little daughter whom he loved tenderly.

The scene, Deutsch continued, met with repression (now being undone), and so too did the child's sexuality and her "hatred for her mother, which in real life she never again betrayed in the same degree."[38]

Deutsch took pains to spell out for her readers how she had construed the scene's significance:

> I do not regard . . . [it] as traumatic in the sense that it produced the subsequent psychic attitude of the patient. . . . The reproach against her mother that she had forbidden masturbation would certainly have arisen in her mind even *without* this scene. The reaction of hatred toward her mother was perceptible also in other situations of childhood and was in accordance with the patient's sadistic constitution. The same was true of her reproach against her father for failing to protect her from her mother. But the scene brought all these trends to the boiling point, so to speak, and thus became the prototype of later occurrences.[39]

After working through her hostility to her mother—that is, after over-coming her hostility to her analyst in the "transference situation"—the patient allowed her father for the first time to appear "on the stage of the analytic play. With him came all the impulses belonging to the Oedipus complex, beginning with the vehement reproach, which the patient had never been able to get over, that he had not been active enough in his love for his daughter." At this point the analysis ended—on Deutsch's urging. In hopes that the revival of the father relation—"above all, . . . the renewed animation and correction of *this* relation"—would produce a "more favor-able . . . outlook for the patient's libidinal future," Deutsch sent her patient to "an analyst of the fatherly type. Unfortunately the transference never went beyond respect and sympathy, and after a short time the patient broke off the analysis."[40] The task of "animation and correction" proved beyond the capacities of male and female analyst alike. The latter, not unhappily, settled for homosexuality: in her view it was far better to love a homosexual object than never to love at all.

Deutsch the narrator presented Deutsch the practicing psychoanalyst as modest in her therapeutic goals; she also presented her as judicious in her research aims. She had collected analytic material about her patient—the first of eleven cases; she had posed to herself the question of how to account for her patient's object-choice; and then, for more than a decade, she lived with a problem "she could not solve." Tact, tolerance, patience: these were her trademarks as therapist and researcher. When Deutsch the narrator, her credibility enhanced by her self-representation as practitioner, turned to drawing "theoretical conclusions . . . important for the understanding of feminine sexuality in general and of feminine homosexuality in particular," she spoke with confidence and authority.[41]

She naturally paid heed to what Freud had written. According to her mentor, one line of development, starting from the castration complex, led the little girl "to cling with defiant self-assertiveness . . . to the hope of getting a penis . . . [and] to her threatened masculinity," with "a manifest homosexual choice of object" as a possible result.[42] Deutsch's patient dis-played ample penis envy. Moreover, the "analysis revealed phases, both in her childhood (before the time of the fateful experiences described) and also at puberty, in which unmistakable signs could be detected of a very marked development of activity, with a masculine bias. Especially at puberty she manifested quite plainly interests which were rather unusual in a girl of her period and social sphere." But, her analyst wrote, penis envy was not "the central part" of her personality. Similarly, Deutsch added, "neither her character nor her attitude toward men indicated that she belonged to the type of woman who has a 'masculinity complex.' "[43] Deutsch resisted the temptation to follow Freud in regarding her patient's homosexuality as an expression of her masculinity. Instead she concluded that her patient did not fit his pattern.

Deutsch took a different tack. Homosexuality, she conjectured, might be a matter not of development gone awry but rather of development arrested. She asked herself—and her reader—whether it would be appropriate "to speak of a primal fixation," to speculate that in her homosexual patients "the libido had always known but *one* object, the mother." Their sexual practices were suggestive. With the first patient "her homosexual relation took the form of a perfectly conscious mother-and-child situation, in which sometimes the one and sometimes the other played the part of mother." In subsequent cases "all the women in question stood in a mother-and-child relation to their homosexual love object and more or less consciously recognized this fact. In all cases the forms of sexual gratification were the same: sleeping in close mutual embrace, sucking one another's nipples, mutual genital and, above all, anal masturbation, and cunnilingus, mainly in the form of sucking, practiced intensively by both parties." Deutsch was prepared to grant that in certain instances a primal fixation might be at work, "but these were quite special cases, in which the whole neurosis had the character of a general psychic infantilism."[44] Not one of her eleven, she maintained, fit this pattern.

The pattern that did fit, Deutsch claimed, was one of "retrogression to the mother-child attitude." (Once again, as in accounting for femininity in the first place, she invoked retrogression.) From what had her patients regressed? From the Oedipus complex, Deutsch answered: it was discovered "in its entirety" in all her cases. So too was frustration, disappointment, and rejection by the father, which her patients experienced as the loss of the love object. Deutsch imagined them saying to themselves, " 'If my father does not want me and such a blow is dealt to my self-love, who will love me now if not my mother?' " In these circumstances the libido turned back to experiences earlier enjoyed. As Deutsch's homosexual patients retreated, they took with them "from the phallic phase the wish for activity"—more specifically the wish to masturbate. A "sanctioning of activity and permission to masturbate" constituted "a motive common to all forms of [female] homosexuality."[45]

The original prohibition had come at the hands of the mother. The childhood scene recollected by Deutsch's first patient represented that prohibition in graphic—indeed lurid—form. It functioned not only as prologue to later occurrences in the patient's sexual life but also as prologue to Deutsch's understanding of her own therapeutic task as well. (In contrast to Deutsch, who stressed the reaction to this prohibition "as the girl's strongest motive for turning away" from her mother, Freud emphasized "the reproach that her mother did not give her a proper penis.")[46] A "sanctioning of activity and permission to masturbate": such could be granted by a "suitable mother-substitute," be she female lover or female analyst. So it had been with Deutsch's patient.

• • • • •

Psychoanalysis, Freud wrote, had set itself the task of inquiring how a woman came into being. Retrogression had been the tale Deutsch told in reply. It was a tale, at least initially, of successive deprivations, with the unattached woman figuring as the most deprived of all. Penis and fecal baby: these losses were the female lot. Heterosexual women might someday acquire a real child; homosexual women might someday be the child; chaste women had nothing—unless, of course, their chastity derived from a masculinity complex in its purest form, in which case they might fantasize that they possessed a penis.

IN THE SERVICE OF MASCULINITY

In 1930 Deutsch published a second book; two years later it appeared in English under the title *Psycho-Analysis of the Neuroses*. It consisted of eleven lectures, which she had delivered in her capacity as director of the Training Institute, addressed specifically to future analysts, and replete with clinical illustrations.

The case that drew most inventively on Deutsch's "insight into the mental processes of the woman in her procreative function" was that of a fifteen-year-old girl whose "neurosis had broken out in puberty in the form of severe fits and twilight states." Deutsch commented that nowadays one did not often meet such patients in analytic practice, and in fact she did not see the girl in her own consulting room; the patient lived in a sanitarium during the treatment. Both Deutsch and the patient relied on sanitarium personnel for information about what happened during the girl's seizures; the patient remembered nothing. The treatment itself did not last long: "for external reasons" the analysis was "broken off after a few months, before we, [that is, Deutsch and the patient working together] were able to penetrate to the bottom of . . . infantile experiences. . . . The making conscious of puberty conflicts," however, "succeeded in restoring the girl to health, at any rate for the time being."[47] It also succeeded in elucidating the thoughts and emotions common to hysterical fits and twilight states alike.

In reconstructing the meaning of her patient's hysterical attacks, Deutsch kept Freud's precepts in mind. For example:

> Hysterical symptoms are—like other psychical structures—an expression of the fulfillment of a wish. . . .
>
> Hysterical symptoms are the realization of an unconscious phantasy which serves the fulfillment of a wish. . . .
>
> Hysterical symptoms may take over the representation of various unconscious impulses which are not sexual, but they can never be without a sexual significance.[48]

Unconscious impulses of a destructive variety had been easy to detect— their "sexual significance" less so. The patient's violent rage had not been completely hidden from her, not even before the analysis; it had been suppressed "until finally the inability to control it provoked the motor discharge of the seizure." Against whom had it been aimed? The patient quite consciously loved mother and hated father, and it was he, she readily admitted, who was the target of her rage. Yet she did not appreciate that her current attitude was simply "a return to a state of feeling which had formerly been present—namely, a primary, excessive love for the mother and a furious protest against the interfering father." She did not appreciate that this return constituted a "reaction to the normal Oedipus relationship" and "represented a complete inversion of the real emotional" situation. And it was here that Deutsch located the unconscious impulses, sexual and destructive alike, which combined in the hysterical fit.[49]

All the patient's accusations against her father, Deutsch reported, and all her "rationalizations of her rage took as their ground his neglect of the family and his brutality to her mother." "Neglect," Deutsch pointed out to both patient and reader, "was identical with 'refusal of love,' and . . . the word 'brutality' was an expression of the patient's view of parental intercourse." Deutsch had difficulty getting her patient to confirm this latter interpretation. She persevered: "the concept of the sexual act as an act of violation was peculiarly noticeable" (how, she left unspecified) in her patient's "defense mechanisms." It was noticeable in her history as well: "during the war the little girl had really been witness to violations." Here was "an actual kernel for the violation fantasy."[50] And here was a fantasy that Deutsch regarded as typical of puberty.

She had now established that the "convulsions procured" the patient "the motor discharge of an attack of rage . . . ; and they represented coitus as well. . . ." Still more it "became clear in the course of the analysis" that they also dramatized "the act of birth." Not the mother, but the patient herself "should be violated by the father and give birth to a child": so Deutsch interpreted.[51] Here was the wish whose fulfillment was expressed in the patient's hysterical fit.

The patient's wish—as interpreted by Deutsch—and Deutsch's theoretical formulation mirrored each other. The patient condensed coitus and childbirth into one; Deutsch expanded the sex act to include childbirth. In her view orgasm and parturition belonged to the same sequence divided by an interval of nine months. That expansion allowed Deutsch to bring in retrogression and give it free rein.

• • • • •

> When the erotogenic susceptibility to stimulation has been successfully transferred by the woman from the clitoris to the vaginal orifice, it implies that she has adopted a new leading zone for the purposes of her later sexual activity.[52]

> The final task of the completely achieved female attitude is not the satisfaction in the sex act of the infantile wish for a penis, but the successful discovery of the vagina as an organ of pleasure.[53]

The first quotation comes from Freud's *Three Essays;* the second, a faithful reproduction, from Deutsch's *Psychoanalysis of the Sexual Functions of Women.* According to Freud "a wave of repression at puberty" overtook "clitoridal sexuality" and along with it a female's "childish masculinity."[54] Deutsch phrased the process in terms of a woman's giving up the "claim of the clitoris to be a penis surrogate";[55] but in her hands this renunciation did not entail the extinction of the female's masculinity. In elaborating her version of the sex act, she managed to revivify that masculinity. In so doing she turned the narrator's "bisexual" (that is, masculine as well as feminine) stance to more than rhetorical account; in effect the medium became the message.

Deutsch started with the standard version—that is, with sexual intercourse—and even with this unpromising point of departure, she managed to preserve a modicum of masculinity for the woman. She started with the vagina, more precisely, with the vexed question of how the exchange of clitoris for vagina took place. The beginning of an answer, she claimed, lay in a direct transfer of libido from the one to the other. This "libidinal component" remained "'male-oriented' even in its vaginal application." The clitoris had "exercised its 'masculinity' in identification with the paternal penis," an identification based on the equation clitoris = penis; the vagina exercised its masculinity "under the aegis of identification with the partner's penis," an identification derived from the introduction into the body from the outside of a real penis, which "in wish fulfillment" became an "organ of the woman's own body."[56] Had Deutsch been satisfied by a sex act so conceived, a woman's masculinity would have been a matter of identification with a male figure (and his organ).

Deutsch began again with the standard version and now found in it a serviceable point of departure for her story of retrogression. She began again with the exchange of clitoris for vagina, this time with indirect transfer of libido to the vagina from the body as a whole. The equation penis = nipple did the trick. Just as the mother's nipple concentrated the infant's body libido in its mouth, so the partner's penis concentrated the woman's body libido in her vagina. The penis performing like a nipple activated another equation, one "prefigured in the whole anatomical structure," that of vagina = mouth. The vagina, in turn, performing like a mouth, constituted the "really passive feminine attitude." The woman had reached "the highest level of libidinal organization (the vaginal phase)." And she had done so by an "intensive mobilization of regressive trends," by the repetition of the "lowest"—that is, Abraham's pre-ambivalent oral—stage.[57] Had Deutsch been satisfied by a sex act conventionally construed, retrogression would have facilitated symbolic trading in body parts, but that trading would not have revivified a woman's masculinity. Retrogression, symbolic bodily equations, and a reconceptualization and expansion of the sex act: all three were necessary to make a woman's masculinity something other than a matter of identification.

The sex act begun in coitus, according to Deutsch, reached its conclusion—for a woman—only with parturition. (How to regard the sex act when the woman did not conceive Deutsch failed to specify.) What then of the interval in between, which figured as part of her expanded version? Here she once again introduced retrogression, alerting her readers to anticipate reactivated traces of "pre-female" or "bisexual" phases—that is, of developmental phases "common to male and female" alike. Coitus reactivated the pre-ambivalent oral phase. Pregnancy reactivated not only oral phases, preambivalent and ambivalent, but anal phases as well. Orality manifested itself in "various 'cravings,'" in "characteristic hunger alternating with complete loss of appetite"; the ambivalence associated with the later oral phase turned up, above all, in morning sickness. Anality manifested itself in the "pregnant woman's very typical temporary character changes . . . e.g., stubbornness, capriciousness, particular cleanliness, thrift bordering on meanness, and a kind of collecting mania"; ambivalence turned up in the symptoms of early labor, and, if intense enough, that ambivalence could lead to miscarriage. Along the way the equation vagina = mouth—and the child, then, as something ingested—promoted the revival of the classic Freudian equation feces = baby; feces, after all, were "orally introduced in food."[58] Freud's equation, as Deutsch and her audience fully appreciated, included a middle term: feces = penis = baby. Retrogression was in the course of revivifying a woman's masculinity.

"In the tremendous disturbance of the libidinal economy" that took place in pregnancy, Deutsch wrote, "the path of regression once entered upon" led "to all abandoned libidinal trends being sought out"—the phallic included. With the beginning of the fifth month of pregnancy, with the child's first stirrings in the womb, it lost its anal meaning, and its phallic significance came to the fore. In the happiest circumstances the child as penis figured as a component of the woman's ego. And as long as those circumstances obtained, the woman experienced "increased self-feeling, self-satisfaction"; she reached her "physical and psychical prime." The equation child = penis thus offered the woman "a direct substitute" for the male organ earlier missed.[59]

Such circumstances could not last:

> The stimulus proceeding from the foetus becomes intolerable and presses for discharge. In this final struggle all the hostile impulses that have been mobilized in the course of the pregnancy reach their greatest intensity. In the physical respect this struggle manifests itself in the contracting activity of the musculature and its tendencies to retain and to expel. The latter finally gain the upper hand. The introjected object is projected into the outside world, and by the route by which it was introjected in coitus.

Coitus had been merely the start, and it was pleasurable, Deutsch suggested, "chiefly because of the psychological fact" that it represented "an attempt at and a beginning of the act of parturition." The "orgastic activity of the vagina" Deutsch regarded as tantamount to a "'missed labour.'" The orgastic activity of the vagina she also considered "analogous to that of the penis"—in a "much moderated form."[60] Childbirth knew no moderation. It occasioned, she claimed, the most intense sexual pleasure and a novel equation: vagina = penis.

The sex act had reached its climax and conclusion, but Deutsch's tale of symbolic trading in body parts had a sequel. It followed immediately upon the climactic event and entailed a repetition of sexual intercourse "with a reversal of roles. . . . As the penis took control of the vagina in coitus," so did "the erect mammary gland now take control of the infant's mouth. The part of the seminal fluid" was "played by the flow of milk." Here Deutsch offered a clinical vignette:

> A young mother with a very ambivalent relationship to her child had to give up breast-feeding even though she wished to continue and possessed an amply functioning mammary apparatus. What happened was that in the interval between the child's feeding times the milk came gushing out, with the result that the breast was empty when the child was put to it. The practices to which she resorted to circumvent this unhappy state of affairs recalled the behaviour of a man suffering from premature ejaculation who desperately tries to accelerate the sex act but is always overtaken with the same lack of success—she was invariably too late.[61]

Once more nipple equalled penis.

Deutsch's tale of retrogression had a sequel as well. Menopause, she wrote, represented "a retrogressive phase in the history of the libido." Under the pressure of failure—and the vagina inevitably failed; that is, it experienced "greater difficulty in object-finding"—it gave up the struggle, and a regressive attachment to "the clitoris as a centre of excitation" occurred—in short, a regression to the phallic phase. Biology, Deutsch argued, now revived a "bisexual constitution," and women re-entered a phase in which male and female did not exist.[62] Biology now gave its seal of approval to what had all along been a psychological possibility.

Deutsch's equations, she admitted, might be "complicated and . . . seem far-fetched,"[63] but they provided a woman with penis surrogates during her reproductive years when her clitoris had renounced that particular function. No surrogates, no masculinity: a bodily representation figured as an essential requirement. And although both the bodily representation and a woman's masculinity ranked as psychological, they were construed as leaning on biology. "Among lower animals," Deutsch wrote, one found "processes in which the close connection between the mouth and genital apparatus" was plain; "similarly, the connection between . . . execretory processes . . . and the genital function" was extremely frequent. Like Abraham she drew an analogy between "actual phylogenetic forms of development . . . and pre-genital phases of the libido."[64] Like him she used biology as a crutch—in her case to justify symbolic trading in body parts.

• • • • •

Female analysts, Freud had suggested, might take comfort from the notion that they were more masculine than feminine. In his view that combination made them an exception; in Deutsch's view they were the rule. Her tale of retrogression, having initially transformed the Freudian "child with a bisexual disposition" into a woman, subsequently restored a woman's masculinity. The first installment featured deprivation, the second installment emphasized restitution.

CODA: PORTRAIT OF A LADY

Here is a book [*The Psychology of Women*] based on experience, the experience of "feeling as one's own" the emotions of a great number of girls and women. In her role as counsellor for many girls in difficulties, as psychoanalyst for a great many women suffering from neurosis, and as hospital psychiatrist, Dr. Deutsch has had an extraordinary opportunity to observe the behavior of women of all ages and sorts. Trained by Freud and working closely with him for years, she speaks the psychoanalytical language; but with her, understanding always comes first, with interpretation and theory following in secondary roles.[65]

Stanley Cobb, Bullard Professor of Neuropathology at the Harvard Medical School, wrote these words in his foreword to Deutsch's *Psychology of Women*, published in 1944. Deutsch had been living in Cambridge, Massachusetts, for the better part of a decade and had been maneuvering, by and large successfully, in analytic and medical circles. Note the plural. The move to the United States had caused a shift in Deutsch's allegiance. Her loyalty to psychoanalysis—and her ties to the Boston Psychoanalytic Institute—remained strong, but not exclusive. By the same token, in her writing she was no longer addressing the psychoanalytic community alone. As Cobb further remarked: "Anyone reading this book will realize that Helene

Deutsch has great knowledge of what women do and great insight into why they do it." He also made clear that "anyone" referred to "parents, teachers, authors, . . . [and] psychiatrists."[66]

Deutsch had acquired "great knowledge," Cobb declared, by means of a "clinical approach"—that is, by talking to people about their thoughts and feelings.[67] She had been aware, she wrote in her preface, that the "empiric data" for her *Psychoanalysis of the Sexual Functions of Women* had been insufficient. Thanks to "case and life histories recorded by other observers—physicians and social workers—not prejudiced in favor of any psychologic theory," to material "taken from the files of various social agencies," to "routine hospital records," as well as to her "personal observations in the course of psychoanalytic therapy," she now felt prepared to remedy her deficiency.[68] She likewise felt prepared to present what amounted to a portrait of a lady, a portrait which owed little to her "empiric data."

Deutsch had also, so Cobb declared, "great insight" into women. Of the two—knowledge and insight—the latter loomed larger. Deutsch regarded an "introspective contemplation of her psyche," a "capacity for identification with other women," as "positive factors" that could "abundantly compensate for a feminine observer's lesser degree of objectivity."[69] Here the femininity of the narrator became crucial to enhancing her stature as a teller of truth, of her own truth.

Femininity was not uniform; even the "normal psychic life of women and their normal conflicts," which Deutsch's book set out to explain, were not uniform.[70] Yet the persona of the narrator did not reflect the diversity of female types in the text. From that diverse population, the feminine-active woman stood out. A creation within the text, she figured as very nearly identical with the narrator herself.

How was this identity or near-identity achieved? By a process of elimination. The rivals, the other feminine types sketched in the text, were simply not up to the task. It was not the case that feminine-passive women lacked "positive factors." Women of this sort, Deutsch claimed, developed "their deepest natures" completely when they engaged in occupations that gave "full play to their intuition—that is to say, artistic and psychologic work," or when, "silent and in the background," they inspired "their husbands, always stimulating, encouraging, and understanding them." Nor was it the case that feminine-active-moral women lacked "positive factors." Women of this kind, Deutsch maintained, were "usually the center of the home,

leaving all activity outside . . . to the man, on condition that they themselves direct the education of the children." They set the moral standard for
the household, and they expected husbands and children alike to conform
to it.[71] Neither type showed much inclination to make her mark in the
world of science.

Masculine women, yet another category, also came up short. In her 1944
book, as opposed to her earlier work, Deutsch relegated such women, and
more generally the masculinity complex in women, to a marginal position.
Where previously she had considered that complex a permanent component of a woman's personality, a memorial to a biogenetically conditioned
masculine phase, here she viewed it as signalling "a fear of the feminine
functions. . . . In its most primitive manifestations," the masculinity complex looked like "the direct enemy of feminine tendencies," disturbing a
woman in "all specifically feminine phases of life (menstruation, pregnancy,
childbirth, etc.)." Or its enmity might be indirect, disturbing self-esteem,
as, for example, when a woman regarded the feminine components of her
personality as hindering her worldly pursuits and concluded that as a
woman she would "never achieve her ends."

> More complicated and veiled is the masculinity complex in those women who
> have brilliantly succeeded in sublimating their masculine activity but are not
> aware of the fact that they have paid a high price for it in their feminine values.
> Woman's intellectuality . . . feeds on the sap of affective life and results in
> impoverishment of this life either as a whole or in specific emotional quali-
> ties. . . . All observations point to the fact that the intellectual woman is mas-
> culinized; in her, warm intuitive knowledge has yielded to cold unproductive
> thinking.[72]

Hardly the description of someone capable of comprehending other
women.

With these three types out of the way, Deutsch had cleared the field for
the feminine-active woman. Balance figured as her most striking characteristic. She was "capable of love ecstasy," but proved "willing to choose a
life companion according to the . . . objective value of her choice, his social
position, etc." She was capable of activity but eschewed aggression. She was
a creator and organizer "in all the departments of peaceful life. Destruction
and preparation for destruction" were not in her "domain." One recognized "this type . . . even in prehistoric times," a woman in whom dwelt the
feeling of right and wrong, who was "wise and understanding even though
lacking that strength of intellect" which was "man's instrument for acquir-

ing knowledge."[73] And here one also recognized the narrator's voice, and in that voice making her own contribution to science.

• • • • •

In her preface Deutsch sought to demarcate not only a woman's domain but a psychological one as well. Where earlier she had noted a tendency (in which she shared) to call upon the biological and anatomical to "explain the differentiated psychologic behavior of the sexes," she now observed that explanatory primacy was passing to educational and cultural factors. In contrast she declared her intention to emphasize "individual emotional experiences and the conflicts connected with them," which, she maintained, could not "be reduced to either . . . biologic or sociologic influences."[74] Her aim to respect disciplinary boundaries may not have been fully realized, but its mere avowal pointed to her consciousness that she had mentally, as well as physically, emigrated to America.

This aim had a strange effect on the story she told: it lost its narrative plot. To be sure, Deutsch proceeded chronologically, beginning oddly enough with pre-puberty—thereby avoiding discussion of the vicissitudes of infantile and childhood instinctual life and screening out the male, on whom the psychoanalytic model of those vicissitudes was based. Yet chronology by itself failed to provide a plot. The real story lay not in evolution but in a search for equilibrium between competing dualisms. Some were staples of psychoanalytic parlance: passive-active, feminine-masculine, heterosexual-homosexual; a couple ranked as recruits from other discourses: nature-culture, species-individual; and two stood out and summed up Deutsch's own contribution: masochism-narcissism, motherliness-eroticism.

Her masochism-narcissism pair took off from Freud's interpretation of beating fantasies as signifying being castrated, copulated with, or giving birth. As early as 1930, in a paper entitled "The Significance of Masochism in the Mental Life of Women," she had argued that the female child began to be a woman when she turned toward masochism: at one and the same time she conceived "the desire to be castrated and raped" and also "the fantasy of receiving a child from her father."[75] Deutsch's 1944 account fleshed out the father's role.

> He appears, without being conscious of it, as a seducer, with whose help the girl's aggressive instinctual components are transformed into masochistic ones. The

masochistic ingredient in the relation to the father appears in the active games with him, which later assume an increasingly erotic character. It is enough to observe the little girl's fearful jubilation when the father performs acrobatic tricks with her that are often painful, when he throws her up in the air, or lets her ride "piggy back" on his shoulders.

That transformation, Deutsch claimed, proved crucial: after all, the reproductive function, "from beginning to . . . end," even where it most served "the purposes of pleasure," required "toleration of considerable pain," and masochism prompted a ready consent to it. But a woman could have too much of a good thing: "an excess of masochism" provoked "a defense," and fleeing from its dangers, a woman turned away "from her tasks, from her femininity."[76] In short, a woman needed to rule her masochism rather than be ruled by it.

Here narcissism came to the rescue. Psychoanalysts, Deutsch wrote, explained the fact—and she assumed it was a fact—that woman's narcissism was "stronger than man's on the basis of her mortification over her organic genital inferiority," which she expressed "by constantly demanding compensations for her offended self-love." This explanation, Deutsch maintained, was not only incomplete; it missed the essential point: narcissism figured as a protective reaction, and it came into play in all situations "marked by intensified masochistic tendencies." Sex produced such a situation. No wonder, then, that the woman's endangered ego strengthened "its inner security by intensifying its self-love." Again, a woman could have too much of a good thing. Excessive self-love might result in an abnormal sensitivity to pain, and along with it, "all sorts of disturbances of the feminine functions." The "destiny of woman as the servant of reproduction," Deutsch solemnly announced, depended on the "harmonious cooperation of masochism and narcissism."[77]

So too with motherliness and eroticism. In 1933, in an essay entitled "Motherhood and Sexuality," Deutsch had fastened on a split between the two. In her later work she took care to suggest that such a split did not necessarily entail conflict:

Sexuality and motherliness are sometimes in close harmony, yet at other times they appear completely separate. . . . In many cases the presence of one permits us to infer the presence of the other, and variations in one produce variations in the other. There are women who are both unerotic and unmotherly, and others who combine extraordinary erotic intensity with the warmest motherliness. . . .

The co-existence of such opposing tendencies is normal, and only a marked preponderance of the one or the other leads to complications and neurotic difficulties.[78]

With both pairs, the achievement of balance and the avoidance of pathological conflict depended on the woman's relationship with her own mother. All women who qualified as feminine, Deutsch argued, had experienced the blessing of a positive mother-daughter relationship. That relationship came in a number of sizes and shapes: "the original tender, loving and . . . passive dependence on the mother" might "weather all the stormy periods of hatred that must be expected in the development of every girl"; or the positive tie might be re-established after successfully overcoming a phase of "aggressive animosity."[79] Here Deutsch trumpeted a theme she had not sounded in her *Psychoanalysis of the Sexual Functions of Women*.

Here she also put the finishing touches on her portrait of a lady. The lady was not born feminine; she did not have femininity thrust upon her; she achieved it. From relatively uniform organic factors, from psychological factors that varied "with the individual, according to . . . inner processes" and environmental influences, from their combined effect, the feminine core, understood as psychological, gradually formed.

> Additional elements come to join it, some of which may figure in the constant psychic inventory of the feminine personality. . . . Sometimes a subsidiary element may succeed in occupying the central position and endow the woman with a less feminine character that is not . . . necessarily abnormal or pathologic. . . . [But] if the mental ingredients outside femininity are not in a harmonious relation with the feminine core, insoluable conflicts arise, these being manifested in neurotic phenomena.[80]

With the notion of such a core, Deutsch stood ready to forgo the accolade of masculinity that Freud had bestowed on his female disciples.

Chapter 2 Epigenesis: Erik H. Erikson and Carol Gilligan

"Epigenesis"—the sequential differentiation, during embryological development, of organs from simpler rudiments—has an eighteenth-century pedigree. In biology textbooks one finds mention of a battle waged more than two hundred years ago between preformationists and epigeneticists. The former, the first in the field, "held that the embryo was preformed in the germ . . . as a tiny . . . individual with all its organs and parts already present, and that development was merely the enlarging and unfolding of this minute bud into the newborn baby." None of this, they acknowledged, was visible with the microscopes then available. The opposing camp, the epigeneticists, felt constrained by the facts as they observed them, "facts which showed how the organs of the embryo . . . developed from undifferentiated material, [and] that each stage of the development process prepared the essential way for the following stage."[1] It was this textbook account that Erik H. Erikson drew on when, in *Childhood and Society,* he announced that "the Freudian laws of psychosexual growth," his chosen starting point, could "best be understood through an analogy . . . with *epigenetic* development."[2]

Erikson had first referred to epigenesis in print in 1940. Quoting liberally from Charles R. Stockard's *The Physical Basis of Personality*, he wrote that each organ had its time as well as its place of origin. Its further development was similarly tied to a schedule—if an interruption occurred, it might be lamed or stunted, and in turn "the whole hierarchy of organs" might be endangered.[3] The psyche followed suit. The relation between fetal and psychic development, Erikson implied, was one of correspondence—homology—rather than similarity—analogy—despite the fact that "analogy" was the word he used. How seriously did Erikson take and intend his readers to take his embryological borrowing? Very seriously indeed.

After the publication of *Childhood and Society* in 1950, epigenesis flourished; it quickly established itself in its new, American psychoanalytic environment. It had much to feed on: the readiness of American psychoanalysts to speak of psychopathology in developmental terms—in terms not only of defects and deficits but also of stresses and strains, of conflicts at particular junctures in what was now habitually referred to as the life cycle; the enthusiasm of American psychoanalysts for developmental research, notably child observation, an enthusiasm mingled with hope that such research might provide a much-needed boost to the scientific status of their postulates. In this fashion, epigenesis became a favored psychoanalytic concept.

As for his old, German intellectual—and emotional—environment, Erikson said little. (And not always the same thing: between the two printed versions of his autobiography, he made subtle alterations.)[4] He was fuzzy about his origins[5]—particularly about his Jewish origins.[6] He wrote of not having known his father and of having been raised by his mother and stepfather, the pediatrician Dr. Theodor Homburger, of Karlsruhe in Baden. He described his father simply as a "Dane," his mother as "a native of Copenhagen, Denmark"—that is, in terms of nationality and geography; his stepfather he described as coming from "an intensely Jewish small bourgeoisie [sic] family"—that is, in terms of religion and class. (His mother's maiden name, Abrahamsen, points to a Jewish origin.) He claimed that his childhood identification by others as Jewish had been ambiguous. To his schoolmates he was a Jew; yet because he was "blond and blue-eyed, and grew flagrantly tall," he was nicknamed "'goy'" in his "stepfather's temple."[7] His German-Jewish stepfather gave him his name, Homburger, and he kept it "out of gratitude . . . but also to avoid the semblance of evasion"[8]—as a middle name. In later years he reduced that acknowledgment to the mere initial H. "Erikson" first appeared as the author of an article published in 1939. In fabricating this name, he seemed to suggest that he, Erik, was the son of Erik, that he was his own father, that he was self-created.

About his formal education in Karlsruhe, which did not go beyond "a humanistic gymnasium," Erikson said only that thanks to it he had "acquired classical *Bildung* and a sense for languages."[9] (*Bildung*—cultivation—commonly associated with university study, had a peculiar resonance in German intellectual life: it signified more than "the transmitting of information and the development of analytical capabilities"; it betokened gaining wisdom and virtue through contemplation of properly selected materials. And if cultivation had "a total effect upon the whole personality, the cultivated man almost had to be conceived as a unique work of art.")[10] The seven years following Erikson's abbreviated education could retrospectively be described as a "moratorium." They were years of wandering, as an artist, in the Black Forest, the Alps, and northern Italy. He subsequently cherished the artist in himself, which gave him the possibility of repaying his "debt to the Freuds" in his own "currency."[11]

Erikson arrived in Vienna in 1927 at the age of twenty-five and remained there until 1933. Thanks to the intercession of his boyhood friend Peter Blos, he was offered a teaching position at a private school recently established for the children of American and English analysands. Through Dorothy Burlingham, its organizer, he came to know her great friend Anna Freud. It was Anna who "judged" him "a desirable candidate for psychoanalytic training," particularly for training in child analysis.[12] And it was she who became his analyst. He said practically nothing about her. About her father he merely commented that his audience could "appreciate the complex feelings aroused by the fact" that his "psychoanalyst was the daughter of the then already mythical founder, who was apt to appear in the door of their common waiting room in order to invite his analysand into his study."[13] By his own admission, Erikson had been searching for a "mythical father." By his own admission, his had been an "ambivalent identification" with his stepfather. In its positive guise, the stepson role allowed him to "take for granted" his "truly astounding adoption by the Freudian circle." In its negative guise, this role might lead him to "use his talents to avoid belonging anywhere quite irreversibly; [and] working between the established fields" could mean shirking the discipline necessary for any one of them.[14] The search for the mythical father lapsed; the ambivalence lingered.

Erikson's completion of his psychoanalytic training coincided with his departure from Vienna, accompanied by his wife, Joan, whom he had married in 1930, and their two small sons. As a student, he wrote, he "could not help sensing . . . a growing conservatism and especially a subtle yet pervasive interdiction" of any idea that echoed "the deviations perpetrated by those earliest and most brilliant of Freud's co-workers . . . who had separated from the movement" before the First World War. After immersion in such a "didactic milieu," Erikson found "invigorating" the thought of "moving on and working independently."[15] But he had no intention of separating from the movement.

When Erikson arrived in the United States at the age of thirty-one, after a brief and unsuccessful attempt to establish himself in Denmark, he had his entire mature career ahead of him. Initially at Harvard and Yale in the 1930s, he slipped into a niche in a medical setting, but in close contact with sociologists and anthropologists as well as psychiatrists. During the next thirty years, at Berkeley in the 1940s, at Austen Riggs in the 1950s, and at Harvard again in the 1960s, he maintained his link to social scientists. More than that, he found himself wandering into their domains, "working between . . . established fields." (Though he never became ensconced in a local psychoanalytic institute nor devoted himself exclusively to clinical practice—and by the 1960s he had ceased seeing patients—he remained connected to the American psychoanalytic establishment and publicly identified as a psychoanalyst.) When he summed up the project he had devised for himself—one that allowed him to repay his debt to Freud and to establish credit of his own—he claimed the psychosocial as his domain, with *Childhood and Society* as his first major venture into it.

This book, Erikson noted in his foreword to the second edition, "originally written to supplement the psychiatric education of American physicians, psychologists and social workers," had found its way "into colleges and into the graduate schools of a variety of fields"[16]—and into the hands of Carol Gilligan. A Swarthmore College graduate, class of 1958, Gilligan was already at Harvard studying psychology when Erikson arrived in the fall of 1960 as the newly named Professor of Human Development. ("It was understood from the start that he would not be expected to behave like an ordinary member of the faculty. His teaching load was light: from the time of his appointment to his retirement ten years later, he gave only two regular courses, a lecture course for undergraduates on 'The Human Life Cycle' and a seminar for advanced students on the writing of psychoanalytic biography.")[17] In her capacity as his teaching assistant, Gilligan figured in the circle that gathered around Erikson—now very much a celebrity.[18] She herself acknowledged him as an intellectual progenitor in the article that formed the basis of her own classic, *In a Different Voice.*[19]

And it was her conceptual, not her personal, links that led to the inclusion of Gilligan in the present study. Erikson's postulates functioned as her point of departure. He had charted, quite literally by drawing a chart, epigenetic stages in a manner that Gilligan considered inadequate—inadequate in terms of his own work on women as well as hers. Erikson, she wrote, was unable to incorporate his insights about women "into the mainstream of his . . . theory."[20] At the same time, she implied, his insights were headed in the right direction—that is, the direction in which she herself was going. One might well read Gilligan as amplifying the Eriksonian chart. She did not fashion an evolutionary narrative of her own.

ANOTHER BODY

On the night of July 23–24, 1895, Freud dreamt his celebrated dream of his patient Irma.

> *A large hall—numerous guests, whom we* [Freud and his wife?] *were receiving.—Among them was Irma. I at once took her on one side, as though to answer her letter and to reproach her for not having accepted my "solution" yet. I said to her: "If you still get pains, it's really only your fault." She replied: "If you only knew what pains I've got now in my throat and stomach and abdomen—it's choking me"—I was alarmed and looked at her. She looked pale and puffy. I thought to myself that after all I must be missing some organic trouble. I took her to the window and looked down her throat, and she showed signs of recalcitrance, like women with artificial dentures. I thought to myself that there was really no need for her to do that.—She then opened her mouth properly and on the right I found a big white patch; at another place I saw extensive whitish grey scabs upon some remarkable curly structures which were evidently modelled on the turbinal bones of the nose.—I at once called Dr. M., and he repeated the examination and confirmed it. . . . Dr. M. looked quite different from usual; he was very pale, he walked with a limp and his chin was clean-shaven. . . . My friend Otto was now standing beside her as well, and my friend Leopold was percussing her through her bodice and saying: "She has a dull area low down on the left." He also indicated that a portion of the skin on the left shoulder was infiltrated. (I noticed this, just as he did, in spite of her dress.) . . . M. said: "There's no doubt it's an infection, but no matter; dysentery will supervene and the toxin will be eliminated." . . . We were directly aware, too, of the origin of the infection. Not long before, when she was feeling unwell, my friend Otto had given her an injection of a preparation of*

propyl, propyls . . . propionic acid . . . trimethylamin (and I saw before me the formula for this printed in heavy type). . . . Injections of that sort ought not to be made so thoughtlessly. . . . And probably the syringe had not been clean.

"The dream," Freud wrote, acquitted him "of the responsibility for Irma's condition by showing that it was due to other factors—it produced a wholes series of reasons. . . . The . . . plea—for the dream was nothing else—reminded one vividly of the defence put forward by the man who was charged by one of his neighbors with having given him back a borrowed kettle in damaged condition. The defendant asserted first, that he had given it back undamaged; secondly, that the kettle had a hole in it when he borrowed it; and thirdly, that he had never borrowed a kettle from his neighbor at all. So much the better: if only a single one of these three lines of defence were to be accepted as valid, the man would have to be acquitted."[21]

In 1949 Erikson gave two lectures on the Irma dream at the San Francisco Psychoanalytic Institute, and five years later they appeared, with revisions, in print—much to the annoyance of Anna Freud.[22] He paid particular attention to what he called the "interpersonal configurations in the dream population." The dreamer, he noted, was first "*part of a twosome,* his wife and himself, or maybe a family group, vis-à-vis a number of guests." That twosome, or family group, vanished the moment Irma arrived on the scene. The dreamer was "suddenly *alone* with his worries, vis-à-vis a complaining patient." He became "active in a breathless way": he looked at the patient, he looked into her throat. (Another dreamer, Erikson commented, "might have awakened in terror at what he saw in the gaping cavity.") Something was wrong; the dreamer called Dr. M. urgently. He thus established "a *new twosome*," which was "immediately expanded to include a professional group of younger colleagues, Dr. Otto and Dr. Leopold." They now formed "a small community," and they were "directly aware" of the infection's origin. What to make of this dream population? Was the "cast of puppets on the dreamer's stage . . . a 'projection' of different identity fragments of the dreamer himself, of different roles played by him at different times or in different situations?"[23] Erikson answered in the affirmative.

One identity fragment or role, he claimed, stood at the dream's nodal point. When the dreamer commented that he felt "the infiltrated portion of skin on the [patient's] left shoulder," he meant to convey that he could "*feel this on his own body.*"[24] As the examination was proceeding, the dreamer suddenly felt "as if he were the sufferer and examined, i. e., he, the doctor and man," fused with "the image of the *patient* and *woman.*"

> The dreamer gives in to a *diffusion of roles*. . . . He . . . forfeits his right to vigorous *male initiative* and guiltily surrenders to the inverted solution of the oedipal conflict, for a fleeting moment even becoming the feminine object for the superior males' inspection and percussion.

Erikson continued:

> To overcome mankind's resistance [to his discoveries] the dreamer had to learn to become his own patient and subject of investigation; to deliver free associations to himself. . . . That this, in view of the strong maleness of scientific approach cultivated by the bearded savants of his day . . . , constituted . . . [a] division within the observer's self, a division of vague "feminine yielding" and persistent masculine precision: this, I feel, is one of the central meanings of the Irma Dream.[25]

From his interpretation Erikson drew a lesson:

> This "feminine" aspect of creation causes tumultuous confusion not only because of man's intrinsic abhorrence of femininity but because of the conflict (in really gifted individuals) of this feminine fantasy with an equally strong "masculine" endowment. . . . All in all the creative individual's typical cycle of moods and attitudes which overlaps with neurotic mood swings (without ever coinciding with them completely) probably permits him, at the height of consummation . . . to represent . . . his father's potency [and] his mother's fertility.[26]

About whom was Erikson speaking? About Freud? Or about himself? Here he constructed Erikson the narrator by identifying with his "Freud." Here he displayed a striking feature of the persona he was to recreate time and time again: a sensibility that encompassed masculine and feminine alike.

• • • • •

In chapter 2 of *Childhood and Society*, after having introduced his readers to epigenesis, Erikson set out to review "the whole field of what Freud called pregenital stages and erotogenic zones in childhood" and to reproduce a chart that he had first presented in a 1937 paper entitled "Configurations in Play—Clinical Notes."[27] He warned his readers that the next section would be the most difficult—for them and for himself. (Why for himself?)

Where did the difficulty lie? Where was Erikson differing from or supplanting Freud's (and Abraham's) delineation of pregenital organizations of the libido?

The crucial item was the notion of organ mode. Erikson found it hard to put it into words. In its 1937 appearance—and again in *Childhood and Society*—he resorted to circles and arrows. These were meant to represent "the dynamic principle of the body aperture" in which the impulses were "first centered."[28] For example: ↻ represented the dynamic principle of incorporation by means of the impulse of sucking; ↺ represented the same principle, but now the impulse was one of biting. Employing differently configured circles and arrows, plus short lines and broken arcs, Erikson depicted retention, elimination, and intrusion. A mode, Erikson elaborated, could show up in a wide variety of behaviors. For example: "the spilling of a bottle's contents, . . . throwing objects out of a window, or pushing a person out of one's physical space," in all these acts one could "recognize the mode of elimination,"[29] or, as he phrased it in *Childhood and Society,* of "letting go."[30]

According to Erikson's understanding of epigenesis, organ modes might manifest themselves across a broad range, but they were obliged to wait their turn. "Normal sequence" and "proper rate," these had become his bywords, and he pictured them on his chart by a diagonal upward and to the right. "Progress," he wrote, meant that "the child's libido" moved on "in order to endow with power a second organ mode." And if progress were "impeded, accelerated, or arrested," these deviations could be charted either horizontally or vertically. In this fashion Erikson translated into his own pictorial mode Freud's and Abraham's oral and anal stages. He did the same with the phallic stage, but in so doing he abandoned his single diagonal. The paths of boys and girls diverged:

> Girls have a fateful experience at this stage in that they must comprehend the finality of the fact that although their locomotor, mental, and social intrusiveness is equally increased and as adequate as that of the boys, they lack one item: the penis. While the boy has this visible, erectable, and comprehensible organ to attach dreams of adult bigness to, the girl's clitoris cannot sustain dreams of sexual equality. And she does not yet have breasts as analogously tangible tokens of her future.[31]

This sounded like psychoanalytic orthodoxy. In fact, epigenesis challenged the accepted wisdom—a fact that Erikson seemed reluctant to trumpet. In a footnote he remarked that although his "method of developing the chart was *additive,* as if at each stage something entirely new was emerging," the whole chart could be considered as representing "a *successive differentiation* of parts all of which exist in some form from beginning to end. . . . In this sense the modes added last (male and female generative)" could be "assumed to have been a central, if rudimentary, factor throughout earlier development."[32] For Erikson, in contrast to Freud and Deutsch, a little girl did not start out as a little man.

• • • • •

Our patient is Mary. She is three years old. She is a somewhat pale brunette, but looks (and is) intelligent, pretty, and quite feminine. When disturbed, however, she is said to be stubborn, babyish, and shut-in. Recently she has enriched her inventory of expression by nightmares and by violent anxiety attacks in the play group which she has . . . joined. All that the play group teachers can say is that Mary has a queer way of lifting things and has a rigid posture: and that her tension seems to increase with the routines of resting and going to the toilet. With this information at hand we invite Mary into our office.[33]

With these words Erikson asked the readers of *Childhood and Society* to join him watch his small patient play. They had already met her in his 1940 paper "Studies in the Interpretation of Play: Clinical Observation of Play Disruption in Young Children." In that text (though not in *Childhood and Society*) he vouchsafed that Mary "revealed something of the conflict of the girl who does not know whether she wants to be a boy or a boy's girl"—and she did so, he added, "with more grace and humor than we would expect from the chronic victims of this conflict."[34]

Mary showed up in Erikson's office holding on to her mother. She let go to shake his hand, gave him a brief smile, then immediately turned to her mother, put her arms around her, hid her face in her mother's skirt, and repeated in "a babyish voice, 'Mommy, mommy, mommy.'" Erikson observed; mother participated. Pointing to a doll, Mary asked her mother "several times, 'What that, what that?'" Mother explained, and again Mary repeated in a babyish voice, "'Dolly, dolly, dolly'"—and insisted that mother take off the doll's shoes. Erikson observed mother playing with Mary, and mother became embarrassed. She asked, Was it not time for her to wait outside? and with Erikson's approval, she left the room. Mary suddenly found herself "without anybody to lean on."[35]

She found herself left holding the doll:

> Mary grasps it firmly around its legs. Suddenly she smiles mischievously, her face flushes, and she begins to touch various things in the room with the doll's head. When a toy falls from the shelf, she laughs and begins to push smaller toys, always with the doll's head, in such a way that they fall too. Her excitement increases, manifested by chuckling and laughter. With special glee she pushes (with the doll's head) a toy train which is on the floor in the middle of the room. As one car overturns, she overturns them all. But then she suddenly stops and becomes very pale.
>
> She leans her back against the sofa, holds the doll over her genital region and drops it to the floor. She picks it up again, holds it over the same region, and drops it again. While repeating this from ten to fifteen times, she begins first to whine, then to cry, finally to yell, "Mommy, mommy, mommy."[36]

How did Erikson interpret Mary's performance? He focused on what he called its autocosmic aspect—that is, how "an isolated object" was "used as a means to extend or intensify the mode of expression of an organ or an organ-system."[37] Or, in this instance, the expression of a missing organ. The doll as an extension of an aggressive hand and then "as something lost in the lower abdominal region under circumstances of extreme anxiety"[38] suggested to Erikson that Mary was "dramatizing" the fact that she had no penis.[39] From mother's account Erikson inferred that a play group had given Mary "her first opportunity to go to the toilet in the presence of boys and to see boys' genitals"—thereby precipitating "the conflict of the girl who does not know whether she wants to be a boy or a boy's girl."[40]

It turned out that a missing penis was not all. After the first session mother told Erikson a fact she had forgotten to mention previously: Mary was born with a sixth finger that had been removed when the child was approximately six months old. Just prior to her anxiety attacks, she had been insistently asking "about the *scar* on her hand and had received the answer that it was 'just a mosquito bite.'" (Whether Mary was fooled her mother did not know. She did know that at an earlier age her daughter "could easily have been present when her operation was discussed.") Just prior to those attacks she had been "equally insistent in her *sexual curiosity*," which, Erikson concluded, pointed to the likelihood that Mary was associating, by way of "'scar,'" the "actually lost finger" with the "mythical lost penis."[41] The information about the sixth finger thus confirmed him in his view that play was the royal road, not to the unconscious, but to organ mode.[42]

That happened to be the case when the play fit the category, not only of autocosmic, but also of microcosmic—i.e., "*an arrangement of small objects*" such that their configuration signified "*conflicting forces in the child's life*."[43] That happened when Mary showed up a second time in Erikson's office—after which he made a series of recommendations to her parents, which they scrupulously carried out, and which led to greater physical and social ease on her part:

> Mary goes to the corner where the blocks are on the floor. She selects two blocks and arranges them in such a way that she can stand on them each time she comes to the corner to pick up more blocks. . . . She now collects a pile of blocks in the middle of the room, moving to the corner and back without hesitation. Then she kneels on the floor and builds a small house for a toy cow. For about a quarter of an hour she is completely absorbed in the task of arranging the house so that it is strictly rectangular and at the same time fits tightly about a toy cow. She then adds five blocks to one long side of the house and experiments with a sixth block until its position satisfies her.[44]

In his comments on this second performance, Erikson noted how Mary's play began with "an autocosmic extension—namely creating a base for the feet." The fact that she had to fabricate "a foot extension (protection? overcompensation?) for herself before picking up blocks" reminded him, and he assumed reminded his readers as well, that during the previous session she had had to fashion a hand extension out of a doll before "she pushed the objects in the room." Both these acts, he claimed, pointed to "the association: scar, operation." So too did Mary's microcosmic play: "the five wings, to which (after some doubt as to where to put it)" she added a sixth, again recalled "the amputation of her sixth finger."[45]

That was not all the microcosmic play suggested. The "close-fitting stable," which looked to Erikson like a hand with a sixth finger, expressed, he claimed, "the 'inclusive' mode, a female-protective configuration, corresponding to the baskets and boxes and cradles arranged by little and big girls to give comfort to small things." Here he saw "two restorations in one: the configuration puts the finger back on the hand and the happily feminine pattern belies" the loss of the mythical penis.[46]

> This time, although again beginning with the representation of the extension of an extremity, Mary's play does not lead into an aggressive outbreak (and the subsequent representation of a catastrophe). . . . There is a pervading femininity about today's behavior which serves to underscore in retrospect and by

contrast the danger dramatized during the first contact, namely the loss from the genital region of an object used for aggressive pushing.[47]

Had Mary passed from wanting to be a boy to wanting to be a boy's girl—or father's girl? The next play sequence suggested as much:

> Suddenly Mary looks teasingly at *Ps* [Erikson himself], laughs, takes *M's* [mother's] hand and pulls her out of the room, saying, "Mommy, come out."
>
> *Ps* waits for a while then looks out into the waiting room. He is greeted with a loud and triumphant "Thtay in there!" *Ps* withdraws, whereupon Mary closes the door with a bang. Two further attempts on the part of *Ps* to leave the room are greeted in the same way.
>
> (After a while, *Ps* opens the door slightly, quickly pushes the toy cow into the other room, makes it squeak and withdraws it again. Mary is beside herself with pleasure and insists that the game be repeated again and again until, finally, it is time for her to go home.
>
> When she leaves she looks at *Ps* directly, shakes hands in a natural way, and promises to "come back").[48]

Play had moved, in Erikson's terms, from the microcosmic to the macrocosmic—that is, to the "*rearrangements of the child's relationship to the real persons or the life-sized objects present in the therapeutic situation.*"[49] What had Mary been rearranging? Erikson explained:

> The words which Mary uses when initiating the game somehow resemble the words which the mother told me the father had used when locking the child out of the bathroom during . . . days of irritation. "Stay out of here," had been the father's angry words. "Thtay in there" is probably linked with it, although in addition to the transference to me a double reversal had taken place: from the passive to the active (it is she who gives orders), and in regard to the vector (she "encloses" instead of being excluded). . . . Since it can be expected that she would transfer to me (the man with the toys) a conflict which disturbed her usually playful relationship to her father, it seems possible that in this game she is repeating with active mastery ("You thtay in there") the situation of exclusion of which she has been a passive victim at home ("Stay out of here"). (This possibility came to me only after I had reacted to her play provocation, which, of course, I was prepared to do as soon as she would have chosen the moment and the theme. By my play acts I unconsciously took the role of the "good father" in a specific, symbolic way.)[50]

"To some," Erikson wrote in *Childhood and Society*, this might "seem like a lot of complicated and devious reasoning for such a little girl."[51] He cautioned his readers not to underestimate her. To some, particularly to those versed in psychoanalytic theory, the sequence of Mary's play might seem like a condensation of the "progress" Freud and Deutsch considered standard precisely for a little girl of this age: a "progress" from penis envy to wish for a child to father as the essential object for baby-making. (Erikson had interpreted Mary's dropping the doll from her genital region as the loss of the mythical penis and as a childbirth as well.) But Freud and Deutsch would have been unprepared to interpret the "close-fitting stable" as evidence of an "inclusive" mode already at work. According to both of them, the little girl did not move from clitoris to vagina: the vagina remained undiscovered.

• • • • •

In chapter 2 of *Childhood and Society*, in its last section, Erikson introduced his readers to the "subjects of a developmental study made at the University of California," to the ten, eleven, and twelve year olds who had been interviewed and observed regularly for a decade.[52] The study, conducted under the auspices of the Institute of Child Welfare, had been designed "to continue for years, indeed for a generation, so that discrete observations and measurements made at this or that time in the life of one or another boy or girl could be put into some large context of child development."[53] In 1940 Erikson, having joined the project the previous year, devised an experimental play situation and used it in examining approximately 150 children, roughly half girls and half boys. (Most children made three contributions to the total number of 468, of which 232 were from girls and 236 from boys.) Here is Erikson's description of the play situation, taken from his more extended account in "Sex Differences in the Play Configurations of American Preadolescents":

> On each occasion the child was individually called into a room where he found a selection of toys such as was then available in department stores (122 blocks, 38 pieces of toy furniture, 14 small dolls, 9 toy cars, 11 toy animals). . . . There was no attempt to make a careful selection of toys on the basis of size, color, material, etc. . . . Our family dolls were of rubber, which permitted their being bent into almost any shape; they were neatly dressed with all the loving care which German craftsmen lavish on playthings. A policeman and aviator, however, were of unbending metal and were somewhat smaller than the doll family. There were toy cars, some of them smaller than the policeman, some bigger; but there were no airplanes to go with the aviator.

The toys were laid out in an ordered series of open cardboard boxes, each containing a class of toys, such as people, animals, and cars. These boxes were presented on a shelf. The blocks were on a second shelf in two piles, one containing a set of large blocks, one a set of small ones. Next to the shelves the stage for the actual construction was set: a square table with a square background of the same size.

The following instructions were given: I am interested in moving pictures. I would like to know what kind of moving pictures children would make if they had a chance to make pictures. Of course, I could not provide you with a real studio and real actors and actresses; you will have to use these toys instead. Choose any of the things you see here and construct on this table an *exciting* scene out of an *imaginary* moving picture. Take as much time as you want, and tell me afterward what the scene is about.[54]

With what expectations did Erikson sit at his desk, "presumably busy with some writing," but actually observing "the child's attack on the problem" and sketching "transitory stages in his play construction"?[55] He claimed, though he imagined his audience as skeptical of his claim, that he tried not to anticipate anything in particular, and was, "in fact, determined to enjoy the freshness of the experience of working with so many children, and healthy ones. To be ready to be surprised," he commented, belonged to "the discipline of a clinician; for without it clinical 'findings' would soon lose the instructive quality of new (or truly confirming) finds." About what, then, did he receive instruction and in turn wish to instruct? Once again, organ modes was the answer, or, as he put it, "the power of organ modes in spatial modalities."[56]

Blocks, he claimed, were ideally suited to serve as teachers. Blocks, he claimed, were nothing but blocks. They provided a "wordless medium quite easily counted, measured, and compared in regard to spatial arrangement"; they were so "impersonally geometric as to be least compromised by cultural connotations and individual meanings." What impressed Erikson was the difference between boys and girls "in the *number* of blocks used as well as in the *configurations* constructed."[57] (He gave photographs of the play scenes to two outside observers to see whether they would agree on the presence of particular arrangements. They did. It was then possible to determine how often such arrangements were found in the constructions of boys and in those of girls.) When Erikson spoke of an item built by one sex or the other, he meant (so he took care to inform his readers) that it had appeared more than two thirds of the time in the constructions of the sex specified children and that in the remaining one third special conditions prevailed that could often "be shown to 'prove the rule.'"[58] Here individual meanings began to intrude and to be interpreted. Here a block turned out to be something more than a block.

High structures, Erikson wrote, were prevalent among boys; so too were ruins or fallen-down structures—indeed they were found exclusively in the male sample:

> In connection with the very highest towers, something in the nature of a downward trend appears regularly, but in such a diverse form that only individual examples can illustrate what is meant: one boy, after much indecision, took his extraordinarily high tower down in order to build a final configuration of a simple and low character; another balanced his tower very precariously and pointed out that the immediate danger of collapse was in itself the exciting factor in his story, in fact, *was* his story. In two cases extremely high and well-built façades with towers were incongruously combined with low irregular inclosures. One boy who built an especially high tower put a prone boy doll at the foot of it and explained that this boy had fallen down from its height; another boy left the boy doll sitting high on one of several elaborate towers but said that the boy had had a mental breakdown and that the tower was an insane asylum. The very highest tower was built by the very smallest boy; and, to climax lowness, a colored boy built his structure *under* the table. In these and similar ways, variations of a theme made it clear that the *variable high-low* is a *masculine variable.* To this generality, we would add the clinical judgment that, in preadolescent boys, extreme height (in its regular combination with an element of breakdown or fall) reflects a trend toward emotional overcompensation or a doubt in, or a fear for, one's masculinity, while varieties of "lowness" express passivity and depression.[59]

Not all towers were built by boys. Occasionally girls built them, but when they did so they seemed "unable to make them stand freely in space." Their towers leaned against or stayed close to the background. "The highest tower built by any girl was not on the table at all but on a shelf in a niche in the wall beside and behind the table." To these remarks Erikson again appended a clinical judgment: in preadolescent girls, he wrote, the presence of such towers pointed to "the masculine overcompensation of an ambivalent dependency on the mother."[60] (*Sotto voce* he thus gave a new twist to the notion of a masculinity complex in women: mother fixation—at least in preadolescent girls—figured as crucial.)

Domestic interiors were built by a majority of girls, in many instances interiors of an "expressly peaceful" character:

> Where it was a home rather than a school, somebody, usually a little girl, plays the piano: a remarkably tame "exciting movie scene" for representative preadolescent girls. In a number of cases, however, a disturbance occurs. An intruding pig throws the family in an uproar and forces the girl to hide behind the piano; the father may, to the family's astonishment, be coming home riding on a lion; a teacher has jumped on a desk because a tiger has entered the room. The intruding element is always a man, a boy, or an animal. If it is a dog, it is always expressly a boy's dog. A family consisting exclusively of women and girls or with a majority of women and girls is disturbed and endangered. Strangely enough, however, this idea of an intruding creature does not lead to the defensive erection of walls or to the closing of doors. Rather, the majority of these intrusions have an element of humor and of pleasurable excitement and occur in connection with open interiors consisting of a circular arrangement of furniture.

In Erikson's calculations, domestic interiors counted as inclosures, and inclosures themselves ranked as the most frequent item among the configurations built by girls. Often, he wrote, these inclosures had a "richly ornamented gate"; at other times, openness was counteracted "by a blocking of the entrance or a thickening of the walls." That girls in significantly larger number than boys built open interiors and simple inclosures, that they also emphasized "intrusion into the interiors, . . . elaboration of doorways, . . . and the blocking off of such doorways," seemed to him "to mark *open and closed* as a feminine variable." And once again, Erikson added a clinical judgment: "high and thick walls reflect either acute anxiety over the feminine role or . . . acute oversensitiveness and self-centeredness."[61]

Not all "intrusive" configurations were built by girls. Three were constructed by boys. "Two were built by the same boy in two successive years. Each time a single male figure, surrounded by a circle of furniture, was intruded upon by wild animals." The boy in question—obese and of "markedly feminine build"—was under treatment for a thyroid problem. "Shortly after this treatment had taken effect, the boy became markedly masculine. In his third construction he built one of the highest and slenderest of all towers." Only one other boy portrayed a number of animals intruding into an open interior containing a family—and then only in a preliminary construction. "When already at the door, he suddenly turned back, rearranged the animals along a tangent which led them close by but away from the family circle."[62] These three constructions stood in Erikson's mind as exceptions that proved the rule.

What rule was in the course of being proved?

> Our group of children, developmentally speaking, stand at the *beginning of sexual maturation.* It is clear that the spatial tendencies governing these constructions closely parallel the morphology of the sex organs: in the male, *external* organs, *erectible* and *intrusive* in character, serving highly *mobile* sperm cells; *internal* organs in the female, with vestibular *access,* leading to *statically expectant* ova. . . . [O]ur data suggest that the *two sexes may live, as it were, in time-spaces of a different quality.*[63]

"The evidence of organ-modes in these constructions," Erikson concluded, served as "a reminder of the fact that experience is anchored in the ground plan of the body."[64] In this fashion he arrived at a new version of anatomy as destiny.

• • • • •

In 1964 Erikson published "Inner and Outer Space: Reflections on Womanhood." (Four years later it appeared in revised form in his *Identity: Youth and Crisis.*) First presented at an interdisciplinary conference sponsored by the American Academy of Arts and Sciences, his paper figured as the lead article in a *Daedalus* volume entitled "The Woman in America." Erikson was a frequent participant in Academy conferences and a frequent contributor to its journal, *Daedalus.* Under this establishmentarian aegis, he reached a highly prestigious and overwhelmingly male audience.

In addressing the problem of "woman's nature or nurture," Erikson began by obliquely responding to a question that he had not been asked: What were his credentials for speaking, as the volume's editor put it, on "woman's specific creativity"?[65] Indirectly he answered that no one else was up to the assignment. Women had been found wanting. The vast majority, he wrote, seemed unable "to say clearly what they feel most deeply, and to find the right words for what to them is most acute and actual, without saying too much or too little, and without saying it with defiance or apology." Men had scarcely even tried. Among them, he commented, there existed "an honest sense of wishing to save at whatever cost a sexual polarity, a vital tension and an essential difference which they fear may be lost in too much sameness, equality, and equivalence, or at any rate in too much self-conscious talk. . . . Where men desire," he continued, "they want to awake desire, not empathize or ask for empathy." He, Erikson implied, was different. In words that echoed what he had earlier written of Freud, he pointed to his own special qualifications:

> Now . . . much of the basic schema suggested here as female also exists in some form in all men and decisively so in men of special giftedness—or weakness. The inner life which characterizes some artistic and creative men certainly also compensates for their being biologically men. . . . They are prone to cyclic swings of mood while they carry conceived ideas to fruition and toward the act of disciplined creation.[66]

What was the "schema" that Erikson attributed to women? He started off with the standard psychoanalytic line: children of both sexes sooner or later knew, in their childish fashion, "the penis to be missing in one sex, leaving in its place a woundlike aperture." He quickly shifted from what was absent to what was present: "the female child under all but extreme urban conditions," he wrote, was apt "to observe evidence in older girls and women and in female animals of the fact that an inner-bodily space" existed. (Did boys not make similar observations?) These observations, he claimed, "are given form by kinesthetic experience and by . . . memories which 'make sense'; in this total actuality the existence of a *productive inner-bodily space* safely set in the center of female form and carriage has, I think, a reality superior to that of the missing organ."[67]

Erikson summed up the significance of the step he had taken:

> Many of the original conclusions of psychoanalysis concerning womanhood hinge on the so-called genital trauma, i.e., the little girl's sudden comprehension of the fact that she does not and never will have a penis. The assumed prevalence of envy in women; the assumption that the future baby is a substitute for the penis; the interpretation that the girl turns from the mother to the father because she finds that the mother not only cheated her out of a penis but has been cheated herself; and finally the woman's disposition to abandon [male] activity and aggressivity for the sake of a "passive-masochistic" orientation: all these depend on "the trauma," and all have been built into elaborate explanations of femininity. . . . [A] theory of feminine development which would assume the early relevance of the productive interior . . . would . . . allow for a shift of theoretical emphasis from the loss of an external organ to the sense of a vital inner potential; from a hateful contempt of the mother to a solidarity with her and other women; from "passive" renunciation of male activity to the purposeful and competent activity of one endowed with ovaries and a uterus; and from a masochistic pleasure in pain to an ability to stand (and understand) pain as a

meaningful aspect of human experience in general, and of the feminine role in particular.[68]

For readers of Erikson's earlier work, there was nothing new—just something more explicit—in this "schema." (Nor was there anything new about the evidence presented. His argument rested heavily on preadolescent block constructions.) For someone who claimed to chart the new realm of the psychosocial, he had very little to say about the social side of it. He simply insisted that "since a woman is never not-a-woman, she can see her long-range goals only in those modes of activity which include and integrate her natural dispositions."[69]

· · · · ·

The readers of *Daedalus* might be overwhelmingly male, but Erikson's article, particularly once a revised version appeared in book form, attracted much female attention—mostly negative. As Erikson expressed it, his views were counted "among those deemed inimical to womanhood."[70] The occasion for his comment was a "letter" addressed to Jean Strouse, who, in the course of editing an anthology of psychoanalytic writings about women and commentaries on those selections, had asked Erikson to serve as his own commentator. Hence his contribution, his "letter" to Strouse, dated 1974, now identified as a "former student."

Erikson stuck to his position—he would have changed nothing, he noted, "except a few imprudent words and phrases"[71]—but not to his persona. Gone was the narrator who, as in his account of Freud, managed to contain within himself "vague 'feminine yielding' and persistent masculine precision," or who, as in his paper on "Inner Space," managed, though biologically male, to specialize "in the inwardness and sensitive indwelling (the German *Innigkeit*) usually ascribed to women."[72] The narrator now figured in turn as a man wounded by the mistrust that being a man seemed to arouse, a Freudian scorned as the bearer of unpalatable truths, an aggrieved professor admonishing his former student and her sisters to take another, closer look at the text before them, and a prophet pointing the way toward "what the next *vision* must be." With the shift to prophecy—and the avowal of his belief that "as women take their share in the over-all economic and political planning of affairs so far monopolized by men," they could not fail to pay "attention to the whole earth as an inner space"—Erikson took his leave.[73]

ANOTHER VOICE

In Freud's *Three Essays on the Theory of Sexuality* (1905), Carol Gilligan noted in a paper entitled "The Conquistador and the Dark Continent: Reflections on the Psychology of Love," the "conquistador" claimed that the erotic life of men alone had "become accessible to research." By contrast, that of women remained "veiled in an impenetrable obscurity—partly owing to the stunting effect of civilized conditions and partly owing to their conventional secretiveness and insincerity."[74] Freud's attack on the problem, Gilligan argued, encountered numerous obstacles: "his theory, his times, his conception of science, and the problem of. . . data."[75] Among these she singled out the first as the chief hindrance. In the course of constructing his theory, she asserted, Freud lost track of the stories his women patients told—and along with them, the possibility of penetrating the obscurity.

Freud had started off pursuing his patients' stories—or, rather, his mentor, Josef Breuer, thanks to his experience with Anna O., had pointed Freud in that direction. Gilligan reviewed the case, quoting liberally from Breuer's account in his and Freud's *Studies on Hysteria* (1893–1895). Here is the key passage:

> Throughout the illness . . . the patient fell into a somnolent state every afternoon and . . . after sunset this . . . passed into a deeper sleep. . . . After the deep sleep had lasted about an hour she grew restless, tossed to and fro and kept repeating "tormenting, tormenting," with her eyes shut all the time. It was also noticed how, during . . . *absences* in day-time she was obviously creating some situation or episode to which she gave a clue with a few muttered words. It happened then—to begin with accidentally but later intentionally—that someone near her repeated one of these phrases of hers while she was complaining about the "tormenting." She at once joined in and began to paint some situation or tell some story, hesititatingly at first and in . . . [a] paraphasic jargon; but the longer she went on the more fluent she became, till at last she was speaking quite correct German. . . . A few moments after she had finished her narrative, she would wake up, obviously calmed down.[76]

If for any reason she was unable to tell her story to someone—and the someone soon became Breuer and Breuer alone—she also failed to calm down, and the following day she would have to tell him two stories in order to be quieted.

Freud followed suit, attending to his patients' stories. Gilligan chose for review the case of "a girl suffering from an intolerable *tussis nervosa* which had dragged on for six years"—a case that Freud reported in a single paragraph in *Studies on Hysteria*:

> All she knew was that her nervous cough began when, at the age of fourteen, she was boarding with an aunt. She maintained that she knew nothing of any mental agitations at that time and did not believe that there was any motive for her complaint. Under the pressure of my hand [placed on her forehead] she first of all remembered a big dog. She then recognized the picture in her memory: it was a dog of her aunt's which became attached to her, followed her about everywhere, and so on. And now it occurred to her, without further prompting, that this dog died, that the children gave it a solemn burial and that her cough started on the way back from the funeral. I asked why, but had once more to call in the help of a pressure. The thought then came to her: "Now I am quite alone in the world. No one here loves me. This creature was my only friend, and now I have lost him." She continued her story. "The cough disappeared when I left my aunt's, but it came on again eighteen months later." "Why was that?" "I don't know." I pressed again. She recalled the news of her uncle's death, when the cough started again, and also recalled having a similar train of thought. Her uncle seems to have been the only member of the family who had shown any feeling for her, who had loved her. . . . No one loved her, they preferred everyone else to her, she did not deserve to be loved, and so on. But there was something attaching to the idea of "love" which there was a strong resistance to her telling me. The analysis broke off before this was cleared up.[77]

It was not cleared up in this case nor, according to Gilligan, in any subsequent one. By late 1900, by the time Dora's father "handed her over" to Freud for what was now psychoanalytic treatment,[78] Freud had begun, Gilligan claimed, to impose on his patients a tale of his own. In Dora's case this meant interpreting his patient's symptoms as signs of her sexual longing for Herr K., the husband of his father's mistress; it meant pursuing that line of interpretation until he tracked down Dora's hitherto unconscious regret over her indignant rejection of what Freud regarded as a serious proposition from Herr K.; and finally it meant interpreting Dora's reporting Herr K.'s proposition to her parents as a jealous act of revenge. "Rather than waiting," Gilligan remarked, "as Breuer had done with Anna O., for her to tell her story herself," Freud had proceeded "to tell Dora the story she was attempting to withhold."[79]

But Dora had her own story to relate, Gilligan insisted. Her evidence: Dora's second dream (in Freud's account the "explanations" were "grouped around two dreams");[80] more precisely, an additional piece that Dora had remembered only in the course of associating to the dream. Having discovered that she had no one to listen to her—so Gilligan glossed Freud's interpretation of the dream itself—Dora suggested, through recollecting the detail of a writing-table, that she would tell her story herself. What was that story? It was about "a deeper sexual current running underneath that attached to . . . Herr K."[81] (Freud in fact reproached himself for his failure "to discover in time and to inform the patient that her homosexual . . . love for Frau K. was the strongest unconscious current in her mental life.")[82] It was also about magnanimity—the magnanimity with which she forgave the treachery of her beloved Frau K. (Frau K. had been "the main source of Dora's knowledge of sexual matters" and was "the very person who later on charged her with being interested in those same subjects"—thereby giving Dora's parents grounds for disbelieving her account of Herr K.'s proposition.)[83] "The story *not* heard in the analysis," Gilligan concluded, "was a story of loyalty and love."[84]

Gilligan had heard what Freud had not. To be sure, she extracted the story from his text; her claim, then, was rhetorical, not empirical. In making it, she highlighted the attributes of Gilligan the narrator—a persona that had already figured in her best-selling book, *In a Different Voice.* She had not been hindered, as Freud had been, by trying to fit—in her words—"the vagaries of female anatomy and the stories told by women patients into the scheme that . . . was emerging from his own analysis and interpretation of dreams." She was free of male blind spots, of male distortion, and thus offered no resistance to the transmission of women's stories. And as a conquistador in her own right, she would chart a continent that had "remained . . . largely unmarked in the growing map of human experience."[85]

• • • • •

In the second chapter of her book, Gilligan introduced her readers to Jake and Amy, two "bright and articulate" eleven year olds. Members of the same sixth-grade class, they were also both participants in the "rights and responsibilities study"—a study of "males and females matched for age, intelligence, education, occupation, and social class at nine points across the life cycle" and "designed to explore different conceptions of morality and self."[86] In addition to Jake and Amy, Gilligan introduced Heinz, or rather Heinz's dilemma—one of a series devised by the psychologist Lawrence Kohlberg to measure moral development in adolescence. In this instance a man named Heinz could not afford to buy a drug his wife needed to save her life. Having described Heinz's predicament, his wife's illness, and the druggist's refusal to lower the price, the interviewer then asked Jake and Amy: "Should Heinz steal the drug?"

Jake had no difficulty answering in the affirmative:

> For one thing a human life is worth more than money, and if the druggist only makes $1,000, he is still going to live, but if Heinz doesn't steal the drug, his wife is going to die. (*Why is life worth more than money?*) Because the druggist can get a thousand dollars later from rich people with cancer, but Heinz can't get his wife again. (*Why not?*) Because people are all different and so you couldn't get Heinz's wife again.[87]

For Jake, so Gilligan interpreted his responses, the conflict, a conflict between life and property, could be resolved by logical deduction. "Considering the moral dilemma to be 'sort of like a math problem with humans,'" he set up an equation and proceeded to work out a solution. Because his solution was rationally derived, he assumed "that anyone following reason would arrive at the same conclusion," and thus if Heinz were caught and brought before a judge, the judge would also decide that stealing had been "the right thing for Heinz to do." In this fashion, Jake abstracted the moral problem from the interpersonal situation, finding in the logic of fairness "an objective way" to determine who would win the dispute. And in her own fashion, Gilligan abstracted from this set of exchanges the notion of a hierarchical ordering, with "imagery of winning and losing and the potential for violence" that such imagery implied. Hierarchy, and its attendant dangers, then, became the code-word for Jake's style of "structuring relationships."[88]

In contrast to Jake's, Amy's reply seemed "evasive and unsure":

> Well, I don't think so. I think there might be other ways besides stealing it, like if he could borrow the money or make a loan or something, but he really shouldn't steal the drug—but his wife shouldn't die either. . . . If he stole the drug, he might save his wife then, but if he did, he might have to go to jail, and then his

wife might get sicker again, and he couldn't get more of the drug. . . . So, they should really just talk it out and find some other way to make the money.[89]

The interviewer tried to probe further; Amy stuck to her initial response: "Whether or not Heinz loves his wife, he still shouldn't steal or let her die. . . . Asked again why Heinz should not steal the drug, she simply repeats, 'Because it's not right.' Asked again to explain why, she states again that theft would not be a good solution, adding lamely, 'if he took it, he might not know how to give it to his wife, and so his wife might still die.' "[90]

The interviewer, who apparently was not Gilligan, failed to grasp Amy's answers or regarded them as incorrect—he or she conveyed as much through a repetition of questions. Gilligan supplied the missing gloss:

> Seeing in the dilemma not a math problem with humans but a narrative of relationships that extends over time, Amy envisions the wife's continuing need for her husband and her husband's continuing concern for his wife and seeks to respond to the druggist's need in a way that would sustain rather than sever connection. . . . [S]eeing a world comprised of relationships rather than of people standing alone, a world that coheres through human connection rather than through systems of rules, she finds the puzzle in the dilemma to lie in the failure of the druggist to respond to the wife. Saying that "it is not right for someone to die when their life could be saved," she assumes that if the druggist were to see the consequences of his refusal to lower his price, he would realize that "he should just give it to the wife and then have the husband pay back the money later." Thus she considers the solution to the dilemma to lie in making the wife's condition more salient to the druggist or, that failing, in appealing to others who are in a position to help.[91]

To Amy, Gilligan continued, what had occurred figured as a "fracture of human relationship" that must (with a shift in metaphor) "be mended with its own thread." Consequently, the solution she imagined amounted to communicating—and more communicating. And Gilligan herself imagined "a network of connection . . . sustained by a process of communication," holding out the prospect of peaceful conflict resolution.[92] A web, then, became the code-word for Amy's understanding of morality.

What did Gilligan make of the contrast between Jake and Amy, between Jake's hierarchy and Amy's web, or between his separateness and her connectedness, a second contrasting pair that Gilligan regarded as emotionally related to the first? Jake's outlook, his "voice," she claimed, was the voice long familiar to developmental psychologists, particularly to those influenced by Freud. For them, according to her reading, development amounted to a "narrative of failed relationships—pre-Oedipal attachments, Oedipal fantasies, preadolescent chumships, and adolescent loves"—relationships that stood as markers on the boy's way to an "increasingly emphatic individuation." Amy's "different voice" created problems. The continuity of connection in her life and her sisters' lives did not fit a scheme derived from male experience. As for the relation between the two voices, it was "complementary rather than sequential or opposed": one child's voice was not the precursor of the other. The trajectory for each child followed a different path—and presumably the potential for that difference had been there from the beginning of their lives.[93]

Here Gilligan herself spoke in contrasting voices. The first, tentative and defensive, could be heard in the introduction. "The different voice," she wrote, was "characterized not by gender but theme. Its association with women" was merely "an empirical observation"—and "not absolute." The disparities between male and female voices she presented merely served "to highlight a distinction between two modes of thought and to focus a problem of interpretation rather than to represent a generalization about either sex."[94] The second voice could be heard at the end of the chapter in which Jake and Amy appeared. Gone was the reluctance to generalize about the sexes—particularly about the female sex.

• • • • •

If, as Gilligan claimed from first to last, it was inappropriate to adopt male life as the norm "to fashion women out of masculine cloth," how, then, to devise a female model? Once again Gilligan pursued "the language of woman's moral discourse." To find that language, she sought places where women had the "power to choose" and thus were willing "to speak in their own voice."[95]

What to make of the "place" Gilligan herself chose: to have or not to have an abortion? She at once excluded Jake and his older brothers from her study; she ruled out a sustained comparison between women and men. She also excluded women who had succeeded in preventing an unwanted pregnancy. Among those who failed, Gilligan made "no effort to select a sample that would be representative of women considering, seeking, or having abortions." She apparently did not do the actual selection; she allowed it to be done for her:

Twenty-nine women, ranging in age from fifteen to thirty-three and diverse in ethnic background and social class, were referred for the study by abortion and pregnancy counseling services. The women participated in the study for a variety of reasons—some to gain further clarification with respect to a decision about which they were in conflict, some in response to a counselor's concern about repeated abortions, and others to contribute to ongoing research. . . . Of the twenty-nine women, four decided to have the baby, two miscarried, twenty-one chose abortion, and two who were in doubt about the decision at the time of the interview could not be contacted for the follow-up research.[96]

The women were interviewed twice, initially at the time they were making the decision, in the first trimester of a confirmed pregnancy, and then again at the end of the following year.[97] In the initial interview, the women were asked to discuss "the decision they were considering, their reasons both for and against each option, the people involved, the conflicts entailed, and the ways in which making the decision affected their views of themselves and of their relationships with others." Gilligan focused on their reiterated use of the words "selfish" and "responsible" and their definition of the moral problem "as one of obligation to exercise care and avoid hurt."[98] There was, she confidently affirmed, something distinctively feminine about this formulation. She expressed equal confidence that she discerned in its shadings a marked progression—a sequence of three levels plus transitions between them.

Women operating at the lowest level of the progression—"Level One"—thought only of their individual survival. Betty was such a woman. An adopted child who had a history of disorderly conduct and reform school, Betty was sixteen when she went to a clinic for a second abortion within a period of six months. Her previous pregnancy resulted from being raped while hitchhiking; her second resulted from an ongoing relationship with a boyfriend. He had started out by treating her differently from anyone she had known before: "'He did everything for me. (*What kind of things?*) Called me, picked me up, take me anywhere I wanted to go, buy me cigarettes, buy me beer if I wanted.'" Convinced that if she refused to have intercourse with him, he would break up with her, she consented. And then he had disappointed her: "'[A]fter I went to bed with him, he just wanted me to do everything that he wanted to do. I was more like a wife than a girlfriend, and I didn't like that.'" When she found out she was pregnant, she was near despair: "I wanted to kill myself, because I just couldn't face the fact. I knew that I wanted to get an abortion, but I couldn't face the fact of going through that [the physical pain] again."[99]

Betty was preoccupied with surviving in a world she perceived as exploitative and dangerous. But she also worried about the child she was carrying: "Thinking about the baby makes me feel kind of strange, because I am adopted, and I was thinking, like my mother didn't want me, otherwise she wouldn't have put me up for adoption. But I was thinking if I could have been an abortion or maybe was intended to be, or something, and that kind of gives me strange feelings about it." And she worried about her own future as well:

> In a lot of ways this pregnancy has helped me because I have stopped getting high and stopped drinking, and this is the first time in three years I stopped. And now that I have, I know that I can do it, and I am just going to completely stop. (*How did the pregnancy help you do that?*) Because when I first got pregnant, I wasn't sure what I was going to do, and when I first found out, I thought to myself, "This time it was my fault, and I have to keep the baby." But then, I stopped drinking and stopped getting high because I didn't want to hurt the baby. And then, after a couple of weeks, I thought about it again, and I said, "No, I can't have it, because I have to go back to school."[100]

Betty, Gilligan argued, was beginning to make moral progress; a year later (on the basis of a follow-up interview) she concluded that Betty had moved on to the next stage.

That stage ranked not as a new level but as a transition, during which the words "selfishness" and "responsibility" appeared for the first time—and simultaneously potential conflict between them. So it had been with Anne, a woman in her late twenties struggling to decide whether to have a third abortion: "I think you have to think about the people who are involved, including yourself. You have responsibilities to yourself. And to make a right—whatever that is—decision in this depends on your knowledge and awareness of the responsibilities that you have and whether you can survive with a child and what it will do to your relationship with the father and how it will affect him emotionally." Anne remained conflicted—owing, Gilligan argued, to a "self-image" that was "insistently contradictory."

> (*How do you describe yourself to yourself?*) I see myself as impulsive, practical—that is a contradiction—moral and amoral, a contradiction. Actually the only thing that is consistent and not contradictory is the fact that I am very lazy, which everyone has always told me is really a symptom of something else which I

have never been able to put my finger on exactly. It has taken me a long time to like myself. In fact, there are times when I don't. . . . I am pretty unfaithful to myself. I have a hard time even thinking that I am a human being, simply because so much rotten stuff goes on and people are so crummy and insensitive.[101]

For Gilligan's readers, who never learned what Anne finally did, she remained caught in the to and fro that the very label transition implied.

It was on "Level Two" that the "conventional feminine voice" emerged, defining the worth of the self "on the basis of the ability to care for and protect others." First time round, twenty-five-year-old Denise, impregnated by her lover, a married man with four children, simply could not make a choice, or rather could not acknowledge that she had done so:

> I just wanted the child, and I really don't believe in abortions. . . . I felt like there were changes happening in my body, and I felt very protective. But . . . he [her lover] made me feel that I had to make a choice and there was only one choice to make and that was to have an abortion and I could always have children another time, and he made me feel if I didn't have it that it would drive us apart.

She had the abortion—and soon began to change her tune:

> Afterwards we went through a bad time—I hate to say it and I was wrong—but I blamed him. I gave in to him. But when it came down to it, I made the decision. I could have said, "I am going to have this child, whether you want me to or not," and I just didn't do it.

Second time round, pregnant again by her lover, Denise intended "to claim her own voice and accept responsibility for choice." "Right now I think of myself as someone who can become a lot stronger. . . . I hope to come on strong and make a big decision, whether it is right or wrong." To claim her own voice, rather than, as Denise put it, to "go along with the tide," meant that Denise was heading for the next transitional stage—so Gilligan argued, without informing her readers of the outcome.[102]

Gilligan had characterized the first transition as a movement from selfishness to responsibility; readers might regard the second as a movement back to selfishness. They would have missed the point, Gilligan implied. Was it, she in effect asked, selfish or responsible for a woman "to include her own needs within the compass of her care and concern"? The latter, she answered: for her, re-examining responsibility ranked as crucial to the second transition.

Janet, "a twenty-four-year-old married Catholic, pregnant again two months following the birth of her first child," was more in doubt: "It is taking a life. Even though it is not formed, it is the potential, and to me it is still taking a life. But I have to think of mine, my son's, and my husband's. And at first I thought it was for selfish reasons, but it is not. I believe that, too, some of it is selfish. I don't want another one right now; I am not ready for it." She struggled to determine how to reckon in her own wishes: "I think in a way I am selfish, and very emotional, and I think that I am a very real person and an understanding person, and I can handle life situations fairly well, so I am basing a lot of it on my ability to do the things that I feel are right and best for me and whomever I am involved with. I think I was very fair to myself about the decision. . . . I feel it is a good decision and an honest one, a real decision." At the end, Janet said, " 'God can punish, but he can also forgive.' " What remained "in question for her" was whether "her claim to forgiveness" was compromised by a decision that not only met the needs of others but also was " 'right and best' " for her.[103]

And finally there was Sarah, who stood as Gilligan's example of the third and highest level. Twenty-five years old, she was pregnant a second time by the same man. She had discovered the first pregnancy after her lover had left her, and she had terminated it by an abortion. When, however, he reappeared, she resumed the relationship. "Two years later, having once again 'left my diaphragm in the drawer,' " she again became pregnant." Initially " 'ecstatic,' " her mood changed abruptly when her lover told her that he would leave her unless she aborted the fetus. She considered a second abortion, but found herself unable to keep the appointments she made. The first abortion seemed an " 'honest mistake' "; a second would make her feel " 'like a walking slaughter-house.' "[104]

Where Janet continued to question the morality of taking action she considered "right and best" for herself, Sarah overcame such scruples:

Well the pros for having the baby are all the admiration that you would get from being a single woman, alone, martyr, struggling, having the adoring love of this beautiful Gerber baby. Just more of a home life than I have had in a long time, and that basically was it, which is pretty fantasyland. It is not very realistic. Cons against having the baby: it was going to hasten what is looking to be the inevitable end of the relationship with the man I am presently with. I was going to have to go on welfare. My parents were going to hate me for the rest of my life. I was going to lose a really good job that I have. I would lose a lot of independence.

Sarah's concept of goodness, Gilligan claimed, was expanding:

> I have this responsibility to myself, and you know, for once I am beginning to realize that that really matters to me. Instead of doing what I want for myself and feeling guilty over how selfish I am, you realize that that is a very usual way for people to live—doing what you want to do because you feel that your wants and your needs are important, if to no one else, then to you, and that's reason enough to do something that you want to do.[105]

For Gilligan, the pattern appeared obvious: "Once obligation" extended "to include the self as well as others, the disparity between selfishness and responsibility" dissolved:[106] "What women then enunciate is not a new morality, but a moral conception disentangled from the constraints that formerly had confused its perception and impeded its articulation. . . . Responsibility for care then includes both self and other, and the obligation not to hurt, freed from conventional constraints, is reconstructed as a universal guide to moral choice."[107]

Recall Helene Deutsch, whose *The Psychology of Women* did not appear among Gilligan's references. Gilligan's pair selfishness-responsibility nevertheless bore a strong family resemblance to Deutsch's narcissism-masochism. According to Gilligan, the reconciliation of her pair was accomplished when traditional notions of feminine responsibility (read: self-sacrifice) were recast to include the self; according to Deutsch, the harmonious cooperation of her pair was achieved when narcissism leavened masochism. Where Gilligan charted a progression, Deutsch's account had been one of alternation and a search for equilibrium. Had Gilligan been inattentive to oscillation in the stories of the women she interviewed? Determined not to fashion women's stories to fit schemes devised by men for men, had she succumbed to the temptation to tailor them to her own design?

• • • • •

The Psychology of Women, in contrast to Deutsch's earlier work, did not tell an evolutionary tale. *In a Different Voice* hinted at such a tale, but it was one borrowed from Erikson. When Gilligan thought of the trajectory Amy might follow, when she thought of Betty and the others making progress, she was thinking of Erikson. Not without misgivings. She faulted him for using the male as the model for his epigenetic chart in general and for his mapping of adolescence in particular:

For the female, Erikson . . . says, the sequence is a bit different. She holds her identity in abeyance as she prepares to attract the man by whose name she will be known, by whose status she will be defined, the man who will rescue her from emptiness and loneliness by filling "the inner space." While for men, identity precedes intimacy and generativity in the optimal cycle of human separation and attachment, for women these tasks seem instead to be fused.

Despite his "observation of sex differences," Gilligan continued, Erikson had failed to integrate his insights about women into his chart.[108] Those insights she had now elaborated in a fashion that resonated with Deutsch's *The Psychology of Women.* Epigenesis, then, promised to fill the narrative gap Deutsch had left open.

At the same time, Gilligan implied that her writings filled the visionary gap Erikson had left open:

My own work . . . indicates that the inclusion of women's experience brings to developmental understanding a new perspective on relationships. . . . The concept of identity expands to include the experience of interconnection. The moral domain is similarly enlarged. . . . And the underlying epistemology . . . shifts from the Greek ideal of knowledge as a correspondence between mind and form to the Biblical conception of knowing as a process of human relationship.[109]

Her expectations were not modest, but then great expectations are a feature of a conquistador's persona.

Chapter 3 Sexual Selection:

Karen Horney

As early as the late eighteenth century, animal breeders noted that females showed a preference for the more vigorous males; not until Charles Darwin, however, did the process by which an individual male gained reproductive advantage by being more attractive to individual females acquire a name. In *The Descent of Man* (1871), selection in relation to sex or sexual selection occupied nearly three quarters of the whole work. And then it languished: until recently sexual selection suffered from neglect if not outright rejection. Males and females are crucially different—so the now scientifically respectable argument runs—in their "investment" practices. A female produces relatively few eggs and may "invest much time and resources in brooding the eggs and developing the embryos and in taking care of the brood after hatching." A male, by contrast, "has sufficient sperm to inseminate numerous females, and his investment in a single copulation is therefore very small."[1] No wonder then that the female is choosy about her mate—and competitive with other females as well.[2]

Sexual selection, unlike retrogression and epigenesis, is a concept familiar to the investigator (that is, to me) rather than to the subject, who in this instance is Karen Horney. Had the notion of sexual selection been readily available to her, she might well have grabbed hold of it. (She came tantalizingly close to doing so when she referred to coitus as a "physiologically more momentous matter for women than for men." Then, she asked, expecting an affirmative answer, Would this fact "have psychological representation"?)[3] What justifies calling Horney's a story of sexual selection is that she featured the very issues that concept highlights: tensions between the sexes and tensions within a single sex, in this case the female. In her tale, sexual selection turned out to be scarcely milder than the struggle for existence, proverbially "red in tooth and claw."

Like Deutsch, Horney burst upon the psychoanalytic scene in the 1920s—but in Berlin rather than Vienna. Born in Hamburg in 1885, thus Deutsch's junior by one year, she was the younger child and only daughter of her father's second marriage. Her older brother, in her eyes, ranked as the favorite of both parents. Father (a sea captain and zealous Lutheran) and mother (the daughter of a man grown prosperous through constructing harbors) were separated by an eighteen-year age difference and by differences in temperament as well. As the strife between her parents mounted, Karen felt obliged to side with her mother. And it was her mother who sympathized with Karen's wish to continue her education: in 1900 women in Hamburg gained entrance to the gymnasium, and a year later Karen began working toward her *Abitur;* also in 1900 the University of Freiburg— among the first in Germany—admitted women to its medical faculty, and in 1906 Karen arrived there—one of thirty-four female students. Despite her own successes, she doubted that women would "*ever* be able to achieve intellectually what men do."[4]

From Freiburg Karen moved on to Göttingen. By then she had finished her formal course work and passed her state exams. To continue with clinical training in another venue was not at all unusual among German medical students. Additionally, in Göttingen she could spend time with Oskar Horney, whom she had initially met in Freiburg and who was on his way to a doctorate in political science and then a business career. In October 1909 they were married and ready to move to Berlin. Karen had not yet completed her medical training but had no intention of letting marriage deter her. If few men in Germany at that time were prepared to marry a woman as resolute as she, Karen, despite her resolution, seemed eager—in line with what she subsequently came to regard as a "neurotic need"—to make her partner the "center of gravity."[5] She still doubted her own gravitational—and intellectual—force.

Horney decided to specialize in psychiatry after her arrival in Berlin and after her first contact with psychoanalysis. According to a recent biographer "it was probably psychoanalysis that led her to specialize in psychiatry and not the other way around."[6] In 1910, in Berlin, Karl Abraham stood alone as Freud's representative. He had arrived at the end of 1907 and immediately begun to practice. Writing to Freud in April 1910, he reported that psychoanalysis had "recently been flourishing" in his consulting room; he had started "four new treatments in quick succession." Thanks to a former patient of Freud who had "introduced analysis . . . to a small circle of neurotics," this former patient and three others had appeared: "first of all a very intelligent young woman," who was "doing very nicely in her treatment" and who "soon sent her best friend" and some days later yet another friend. The "very intelligent young woman" was quite likely Karen Horney.[7]

What brought her to psychoanalysis and to Abraham? From Horney's diary, it is clear that "states of exhaustion, the inclination to passivity" that increased "to a longing for sleep—even for death"—acted as spurs. So too did the "great attraction brutal and rather forceful men" exerted on her, "the wanting to blend in with the will of a man who . . . set his foot" on her neck—all, in her view, were part of "the same story." Horney's analyst did not hesitate to trace her "erotic ideal" back to her "first childhood impressions," to the time when she had loved her father "with all the strength" of her passion. Abraham himself did not measure up to that ideal (nor did Oskar Horney). Acknowledging a mass of "contradictory feelings" concentrated on him, she told Abraham that she "no longer had any confidence" that the analysis was doing any good—and suspended treatment.[8] It continued intermittently for more than two years.[9]

In the early 1920s, Horney (now the mother of three daughters) underwent a second analysis. She chose not return to Abraham—who died in 1925. She chose further analysis while still living with Oskar; they separated in 1926. (They did not actually divorce until 1939.) Beyond the identity of her second therapist—Hanns Sachs, a senior analyst who had migrated from Vienna to Berlin in 1920—nothing is known about this further treatment. By the time Horney went to Sachs, she herself ranked as a promising figure; she had given a talk to the Berlin Psychoanalytic Society as early as 1912. (The subject had been "sexual instruction in early childhood," and Abraham had reported to Freud that "for once, the paper showed a real understanding of the material, unfortunately something rather infrequent . . . in our circle.")[10] Shortly after the war, Horney had started seeing patients in her own analytic practice; and when, a few years later, psychoanalytic training became regularized, she served as a member of the Berlin education committee. By the time she finished with Sachs, she was on the verge of challenging Freud's and Abraham's views on women. She was on the verge of affirming confidence in her own intellectual force.

Horney's starting point, however, was recognizably Freudian: the Oedipus complex as Freud had initially formulated it. The Greek tragic figure had turned up, albeit without much fanfare, in a section of *The Interpretation of Dreams* devoted to typical dreams. Under that rubric, Freud had included dreams of the death of parents. A child's sexual wishes awakened very early, he noted, and as he understood it, the boy's wishes were directed toward mother and the girl's toward father—with the child's death wishes directed at the same-sex parent. Freud continued to view boys' and girls' oedipal desires in this symmetrical fashion for the next two and a half decades. As late as 1924 he wrote that, in his experience, the girl's Oedipus complex seldom went beyond "the taking of her mother's place and the adopting of a feminine attitude towards her father."[11]

Between 1923 and 1937 Horney published fifteen papers on the psychology of women. (In 1967 they appeared in a translated collection entitled *Feminine Psychology.*) The last two written before she moved to the United States in 1932 were also the last two published in *The International Journal of Psycho-Analysis.* Horney's views were in the course of becoming less acceptable to the psychoanalytic establishment, and she herself was in the course of seeking other audiences. Along the way she had discarded the instinctual idiom of her early psychoanalytic training. Eventually she discarded Oedipus as well. The first casting aside proceeded gradually: it began as a matter of emphasis, and it began while Horney was still in Germany. The second proceeded more abruptly and after her arrival in the United States.

With her widely acclaimed book *The Neurotic Personality of Our Time* published in 1937, the same year as the last essay included in her *Feminine Psychology,* Horney was on the cusp of her departure from the Freudian fold.[12] She was on the cusp of shifting her focus away from women as well.

THE "STRONGER" SEX

> Like all sciences and all valuations, the psychology of women has hitherto been
> considered only from the point of view of men. It is inevitable that the man's
> position of advantage should cause objective validity to be attributed to his
> subjective, affective relations to the woman, and . . . the psychology of women
> . . . actually represents a deposit of the desires and disappointments of men.[13]

Commenting to a friend about her paper "The Flight from Womanhood," in which the paragraph quoted above figures, Horney noted that she
had originally written "much more aggressively," but since she had planned
her paper as a contribution to a *Festschrift* for Freud, she had taken the
advice of a senior colleague and had pulled her punches. (The *Festschrift* was
never published; Horney's paper appeared in both the *Internationale
Zeitschrift für Psychoanalyse* and *The International Journal of Psycho-Analysis*
in 1926.) She had intended to press the charge that male psychoanalysts had
been unable "to overcome certain deeply rooted prejudices against what was
feminine," and that biased research had been the result; she had intended to
question the psychoanalytic comparisons that again and again turned out
unfavorable to the female sex.[14] She had no intention of claiming to be an
exception among women, of claiming to be "more masculine than feminine"; she had no intention of taking her stand on the "ground of bisexuality."[15] The persona of the narrator (in this paper and elsewhere) came
across as feisty and combative—and also distinctly feminine.

Horney did not in fact pull her punches when she proceeded to draw up
two parallel columns, one labeled "the boy's ideas," the other "our," meaning psychoanalytic, "ideas of feminine development. Here is her chart:

The Boy's Ideas	Our Ideas of Feminine Development
Naive assumption that girls as well as boys possess a penis	*For both sexes it is only the male genital which plays any part*
Realization of the absence of the penis	*Sad discovery of the absence of the penis*
Idea that the girl is a castrated, mutilated boy	*Belief of the girl that she once possessed a penis and lost it by castration*

Belief that the girl has suffered punishment that also threatens him	*Castration is conceived of as the infliction of punishment*
The girl is regarded as inferior	*The girl regards herself as inferior*
The boy is unable to imagine how the girl can ever get over this loss or envy	*The girl never gets over the sense of deficiency and inferiority and has constantly to master afresh her desire to be a man*
The boy dreads her envy	*The girl desires throughout life to avenge herself on the man for possessing something which she lacks*[16]

Horney thus exposed psychoanalytic postulates as the stuff of juvenile male fancies—and made them look ridiculous. How better to deflate the pretensions of her male colleagues!

• • • • •

All of these items, the last most readily, could be teased out of Freud's 1918 paper, "The Taboo of Virginity." It was a paper which Horney referred to a number of times and which she set out, explicitly, to refute.[17]

What is the taboo of virginity? The title might suggest the customary demand that a woman remain a virgin until wed. Whose customs? Freud's own and those of his times, not of all times and places. "Few details of the sexual life of primitive peoples," so he began his essay, were more different from and alien to those of his European contemporaries than their attitude toward a woman's virginity. It was not the case, he continued, that the (male) primitives set no value on it. To them also defloration figured as "a significant act"; but it had "become the subject of a taboo. . . . Instead of reserving it for the girl's bridegroom and future partner in marriage," these alien customs specified that the bridegroom should "*shun the performance of it.*"[18]

How to account for a taboo that was both widespread and diverse? Anthropologists drew attention to the fact that the taboo of virginity constituted part of a more global prohibition. Not only was the first coitus taboo. Not only was intercourse taboo in particular situations arising from a woman's "sexual life such as menstruation, pregnancy, childbirth and lying-

in." Intercourse was taboo whenever a man undertook "some special enterprise, like setting out on a hunt or a campaign." It was taboo because the
man feared it might "paralyse his strength" or "bring him bad luck." Safety
lay in abstinence. It also lay in separation. Sometimes that separation went
so far that the sexes lived apart, women with women, men with men.
Sometimes it went even further: one sex was not permitted "to say aloud the
personal names of members of the other sex," and women developed "a
language with a special vocabulary." The evidence was piling up: "one
might almost say," Freud noted, that women were "altogether taboo."[19]

He felt dissatisfied. He had followed his anthropological mentors in
moving from the specific to the general—in vain. "The general taboo of
women," Freud concluded, threw "no light on the particular rules concerning the first sexual act with a virgin." Where once he had been (seemingly)
content to follow, he now proposed to lead. He promised to solve the
anthropologists' puzzle for them: to determine what psychical danger primitive man was defending himself against by instituting the taboo of virginity. He promised to do so by examining closely women's behavior in his own
"stage of civilization" in similar circumstances—that is, in the first act of
sexual intercourse.[20]

Certain "pathological cases" Freud found illuminating: "after the first
and indeed after each repeated instance of . . . intercourse," the woman in
question gave "unconcealed expression to her hostility towards the man by
abusing him, raising her hand against him or actually striking him." In one
such case, "this happened although the woman loved the man very much,
used to demand intercourse herself and unmistakably found great satisfaction in it."[21] Defloration thus aroused hostility that the prospective husband would have every reason to want to avoid.

These pathological cases allowed Freud to establish the reality of the
psychical danger men, "primitive" and "civilized" alike, ran in deflower-
ing a virgin. They did not, however, explain the hostility itself, and he
recognized that whatever explanation he might devise it had to apply to
women, "primitive" and "civilized" alike. His preferred explanation ran
as follows:

> We have learnt from the analysis of many neurotic women that they go through
> an early age in which they envy their brothers their sign of masculinity and feel at
> a disadvantage because of the lack of it . . . in themselves. . . . During this
> phase, little girls often make no secret of their envy, nor of the hostility toward
> their favoured brother which arises from it.

He continued:

> Some time ago I chanced to have an opportunity of obtaining insight into a
> dream of a newly married woman which was recognizable as a reaction to the loss
> of her virginity. It betrayed spontaneously the woman's wish to castrate her
> young husband and to keep his penis for herself.[22]

What was to be demonstrated had been.

Freud was not alone in appreciating the real psychical danger behind the
taboo of virginity. Poets and playwrights proved equally discerning. Here
Freud cited Friedrich Hebbel's tragedy *Judith and Holofernes*.

> Judith is one of those women whose virginity is protected by a taboo. Her first
> husband was paralysed on the bridal night by a mysterious anxiety, and never
> again dared touch her. "My beauty is like belladonna," she says. "Enjoyment of it
> brings madness and death." When the Assyrian general [Holofernes] is besieging
> her city, she conceives the plan of seducing him by her beauty and of destroying
> him. . . . After she has been deflowered by this powerful man, . . . she finds the
> strength in her fury to strike off his head and thus becomes the liberator of her
> people. Beheading is well-known to us as a symbolic substitute for castrating;
> Judith is accordingly the woman who castrates the man who has deflowered her.

In the Biblical text, there is no mention of Judith's "uncanny wedding
night" nor of her defloration by Holofernes; she boasts in fact that "she has
not been defiled." Freud congratulated Hebbel for sexualizing the patriotic
narrative. "With the fine perception of a poet, he sensed the ancient motive,
which had been lost . . . , and . . . merely restored its earlier content to the
material."[23] With the "fine" perception of a (male) psychoanalyst, Freud
put his finger on the nature of women's hostility to men, which in turn led
men to dread them.

• • • • •

That man had a "dread of woman" Horney regarded as an established
fact. "Always, everywhere," she wrote in a 1932 paper, "the man strives to rid
himself of his dread of woman by objectifying it. 'It is not,'" she imagined
him saying, "'that I dread her; it is that she herself is malignant, capable of
any crime, a beast of prey, a vampire, a witch, insatiable in her desires. She is
the very personification of what is sinister.'" That Freud had fathomed this
dread Horney regarded as doubtful. He had fared no better than Everyman,
she suggested, contenting himself with castration impulses that sometimes

do occur in women. She faulted him for not pressing his analytic inquiry with sufficient rigor:

> Even if defloration invariably aroused destructive impulses in the woman, we should still have to lay bare (as we should do in every individual analysis) the urgent impulses within the man himself which make him view the first— forcible—penetration of the vagina as so perilous an undertaking; so perilous, indeed, that it can be performed with impunity only by a man of might or by a stranger who chooses to risk his life or his manhood for a recompense.[24]

That "so little recognition and attention" had been paid "to the fact of man's secret dread of woman" pointed, in Horney's view, to formidable resistance. It took many apparently contradictory guises—glorification and disparagement of women among them. "The attitude of love and adoration signifies: 'There is no need for me to dread a being so wonderful, so beautiful, nay, so saintly. That of disparagement implies: 'It would be too ridiculous to dread a creature who, if you take her all round, is such a poor thing.'"[25]

How could this resistance be breached? The dreams of male analysands proved once again the royal road to unconscious material. "All analysts," Horney wrote, were familiar with dreams in which "a motorcar is rushing along and suddenly falls into a pit and is dashed to pieces; a boat is sailing in a narrow channel and is suddenly sucked into a whirlpool; there is a cellar with uncanny, blood-stained plants and animals; one is climbing a chimney and is in danger of falling and being killed."[26] Even without relating the patients' associations, Horney interpreted—and assumed that fellow analysts would interpret—these dreams as graphic representations of man's dread of the female genital.

The play of children provided another path to the same material. Horney reported the following experiment:

> The physician was playing ball with . . . children [of an unspecified age] at a treatment center, and after a time showed them that the ball had a slit in it. She pulled the edges of the slit apart and put her finger in it, so that it was held fast by the ball. Of 28 boys whom she asked to do the same, only 6 did it without fear and 8 could not be induced to do it at all. Of 19 girls 9 put their fingers in without a trace of fear; the rest showed a slight uneasiness but none of them serious anxiety.[27]

At this point Horney's orthodox readers might well have paused. After all, the phallic phase, as Freud had conceptualized it, consisted in "the fact that, for both sexes, only one genital, namely the male one," came into account.[28] "The truly feminine vagina," he argued, remained "undiscovered for both sexes"—and by implication remained psychically unelaborated.[29] Horney objected—vigorously: the "undiscovered" vagina was a "denied vagina."[30] The little girl did not begin as a little man, and the boy was painfully aware of this difference.

Horney started with the body, or rather with the meaning of bodily experiences, in this instance the fantasies and wishes that accompanied penile sensations. So too had Freud when he had imagined five-year-old Hans puzzling over childbirth:

> But his father not only knew where children came from, he actually performed it—the thing that Hans could only obscurely divine. The widdler [penis] must have something to do with it, for his own grew excited whenever he thought of these things. . . . If he listened to these premonitory sensations he could only suppose that it was a question of some act of violence performed upon his mother, of smashing something, of making an opening into something, of forcing a way into an enclosed space—such were the impulses he felt stirring within him.

At this point, Freud assumed, Little Hans's meditations reached a deadend: "Although the sensations of his penis had put him on the road to postulating a vagina, yet he could not solve the problem, for within his experience no such thing existed as his widdler required."[31] Not so Horney. She assumed that a boy's phallic impulses bade him "instinctively to search for an appropriate opening in the female body"—an opening, moreover, that he himself lacked. The boy pictured "in fantasy a complementary female organ."[32]

What made this genital difference painful and/or anxiety-provoking? Here Horney ushered the oedipal mother onto the stage. The boy, she wrote, "instinctively" judged that his penis was "much too small for his mother's genital."[33] (Freud tacitly agreed: he imagined Hans musing on a "big widdler . . . , bigger than his own," which performed the act he "could only obscurely divine.")[34] The boy reacted, Horney emphatically believed, with a sense of "inadequacy, of being rejected and derided." Organ sensations and fantasies combined to produce a "menace" to the boy's "self-respect" and along with it his dread of women.[35]

How did the boy react to this dread—for Horney, the most fundamental of all anxieties? His reaction, she wrote, displayed two aspects. The first amounted to a heightening of sadism. The foiling of a boy's phallic impulses would, Horney assumed, provoke anger; it would also trigger "old resentment springing from pregenital frustrations." The boy's "impulses to penetrate" would "merge with his anger and frustration," and the impulses themselves would "take on a sadistic tinge." (The sadistic admixture, through fear of retaliation, would make the mother's genital even more dreadful—as a source of castration anxiety.) The second aspect amounted to a strengthening of the boy's phallic narcissism. He withdrew his libido from his mother and concentrated it "on himself and his genital."[36] The female genital no longer existed for him. Now, and only now, did he conform to the infantile genital organization postulated by Freud—that is, the "primacy of the *phallus*."[37]

• • • • •

The story that boys told themselves about feminine development, and psychoanalysts echoed—the story of organ deficiency and a lifelong sense of inferiority—stood revealed as their own. It had simply, Horney implied, been disavowed and displaced. The final item of her exegesis concerned envy, not boys' obvious and persistent envy of paternal potency, but rather their hidden and equally persistent envy of maternal fecundity. It turned out that boys and men dreaded women and envied them as well.

Small boys, Horney argued, expressed "without embarrassment . . . the wish to be a woman."[38] Here she might have cited Little Hans's conviction about his childbearing capacity. On this point his father had been explicit: "You know quite well that boys can't have children." Hans had replied: "Well, yes. But I believe they can, all the same."[39] Grown men no longer uttered such thoughts, but, as Horney learned, they harbored wishes, all the same: "When one begins, as I did, to analyze men only after a fairly long experience of analyzing women, one receives a most surprising impression of the intensity of the envy of pregnancy, childbirth, and motherhood, as well as of the breasts and of the act of suckling."[40] All the more painful, then, the reality that theirs was only a "minute share in creating new life."[41]

This differing parental investment, to use the language of contemporary sexual selection theory, Horney regarded as a continuing source of tension between the sexes. (She also regarded it as an "incitement" to men "to create something new" of their own. "State, religion, art and science," she wrote, were their "creations.")[42] At the same time men sought "to deny or conceal the existence of a . . . power struggle . . . between the sexes." To that end, they, the more powerful, had constructed an ideology that interpreted "the differentness of the weaker . . . as inferiority" and claimed that these differences were "unchangeable, basic, or God's will."[43]

THE "WEAKER" SEX

In an article published in 1923, Horney made special mention of Freud's essay of 1920 entitled "The Psychogenesis of a Case of Homosexuality in a Woman." It was just this paper, she wrote, that helped her to understand the masculinity complex in women.[44] His paper provided her with the conceptual elements she was to deploy. It was her paper that figured in retrospect as opening the psychoanalytic debate about feminine psychology.[45]

The patient Freud reported on stayed in treatment with him only briefly. (After careful study, he "advised her parents that if they set store by the therapeutic procedure it should be continued by a woman doctor.")[46] "A beautiful and clever girl of eighteen, belonging to a family of good standing," she had aroused her parents' "displeasure and concern . . . by the devoted adoration with which she pursued a certain 'society lady'" about ten years her senior. It was well known, the parents informed Freud, that "in spite of her distinguished name, this lady was nothing but a *cocotte* . . . , that she lived with a friend, a married woman, and had intimate relations with her, while at the same time she carried on promiscuous affairs with a number of men." None of "these evil reports" interfered with the girl's "worship of the lady. . . . No prohibitions and no supervision hindered the girl from seizing every one of her rare opportunities of being together with her beloved, of ascertaining all her habits, of waiting for her for hours outside her door or at a tram-halt, of sending her flowers, and so on. . . . [T]his one interest had swallowed up all others in the girl's mind."[47]

His careful study equipped Freud to give a "concise summary" of the girl's sexual history. That summary consisted of two distinct conceptual elements. The oedipal stood out as the more prominent. "In childhood," Freud wrote, "the girl had passed through the normal attitude characteristic of the feminine Oedipus complex in a way that was not at all remarkable."[48] By that he meant that she had been attached to her father, that she had chosen him as her love object, and that, again in a fashion characteristic of the feminine Oedipus, she had later found a substitute in a brother slightly older than herself. Freud's conciseness bordered on the meagre, and he acknowledged as much. ("The girl," he wrote, "had never been neurotic, and came to the analysis without even one hysterical symptom, so that opportunities for investigating the history of her childhood did not present themselves so readily as usual." The task to be carried out amounted not to "resolving a neurotic conflict" but to "converting one variety of the genital organization of sexuality into the other . . . never an easy matter.")[49]

In contrast the girl's adolescent oedipal history was altogether remarkable, and Freud proceeded to elaborate aided by a "series of dreams, interrelated and easy to interpret." One event figured as the turning point. When the girl was about sixteen, her mother gave birth to a son. Before her mother became pregnant, the girl, from roughly the age of thirteen or fourteen, had "displayed a tender and, according to general opinion, exaggeratedly strong affection for a small boy, not quite three years old." With her mother's pregnancy, she became cool to the boy and "began to take an interest in mature, but still youthful, women." It was evident, Freud wrote, that at "this point a number of very different things might have happened." What actually happened—the girl's repudiating "her wish for a child, her love of men, and the feminine role in general"—he regarded as "the most extreme case."[50]

How, he asked rhetorically, was one "to understand the fact that it was precisely the birth of a child who came late in the family (at a time when the girl herself was already mature and had strong wishes of her own) that moved her to bestow her passionate tenderness upon the woman who gave birth to this child—i.e., her . . . mother—and to express that feeling towards a substitute?"

> The explanation is as follows. It was just when the girl was experiencing the revival of her infantile Oedipus complex at puberty that she suffered her great disappointment. She became keenly conscious of the wish to have a child, and a male one; that what she desired was her *father's* child and an image of *him*, her consciousness was not allowed to know. And what happened next? It was not *she* who bore the child, but her unconsciously hated rival, her mother. Furiously resentful and embittered, she turned away from her father and from men altogether. After this first great reverse she . . . sought another goal for her libido.[51]

What about that goal? Why should the girl pursue a mother-substitute when her own mother stood as a "hated rival"? (The mother, "still youthful herself, saw in her rapidly developing daughter an inconvenient competitor; she favoured the sons at her expense, limited her independence as much as possible, and kept an especially strict watch against any close relation between the girl and her father.")[52] From the beginning, Freud surmised, the girl's tie to her mother had been loving as well as hating. She simply revived that love, but since "there was little to be done with the real mother," she transferred it to a substitute "to whom she could become passionately attached." That was not all:

> The first objects of her affection after the birth of her . . . brother were really mothers, women between thirty and thirty-five whom she had met with their children during summer holidays or in the family circle of acquaintances in town. Motherhood as a *sine qua non* in her love-object was later on given up, because that precondition was difficult to combine in real life with another one, which grew more and more important. The specially intense bond with her latest love had still another basis which the girl discovered quite easily one day. Her lady's slender figure, severe beauty and downright manner reminded her of the brother who was a little older than herself. Her latest choice corresponded, therefore, not only to her feminine but also to her masculine ideal; it combined satisfaction of the homosexual tendency with that of the heterosexual one.[53]

To Freud the oedipal story seemed sufficient to account for the girl's choice of object—at least retrospectively. It was not sufficient to account for "the fact that in her behaviour to her adored lady the girl had adopted the characteristic masculine type of love."

> Her humility and her tender lack of pretensions, . . . her bliss when she was allowed to accompany the lady a little way and to kiss her hand on parting, her joy when she heard her praised as beautiful . . . , her pilgrimages to places once visited by the loved one, the silence of all more sensual wishes—all these little traits in her resembled the first passionate adoration of a youth for a celebrated actress whom he regards as far above him, to whom he scarcely dares lift his bashful eyes. . . . When the girl learnt later . . . that . . . her adored lady lived simply by giving her bodily favours, her reaction took the form of great compassion and of phantasies and plans for "rescuing" her beloved from these ignoble circumstances. . . . All that is enigmatic in this attitude vanishes when we remember that in the . . . *masculine* type of object-choice derived from the mother it is a necessary condition that the loved object should be in some way or other "of bad repute" sexually—someone who may be called a *cocotte*.[54]

To explain this type of love Freud turned to a second conceptual element: the girl's penis envy and her consequent "strongly marked 'masculinity complex'":

> A spirited girl, always ready for romping and fighting, she was not at all prepared to be second to her slightly older brother; after inspecting his genital organs she

had developed a pronounced envy for the penis, and thoughts derived from this envy continued to fill her mind. She was in fact a feminist; she felt it to be unjust that girls should not enjoy the same freedom as boys, and rebelled against the lot of women in general.[55]

How object-choice and what Freud referred to as "mental sexual character" fit together he claimed not to know. ("A man in whose character feminine attributes obviously predominate, who may, indeed, behave in love like a woman, might be expected from this feminine attitude, to choose a man for his love-object; but he may nevertheless be heterosexual, and show no more inversion in respect to his object than an average normal man.")[56] How the oedipal story and penis envy fit together he neglected to ask.

Five years later he remedied this neglect. In a paper entitled "Some Psychical Consequences of the Anatomical Distinction Between the Sexes" (1925), he located penis envy in the prehistory of the Oedipus complex and for the first time conceptualized that prehistory. The scene unfolded as follows: little girl noticing, glancing at, or examining the penis of brother or playmate. She had seen it, knew she was without it, and wanted it—all "in a flash."[57] From this scene the masculinity complex branched off. Other branchings included the little girl's turning her back on sexuality altogether and finding her way along a roundabout path to her father as love object and thus to the positive female Oedipus complex.[58] By the time Freud enumerated these trajectories, Horney's paper had already appeared in print.[59]

· · · · ·

Horney began her 1923 article "On the Genesis of the Castration Complex in Women" by paraphrasing a text of her former analyst, Abraham. "Many females," her rendering went, suffered "either temporarily or permanently from the fact of their sex." Their "objection" to being women could be traced to "their coveting a penis when they were little girls." Abraham's formulation, Horney was quick to point out, assumed as an "axiomatic fact" that females felt "at a disadvantage because of their genital organs." Thanks to "male narcissism,"[60] female penis envy had seemed so self-evident, so obviously to constitute "bedrock," as Freud was to put it, that it had not prompted a demand for explanation.[61] Horney insisted that the question be posed: Was it the case, she asked, that the masculinity complex in women derived solely from their "coveting a penis"?[62] The reader had reason to expect an answer in the negative.

Horney was ready to acknowledge that penis envy was "an almost invariable typical phenomenon," even when there was "no favored brother to make envy of this sort comprehensible," and when no particular experiences had caused "the masculine role to seem the more desirable." She was not ready to acknowledge that this envy derived, in unmediated fashion, from anatomical difference. Instead she focused on the fantasies and wishes that accompanied infantile sexual impulses. They could, she claimed, be sorted into three categories: "fantasies of omnipotence, especially those of a sadistic character"—they were "more easily associated with the jet of urine passed by the male"; exhibitionistic and voyeurist wishes—they could be satisfied by the boy, "at least as far as his own body" was concerned, every time he passed urine; and masturbatory wishes—the license granted boys "to take hold of their genital when urinating" might be "construed as permission to masturbate."[63] Horney then located the starting point for what she referred to as primary penis envy in a little girl's wish to urinate like a boy. Having located it, she quickly dismissed it as of scant consequence for explaining the masculinity complex.

Here Horney broke off her discussion of primary penis envy and introduced the Oedipus complex—this time, its female version. Recall the components she had brought together in elaborating on the male counterpart: the boy's phallic sensations coupled with his fantasies of a complementary female organ; the oedipal mother coupled with the boy's sense of genital inadequacy; the dread of women; sadism and/or phallic narcissism as sequelae. Each of these elements now turned out to come in female guise, and as she lined them up, Horney challenged the causal connection Freud had postulated between penis envy and the masculinity complex.

First came childhood vaginal sensations. Horney did not speculate about them in print until 1926. In "The Flight from Womanhood," she deemed the occurrence of such sensations highly probable. Childhood female fantasies—"an excessively large penis . . . effecting forcible penetration, producing pain and hemorrhage, and threatening to destroy something, . . . and also the logically ensuing dread of an internal . . . injury"—suggested, she claimed, "that the vagina as well as the clitoris" played "a part in the early infantile genital organization of women."[64] Seven years later, in a paper entitled "The Denial of the Vagina," she sounded more convinced. To make her case she used an argument from Freud to arrive at a distinctly un-Freudian conclusion. If, she reasoned, one accepted his view that the child's sexual theories were modeled on the child's own psychosexual constitution,[65] meaning that the theories traversed a path "marked out and determined by spontaneously experienced impulses and organ sensations," then the genital fantasies and anxieties of little girls must be "based on vaginal organ sensations (or the instinctual impulses issuing from these)."[66] Both Freud and Horney worked back to bodily experiences from the psychical elaboration of them. Horney, however, found her way back to two bodies rather than to only one.

Next came the oedipal father himself (and he had already figured in her 1923 paper). Horney reported that girls and women who manifestly desired to be men had "at the very outset of life passed through a phase of extremely strong father fixation." They had tried "to master the Oedipus complex" in what she regarded as the normal way "by retaining their original identification with the mother, and like the mother, taking the father as love object."[67] (Note how Horney took for granted an original identification with mother. Note also that Horney, like Deutsch, assumed that the identification derived not from anatomy but from an understanding of the mother's position in intercourse.) Thanks to love of father and identification with mother, the little girl constructed the fantasy that she had experienced "full sexual appropriation by the father." So it had been with a patient Horney identified merely as X:

> At times she [X] was under a compulsion to eat salt. Her mother had been obliged to eat salt on account of hemorrhages of the lungs, which had occurred in the patient's early childhood; she [X] had unconsciously construed them as the result of her parents' intercourse. This symptom therefore stood for her unconscious claim to have suffered the same experience from her father as her mother had undergone. It was the same claim that made her regard herself as a prostitute (actually she was a virgin).[68]

Love of father and identification with mother also produced anxiety: the little girl knew or felt that her genital was "too small for her father's penis"; she feared that "if her wishes were fulfilled, she herself or her genital would be destroyed."[69]

Then reality supervened, and with it frustration, which, Horney claimed, often changed into "a profound *disappointment*"—at least it had done so in those women who desired to be men. These patients felt as if "their fathers had actually once been their lovers and had afterward been false to them or deserted them."

In the patient X, who used to revel in numerous recollections of that earliest period of her life, which she called her childhood's paradise, this disappointment was closely connected in her memory with an unjust punishment inflicted on her by her father when she was five or six years old. It transpired that at this time a sister had been born and that she had felt herself supplanted by this sister in her father's affections. As deeper strata were revealed, it became clear that behind the jealousy of her sister there lay a furious jealousy of her mother, which related to her mother's many pregnancies. "Mother *always* had the babies," she once said indignantly. More strongly repressed . . . was sexual jealousy of her mother dating from her witnessing parental coitus. . . . It was a mishearing on her part that put me on the track of this last source of her feeling. Once as I was speaking of a time "nach *der Enttäuschung*" (after the disappointment), she understood me to say "Nacht *der Enttäuschung* (the night of the disappointment).[70]

What sequelae did this disappointment produce? The first, the masculinity complex—that is, the desire to be a man—has already been hinted at. Horney elaborated: the disappointed little girl renounced her claim upon her father and renounced her desire for a child as well. (Here Horney challenged the Freudian notion that a woman's wish for a baby represented a displacement from her wish for a penis.)[71] Having given up the father as a love object, the little girl, Horney claimed, "regressively replaced" the object relation "by an identification with him."[72] (Here Horney exploited a "mechanism" postulated by Freud. And here her accounts of boys and girls did not map onto each other: in a man, identification with mother implied the fulfillment of his castration fears—hence he repudiated it; in a woman, identification with father could draw on primary penis envy.)

What had happened to penis envy? For Freud it lay at the root of the masculinity complex and could not be extirpated. For Horney, (disappointed) love of father figured as crucial, and should it give way to an identification, a secondary form of penis envy would follow. Revived by and dependent upon the identification with father the little girl's penis envy now reached Freudian proportions. Now and only now did she brood over her lack of that organ and wonder whether her genitals had been injured.

In . . . [one] patient . . . this feeling of having sustained a wound was displaced on to other organs, so that . . . the clinical picture was markedly hypochondriacal. . . . Her resistance took the following form: "It is obviously absurd for me to be analyzed, seeing that my heart, my lungs, my stomach, and my intestines are evidently organically diseased." . . . Her associations constantly brought the idea that she had been struck down (*geschlagen*) with illness by her father. As a matter of fact, when these hypochondriacal symptoms cleared up, fantasies of being *struck* (*Schlagephantasien*) became . . . prominent . . . Their main features . . . [are] perfectly clear if we regard them as an effect of the impulse to experience anew, after a compulsive fashion, the suffering undergone at the hands of the father and to prove to herself the reality of the painful experience.[73]

(Note how even now love of father came to the fore, displacing penis envy from its preeminent Freudian position.)

Recall how Freud had carefully distinguished between "mental sexual character" and object-choice; Horney ran them together—or rather envisaged the masculinity complex as eventuating in homosexuality. A "completely successful . . . repression of the love attitude toward the father," she claimed, and "identification with him"—that is, playing the "father's part"—always amounted to "desiring the mother in some sense."[74] At this point she reached the end of her remarks about the masculinity complex.

A second sequel to (disappointed) love of father—a revengeful attitude toward men, "directed with particular vehemence against the man" who performed "the act of defloration"—required further comment.[75] In a paper of 1931 entitled "The Distrust Between the Sexes," she spelled out just how disturbed relations to men could be:

The little girl who was badly hurt through some great disappointment by her father, will transform her . . . instinctual wish to receive from the man, into a vindictive one of taking from him by force. Thus the foundation is laid for a direct line of development to a later attitude, according to which she . . . will have only one drive, i.e., to harm the male, to exploit him, and to suck him dry. She has become a vampire. . . . Let us further assume that the . . . wish [to suck him dry] was repressed due to anxiety from a guilty conscience; then we have here the fundamental constellation for the formation of a certain type of woman who . . . fears that every male will suspect her of wanting something from him. This really means that she is afraid he might guess her repressed desires. Or by completely projecting onto him her repressed wishes, she will imagine that every male merely intends to exploit her, that he wants from her only sexual satisfaction, after which he will discard her. Or let us assume that a reaction formation of excessive modesty will mask the repressed drive for power. We then have the type of woman who shies away from demanding or accepting anything from her husband. . . . Quite often the repression of aggression against the male drains all her vital energy. The woman then feels helpless to meet life. She will shift the entire responsibility for her helplessness onto the man, robbing him of the very breath of life. Here you have the type of woman who, under the guise of being helpless and childlike, dominates her man.[76]

Once again Horney was intent on bringing into the open the power struggle between men and women.

• • • • •

In her paper "The Overvaluation of Love" (1934), Horney demanded an explanation for yet another phenomenon that male narcissism made it easy to take for granted: women's or certain women's "exclusive concentration upon men." Her questions, and the answers she offered, were based on seven analytic cases of her own as well as a number of cases familiar to her through analytic conferences. By and large, "these patients had no prominent symptoms." All, however, complained about difficulties in their relations to men. After "somewhat prolonged analytic work," it emerged that "these women were as though possessed by a single thought, 'I must have a man'"—so obsessed "that by comparison all the rest of life seemed stale, flat, and unprofitable. The capabilities and interests" with which most of them were well equipped "either had no meaning . . . for them or had lost what meaning they once had." In short, "their estimate of a heterosexual relationship as the only valuable thing in life" represented "a compulsive overvaluation."[77]

"The transference situation" with a woman analyst, Horney wrote, was "dominated throughout by two attitudes." The first consisted in pushing relations with men "into the foreground." As in life, so now in the analysis—but now it might be interpreted as acting out. "Often one man after another" played a part, "ranging from mere approaches to sexual relations," while accounts of what he had done or not done, whether he loved or disappointed her patient, and of how she had reacted to him took up "at times the greater part of the hour" and were "tirelessly spun out to the smallest detail."[78]

Horney raised the possibility—one that would have immediately occurred to her psychoanalytic audience—that the key to her patients' behavior lay in "a strong and at the same time dreaded homosexuality." She had, however, been taken aback—and she expected her audience to respond similarly—by finding that "in all these cases an interpretation based upon unconscious homosexual tendencies and flight therefrom" remained "completely ineffectual therapeutically." She had continued her search for "a more correct one." A clinical example had put her on the right track and would, she assumed, induce her audience to follow her along it:

> A patient at the beginning of her treatment repeatedly sent me flowers, at first anonymously and then openly. My first interpretation, that she was behaving like a man wooing a woman, did not alter her behavior, although she admitted it laughingly. My second interpretation, that the presents were intended as a compensation for the aggression she abundantly exhibited, was equally without effect. . . . [T]he picture changed as if by magic when the patient brought associations that stated unequivocally that by means of presents one can make a person dependent upon one. A fantasy that followed brought to light the deeper destructive content behind this wish. She would like, she said, to be my maid and do everything for me to perfection. Thus I would become dependent on her, trust her completely, and then one day—she would put poison in my coffee. She concluded her fantasy with a phrase that is absolutely typical of this group of individuals: "Love is a means of murder."[79]

How did this example serve Horney's purposes? It illuminated what distinguished her sample of patients from homosexuals and why her interpretation of homosexuality had proved ineffective. Homosexual women, she wrote, not only exploited their masculinity; they also loved with an intensity that overcompensated for their destructive impulses. This amounted to rendering such impulses "harmless by means of libidinal ties." This amounted, as well, to giving up on men or to having given up on them so early and so thoroughly that "erotic rivalry with other women" had receded into the background.[80] (Here Horney added to her earlier stress on the little girl's disappointed love of father a new emphasis on the competition with mother and/or sister that she had foresworn.) In the case Horney cited, the overcompensation had not materialized—rivalry had instead.

Within her sample, she claimed, rivalry figured as a second attitude that dominated the transference. The patients saw the (woman) analyst as interfering in their relations to men; they saw the analyst as a jealous mother or sister who would not "tolerate a feminine type of development or success in the feminine sphere." A struggle was being enacted:

> When the analyst insists upon analyzing instead of allowing the acting out of the relations to the man, this is unconsciously interpreted as a prohibition, as opposition, on the part of the analyst. If on occasion the analyst points out that

without analysis these attempts to establish a relationship with a man cannot possibly lead anywhere, this signifies . . . to the patient a repetition of attempts by the mother or sister to suppress the patient's feminine self-esteem—as if the analyst had said: You are too little, or of too little account, or not sufficiently attractive; you cannot attract or hold a man. And comprehensibly enough, her reaction is to demonstrate that she can.[81]

At this point Horney felt obliged to ask: What had "so tremendously" increased the rivalry and imparted to it "such an enormously destructive character"?[82] (She suspected that "not infrequently the family situation"—that is, "the Oedipus complex"—was being played out in the transference "in almost unchanged form.")[83] From the previous histories of her sample, she deduced a marked exacerbation of a typical oedipal experience: as children these women had suffered a greater than usual sense of defeat thanks to the presence of a mother or sister whose domination appeared well-nigh total.

> In one of these cases the mother was a particularly attractive woman, surrounded by a crowd of male acquaintances, and [she] kept the father in a state of absolute dependence upon her. In another instance not only was the sister preferred, but the father had a love affair with a relative living in the house and in all probability with other women. In yet another case the still young and unusually beautiful mother was the absolute center of attention on the part of the father as well as of the sons and the various men who frequented the house. . . . In still another case the father had made sexual advances to the patient from her fourth year, which became more outspoken in their character at the approach of puberty. At the same time he not only continued to be extremely dependent upon the mother, who received devotion on all sides, but was likewise very susceptible to the charms of other women, so that the girl got the impression of being merely her father's plaything, to be cast aside at his convenience or when grownup women appeared on the scene.[84]

To compete or not to compete: that was the choice, and a painful one, that Horney's patients confronted after their (failed) struggle. In all her cases, she found either "a partial or complete avoidance or inhibition in regard to rivalry with women, or . . . compulsive rivalry of exaggerated proportions—and the greater the feeling of being worsted, the more intent" was "the victim . . . upon the death of the rival, as though to say: Only when you are dead can I be free."[85]

And those who chose to compete did not succeed: they did not establish a satisfactory relationship with a man. How could it be otherwise, when the man being chased was merely a trophy in a war with other women?

• • • • •

Horney had begun her work intent on rescuing the psychology of women from the condescension of men. She had pursued her goal by telling an unsentimental tale. Nowhere did she imply that women were less egotistical than men, that they were less competitive, that they might somehow lead the way, if only men would follow, toward the light. On the contrary she fastened on the tension between the sexes, derived from man's fear of mother's genital and woman's disappointment in father's love, and on rivalry among women for the frustrating father. She highlighted the very issues that the theory of sexual selection featured and hence suggested that theory as a title for her story. At the same time she hinted at how her tale might account for the "patriarchal ideal" she deplored, more particularly how competition among women—how females maximizing their chances for (reproductive) success vis-à-vis other females—perpetuated the ideal image of "woman as one whose only longing" was "to love a man and be loved by him, to admire him and [to] serve him."[86]

CODA: *THE NEUROTIC PERSONALITY* *OF OUR TIME*

In the autumn of 1935, three years after her arrival in the United States and a year after her move to New York City, Horney delivered a series of lectures at the New School for Social Research. The series, entitled "Culture and Neurosis," led first to an article with the same title, which appeared the following year in the *American Sociological Review*,[87] and second to a book published in the spring of 1937. When the book, *The Neurotic Personality of Our Time,* came out, the professional reviews were mixed: the anthropologist Ruth Benedict praised it for throwing "into sharp relief the interdependence of psychological and sociological work";[88] the psychoanalyst Ernest Jones also recognized Horney's "predominantly social conceptions," but those conceptions did not meet with his approval. A number of her observations he regarded as either dangerous half-truths or examples of throwing out "the baby with the bath."[89] Jones's response suggested that Horney had not intended her work primarily for the psychoanalytic community.

In her introduction, she made it clear that she aimed her book at a diverse audience. Her work, she declared, was addressed to those who dealt "professionally with neurotic persons" and were "familiar with the problems involved." Among them she counted psychiatrists, social workers, teachers, and in addition, "anthropologists and sociologists" who had become "aware of the significance of psychic factors in the study of different cultures." It was also addressed, she announced, to the "interested layman." For this diverse audience, she had taken pains to avoid "technical terms" and to write in "plain language." In return she expected her readers to be actively engaged. "The specialist and even the layman," she hoped, would "test the validity" of her statements, not against detailed case histories—to keep the book from being "unduly cumbersome," she provided none—but against their "own observations and experience, and on this basis reject or accept, modify or underscore" what she had said.[90]

From one group of readers—those who themselves were neurotic—Horney expected most in the way of active engagement. If they did not oppose "psychological thinking as an intrusion and an imposition," she wrote, they often possessed in their "own suffering a keener and finer understanding of psychological intricacies" than their "more robust brothers." They were far more likely to appreciate that "psychological problems" were "necessarily . . . subtle" and not reducible to "ready formulae."[91] Unfortunately, she continued, they also tended to recognize such intricacies in others more readily than in themselves. Here, without using technical language, Horney pointed out projection at work and made a clinical intervention. Here the narrator appeared in the role of sympathetic therapist.

And she received an appreciative response: in the decade following its publication, *The Neurotic Personality of Our Time* went through thirteen printings.[92]

• • • • •

In contrast to her earlier writings, in which Freud's initial formulation of the Oedipus complex figured as central, Horney now pushed that complex to the margins. Already, in a publication of 1935, she had referred in passing to "ethnological studies," which showed that the "peculiar emotional pattern in the relations between parents and children . . . denoted by the term Oedipus complex" arose "only under certain cultural conditions."[93] In *The*

Neurotic Personality of Our Time she insisted far more on its peculiarity: "I believe that the Oedipus complex is, instead of a primary process, the outcome of several processes which are different in kind. . . . In fact a fully developed Oedipus complex . . . is not . . . the origin of the neurosis, but is itself a neurotic formation."[94]

Along with Oedipus, sexuality beat a retreat. " 'All is not gold that glitters,' " she wrote, "so also 'all is not sexuality that looks like it.' " "Many phenomena are accepted as sexual which are really the expression of complex neurotic conditions. . . . For example, sexual desires concerning the analyst are usually interpreted as repetitions of a sexual fixation on the father or mother, but often are not genuine sexual wishes at all, but a reaching out for some reassuring contact to allay anxiety."[95] Horney both reduced sexuality to its pre-Freudian dimensions, and in denying its infantile variety—the tenderness between mother and child, she claimed, was not sexual in nature[96]—deprived sexuality of its lengthy and complex history.

What came to the fore—a coupling of hostility and anxiety—ranked as ingredients of the oedipal drama, but in Horney's new account these powerful emotions derived from the parents' actual behavior rather than the child's sexual fantasies. From examining the histories of "great numbers of neurotic persons," she drew a profile of their childhood environment:

> The basic evil is invariably a lack of genuine warmth and affection. A child can stand a great deal of what is often regarded as traumatic—such as sudden weaning, occasional beating, sex experience—as long as inwardly he feels wanted and loved. . . . The main reason a child does not receive enough warmth and affection lies in the parents' incapacity to give it on account of their own neuroses. More frequently than not, in my experience, the essential lack of warmth is camouflaged, and the parents claim to have in mind the child's best interest. Educational theories, oversolicitude or the self-sacrificing attitude of an "ideal" mother are the basic factors contributing to an atmosphere that more than anything else lays the cornerstone for future feelings of immense insecurity.

> Furthermore, we find various actions or attitudes on the part of the parents which cannot but arouse hostility, such as a preference for other children, unjust reproaches, unfulfilled promises, and not least important, an attitude toward the child's needs which goes through all gradations from temporary inconsideration to a consistent interfering with the most legitimate wishes of the child, such as disturbing friendships, ridiculing independent thinking, spoiling its interest in its own pursuits, whether artistic, athletic or mechanical—altogether an attitude of the parents which if not in intention nevertheless in effect means breaking the child's will.[97]

Horney fastened on two measures frequently adopted to protect against the "basic anxiety" that such a childhood environment engendered. The first amounted to a quest for affection—on the assumption that if a person is loved by someone, that someone would not hurt him or her. In acquiring a protective function, she argued, an otherwise normal wish became "entirely different": where no pathology impinged, the primary feeling was one of fondness; where neurosis held sway, the primary feeling was "the need for reassurance, and the illusion of loving" was "only secondary."[98] (Why illusion? The neurotic's affectionate attitude, Horney claimed, was "born of a fear" that he would "lose the other, or of a wish to get the other person under his thumb." This, she insisted, was not love.)[99] As a clinician she considered a patient's "enchanced need for affection . . . [as] an alarm signal" indicating that some anxiety and/or hostility, the two being inextricably interwoven, had come close to the surface. A familiar sequence went like this: "a problem comes up, discussion of which provokes an intense hostility against the analyst; the patient starts to hate the analyst, to dream that he is dying; he represses his hostile impulses immediately, becomes frightened and out of a need for reassurance he clings to the analyst; when these reactions have been worked through, hostility, anxiety and with them the increased need for affection recede into the background."[100]

The second protective measure, already hinted at, amounted to a quest for power—on the assumption that if a person had power, no one could hurt him or her. Again such a quest came in a normal as well as a pathological variety. The latter might serve as protection against feeling helpless or "against the danger of feeling or being regarded as insignificant"; a cousin to it, the quest for prestige, protected against humiliation; and still another cousin, the quest for possession, protected against fear of "impoverishment, destitution, dependence on others." Taken together these *cousinages* ruled out relationships of mutuality and in so doing severely handicapped analytic work:

> Patients of this kind may ask desperately for help, yet not only will they fail to follow any suggestion, but they will express resentment at not being helped. If they do receive help by reaching an understanding of some peculiarity, they immediately fall back into their previous vexation and, as if nothing had been done, they will manage to erase the insight which was the result of the analyst's hard labor. Then the patient compels the analyst to put in new efforts which again are doomed to failure.
>
> The patient may receive a double satisfaction from such a situation: by presenting himself as helpless he receives a sort of triumph at being able to

compel the analyst to slave in his service. At the same time this strategy tends to elicit feelings of helplessness in the analyst, and thus since his [the patient's] entanglements prevent him from dominating in a constructive way, he finds a possibility of destructive domination. Needless to say, the satisfaction gained in this way is entirely unconscious, just as the technique used in order to gain it is applied unconsciously.[101]

The neurotic, Horney argued, did not engage in a single quest. Instead he set out on two incompatible missions simultaneously: he coupled "an aggressive striving for a 'no one but I dominance'" with an "intense desire to be loved by everyone." Here was an obvious dilemma: one could not step on people and be loved by them at the same time. Still the neurotic persevered: as a result he feared both failure and success. Failure represented catastrophe, all the more powerfully if it came after the neurotic had shown in any way that he did "indeed want success" and had tried to get it. How could it be otherwise, since he felt himself "surrounded by a horde of persecuting enemies," who lay in wait "to crush him at any sign of weakness"? Success also figured as dangerous. It would surely prompt, so the neurotic feared, "the begrudging envy of others and thus . . . the loss of their affection." Back and forth he went between "a frantic and compulsive wish to be the first in the race . . . and . . . an equally great compulsion to check himself" as soon as he made "any progress."[102]

Horney summed up: "a crushed self-esteem, destructiveness, anxiety, enhanced competitiveness entailing anxiety and destructive impulses, and excessive need for affection."[103] This was "the neurotic personality of our time." Narcissus rather than Oedipus might serve as its Greek prototype.

• • • • •

Horney's book overflowed with generalizations: she was intent on sketching permutations and combinations of personality structure—not their childhood genesis so much as their adult modes of action. (Hers, one commentator noted, was "a theory of the 'functional autonomy' of character trends formed early in life.")[104] Among Horney's generalizations those derived from sexual difference were notable by their absence. Her interests had shifted from the construction of womanhood to the construction of neurosis. What had once figured as disturbing in women—a craving for affection and intense competition—now figured as the common lot of neurotics across the board.

Chapter 4 Artificial Selection:
Robert J. Stoller and Nancy
Chodorow

After his return to England in 1837, Charles Darwin began "collecting all facts which bore in any way on the variation of animals and plants under domestication"—in hopes, as he commented in his *Autobiography,* that some light would be thrown on the subject of species modification. Thanks to the writings of animal breeders, he soon came to recognize the power of judiciously selecting males and females to propagate. Artificial selection, he noted, was "the keystone of man's success in making useful races of animals and plants." Thus, he continued, happening "to read for amusement Malthus on *Population,*" he was "well prepared to appreciate the struggle for existence" which went on everywhere.[1] The role of artificial selection in Darwin's theory building has been questioned;[2] its role in the modification of domesticated species has long been established.

Artificial selection, unlike sexual selection, remained ready at hand and could be reckoned as background knowledge shared by Robert J. Stoller and Nancy Chodorow—and by their readers as well. Yet neither explicitly referred to it. What justifies using artificial selection as a title for their stories is that they featured the issue the concept highlights: the role of intelligent manipulation (in this instance not always fully conscious). As for those being domesticated—that is, children—in the tales Stoller and Chodorow told, they figured as passive creatures.

Their narratives took off from a common Freudian starting point. In a series of papers published between 1925 and 1933, Freud revised his initial symmetrical view of girls' and boys' oedipal desires—that girls' wishes were directed toward father and boys' toward mother.[3] For girls as well as for boys, he now argued, mother figured as the original love object. In Stoller's judgment, Freud merely broached the subject: he "did not have time to follow through on his awareness . . . that a huge domain—the preoedipal relationship with mother—lay behind what he had discovered in the oedipal period."[4] By the time Stoller began writing in the 1960s, the preoedipal mother was becoming a much-studied parent indeed.

By that time, Stoller had been doing analytic work for roughly a decade. Born in 1924 and educated in New York, Stoller, like many of his agemates, had had his education interrupted by the Second World War. After only a year's study at Columbia University, he had been inducted into the army. He had not seen combat; instead, he had been shunted into a speeded-up medical program. By 1948 he had finished his medical training at the University of California, San Francisco, with an obligation for government service still outstanding. That debt he paid off by functioning as head of psychiatry at Travis Air Force Base from 1951 to 1953. A year later, his psychiatric residency completed, he moved with his family to Los Angeles, with the aim of pursuing psychoanalytic training at the Los Angeles Institute.[5]

The Institute had been founded in 1946, and the tripartite education it offered—training analysis, supervised control cases, and courses in theory and practice—conformed to the regulations of its parent organization, the American Psychoanalytic Association. Psychoanalytic candidates in the United States in the 1950s dutifully read Freud and were exposed to the "ego psychology" then being elaborated, to the work of Heinz Hartmann and his colleagues, who had come to dominate the New York Psychoanalytic Institute in particular and the American psychoanalytic scene more generally. One finds an echo of Hartmann's emphasis on the ego's conflict-free sphere in Stoller's insistence on the possibility of conflict-free development. One also finds a tuning out of much ego psychological discourse in Stoller's frequent strictures against the kind of psychoanalytic terminology and jargon that had become *de rigueur* in New York.

The position Stoller occupied within the psychoanalytic community was marginal: though highly respected in the Los Angeles Institute and sporadically teaching there, he never became a training and supervising analyst. His position position within the UCLA department of psychiatry was marginal as well. He had accepted a faculty appointment in 1954, upon moving to Los Angeles and beginning his analytic training. He continued on the faculty, ascending the University of California's professorial ladder— the one practicing analyst in a department not noted for its friendliness to psychoanalysis. But he was secure, and his security coupled with his marginality gave him the independence he so evidently relished.

How, then, did Stoller come to study "core gender identity"—the concept for which he is best known? His psychoanalytic training, he made clear, did not act as a spur. On the contrary: in the 1950s what he was being taught contributed to a complacent sense that in matters of sexuality, his patients would not baffle him. At that time, he noted, "analysts were raising few questions about the origins or maintenance of gender behavior; analytic theory seemed sophisticated enough to account for any clinical event, any observation, any data collected by another method." Despite the fact that his colleagues at UCLA had started a project on transsexualism, Stoller remained unmoved. The one patient those colleagues asked him to interview, "an anatomically normal man who needed to put on women's clothes and be enchained in order to become sexually excited," he found to be "no more than a pervert, readily enough understood by considering the vicissitudes of instincts, libidinal fixations, and oedipal traumas." Stoller awakened from his dogmatic slumber "one day in 1958, literally in a single moment." His colleagues had completed their work and had asked him to see a final patient simply to tell her—she had been categorized a " 'transsexual woman' "—that the research was finished.

> Shortly before the appointment hour, I was approaching stupor at a committee meeting in a conference room with a glass wall that allowed us to see people pass. A man walked by; I scarcely noticed him. A moment later, a secretary announced my eleven o'clock patient. And to my astonishment, the patient was not what I expected—a woman who acted masculine and in the process was a bit too much, grimly and pathetically discarding her femininity. Instead it was a man, unremarkable, natural appearing—an ordinary man (and eight years' follow-up until his death never changed that impression). Analytic theory,

though it can explain everything, did not, I felt, account for the naturalness of his masculinity, its presence since earliest childhood (confirmed in photographs from the family album), his nonhistrionic quality, and his unquestioned acceptance in society as male.[6]

Stoller was caught. The first patient "referred a friend, a butch homosexual 'female' who turned out to be a male pseudohermaphrodite." Then an intersexed patient turned up "who years later was revealed as really a male transsexual." Over the next twenty-five years Stoller "saw hundreds of patients and their family members in consultation or treatment. Anyone who came, by whatever way of referral, was worked up, and all those who asked for help were treated, as were their families." Stoller had neither a shortage of patients nor a shortage of questions. Over the course of those years he gradually discerned "several categories of cross-gender behavior," which he pressed into service for "studying the development of masculinity and femininity." And he slowly came to think that not all aberrations could be understood as psychoanalysts understood "perversions"—that is, as "attempts to resolve traumas, frustrations, intrapsychic conflicts."[7]

When he subsequently shifted his focus to sexual excitement, perversion, pornography, and sadomasochism, Stoller again had neither a shortage of patients nor a shortage of questions. He continued as a "naturalistic observer"—a notion to which he frequently resorted:

> I sightsee. The purpose is to get acquainted, look around, find interesting questions, ask people what they think the answers are, and keep at it for as long as I am interested. Those who say there is nothing left to be found by simple exploration, going there and looking, and that only experimental science can make the discoveries, are premature. The stories people can tell of what they have experienced and what they make of it have scarcely been heard.

And he introduced the notion of being an ethnographer as well:

> What I have not done until recently . . . is to go out into the world and do as the ethnographer does: not just to bring the specimens to the zoo or the museum, but to go into the forest and observe. That's a very tricky business, especially for a psychoanalyst. But being curious, adventuresome, and nonphobic, I did eventually wander out of the office and into the field, first for a study of the gender and erotic life of a New Guinea tribe, and later for the study of the X-rated industry and . . . of consensual sadomasochism. . . .
>
> In doing this work, I see myself, though an amateur, as working up a kind of ethnography that will be available to another motivated amateur. . . . The technique is, first, to ask all possible questions, and second, to use good judg-

ment and have good luck in finding informants who, singly or *en masse,* have answers. When you embark on a study such as this, know it has no end: there will always be more valuable informants, more facts, more questions, more theory, more wandering into other areas of study to surprise you with their centrality to your original interest. You must be prepared for unending amusement. (A sense of humor will protect you from the otherwise excessive stimulations of reality.)[8]

Stoller published this statement in 1991. Later that same year he was killed in an automobile accident.

• • • • •

In the 1970s and 1980s the concept of gender figured crucially in second-wave feminism. "From genetic differences in mathematics ability of boys and girls, the presence and significance of sex differences in neural organization, the relevance of animal research to human behaviors, the causes of male dominance in the organization of scientific research, sexist structures and use patterns in language, sociobiology debates, struggles over the meanings of sex chromosomal abnormalities, to the similarities of racism and sexism"[9]—in all these controversies, gender did yeoman service. Stoller himself did not enter the fray—in which Nancy Chodorow ranked as a key participant.

Had Stoller been interested in feminism, he might have appreciated that he and Chodorow belonged to the same conceptual lineage.[10] (The directors of the Stoller Foundation implicitly recognized the family resemblance when in 1993 they asked her to deliver the first Stoller Memorial Lecture.) Chodorow had worked out her own position independently of Stoller. She had been connected with "the feminist subculture that developed out of the New Left," and it was dissatisfaction with Marx, not with Freud, that had prompted her to intellectual exploration. As "an alternative to the Marxist account of women's oppression," Chodorow turned to the psychoanalytic theory she had encountered in the 1960s and early 1970s, first as an undergraduate studying anthropology at Harvard and then as a graduate student in sociology at Brandeis. By the time she had completed her classic, *The Reproduction of Mothering,* she was teaching sociology at the University of California, Santa Cruz—she later moved to Berkeley—and, as she put it, was "'hooked on'" psychoanalytic theory.[11] The addiction progressed: by the late 1980s she was undertaking training at the San Francisco Psychoanalytic Institute.

One might read Stoller and Chodorow as telling the same evolutionary narrative, each having constructed it on his or her own. One might also read Chodorow as exploiting Stoller's work on core gender identity for a feminist assault on the existing "sexual division of labor," which, she wrote, perpetuated male dominance.[12]

THE PRODUCTION OF GENDER IN MALES

Here is Stoller, in a this-is-your-author-speaking passage, making fun of what he labeled Rule Number 1 for playing the presenting and publishing game:

> Use the rhetoric of science, a formal not a conversational, writing style. . . .
>
> Heavy use of technical language (*cathexis, deneutralization, projective identification, narcissism*), for which we have less agreement on definitions than we admit publicly or to ourselves.
>
> Ponderous tone ("a function of the narcissistic libido which is amalgamated with the object cathexes").
>
> Replacing modest truths such as "I think" or "I guess" with prouder statements such as "I submit" or "The analysis of a number of such cases reveals the likelihood that it is substantially true, as Hartmann has conclusively shown, that . . . "
>
> Using pseudoquantifying words to bring science to one's declaration (*extreme, overwhelming, normal, archaic, healthy, borderline;* "in a *considerable number* of cases I have found that . . . "; "the patient was *obviously extremely* narcissistic, *almost* psychotic"; the fixation *points* of the central psychopathology of these cases are *located* at *a rather early* portion of the time axis of psychic development").[13]

Stoller the narrator intended to devise a different set of rules. Believe me—he, in effect, told his readers—precisely because I am not like other analysts, because I do not hide behind the usual jargon that dehumanizes what it describes, because I will not deny "the subjectivity out of which we [analysts] create both our data and our theory."[14] He expected his readers to find his account credible because they found him, the narrator, a trustworthy witness.

> I have tried to rely primarily on what one can observe in the patients. . . . Unhappily there is no way around the problem that one cannot know what an author really has observed unless one has been able to see the author's patients with him. That being impossible the author is under special obligation to try to

choose words that will come as close as possible to approximating what he actually observed. Since that requires the skill of an artist (with all the dangers that are latent in poetic privileges with language), and since I am not an artist, I must make do with relatively simple, nonabstract, nonimaginative language.[15]

His trustworthiness was reinforced by the tone: always conversational, frequently humorous—the result in part of dictating and then revising and revising the typed version.[16] It was as though the narrator were striking a bargain with his readers. He would reward their tolerance of his subjects' bizarre behaviors by presenting them in a fashion that was both accessible and compelling. At the same time, it was as if the narrator had struck a similar bargain with his subjects. He would reward their self-exposure by making certain that the self exposed remained recognizable to them: he let "patients and informants read the . . . material at each stage of its development toward publication"—he audiotaped most interviews let them "correct" the transcripts as they wished.[17] In two directions—toward readers and toward subjects—Stoller strove to reduce the emotional distance between him and them.

• • • • •

The patient is a 19-year-old, white, single secretary. . . . She was born a boy, with normal-appearing male genitalia. A birth certificate was issued for a male and she was appropriately named. . . .

With puberty began the development of secondary sex characteristics of a feminine nature. Her increasing fantasy life concerned the desire to be a girl, and with the increasing embarrassment over the need to continue to play the role of a boy, she became rather withdrawn and secretive. . . . Finally, at the age of 17, her appearance (37–25–37, as she proudly and accurately states) and the pressure of the desire to change sex became too great. She dropped out of school. During a vacation to relatives in a different state, she decided that this was the time to make the change. She accomplished this very abruptly by leaving her hotel as a male, buying clothes for a girl (alleging these were gifts), visiting a beauty parlor to have her already longish hair waved, and emerging from these procedures looking like a female. . . . The two years that have elapsed since have been filled with the patient's searching out and learning how to take over the role of female.[18]

In 1958 the patient, pseudonymously named Agnes, came to UCLA in the hope that by participating in a study on intersexuality he/she would be able to obtain corrective plastic surgery—removal of the penis and testes and fabrication of a vagina—at minimal cost. The group of researchers included Stoller, and he and his co-workers insisted on using the feminine pronoun:

> The most remarkable thing about the patient's appearance when she was first seen by us was that it was not possible for any of the observers, including those who knew of her anatomic state, to identify her as anything but a young woman. She was tall, slim, though of female build. Her hair, which was long, fine, and pulled back from her face across her ears, was touched a blond-brown from its normal brown. Her face was young-appearing, with a "peaches-and-cream" complexion. There was no facial hair. Her eyebrows were subtly plucked. . . . She was dressed in a tight sweater, which revealed her shoulders, ample breasts, and a narrow waist. Her hips and buttocks were larger than those to be expected in a 19-year-old youth and compatible with those seen in a woman of that age. Only her feet and hands seemed larger than usual for a woman, but . . . these were not so large as to be remarkable.
>
> She was dressed in a manner indistinguishable from that of any other typical girl of her age in this culture. There was nothing garish, outstanding, or abnormally exhibitionistic in her attire, nor was there any hint of poor taste or that the patient was ill at ease in her clothes. . . . All her mannerisms seemed appropriately feminine, though there was a touch of awkwardness about her reminiscent of a gawky adolescent who had not yet developed the full, subtle, feminine control of her body that would come in later years.
>
> Her voice was rich, soft, pitched at an alto level, with a lisp similar to that affected by feminine-appearing male homosexuals.[19]

Agnes was a medical mystery. She had feminine hair distribution and body build but a "normal-sized penis and atrophied testes"; laparotomy disclosed "no internal female organs, but the presence of all male anatomic structures. . . . Chromatin staining of buccal smear and of skin revealed a male pattern."[20] An endocrinological work-up showed evidence of continuing estrogen influence from a source that could not be determined— despite careful exploration of Agnes's abdominal cavity for an estrogen-producing tumor and microscopic examination of her testicular tissue for estrogen-producing cells. The endocrinologist concluded that Agnes presented a clinical picture suggesting "a superimposition of an excess of estrogen upon the substratum of a normal male."[21] What made her unique in the endocrinological literature was that, notwithstanding the presence of enough estrogen to produce completely feminine secondary sex characteristics, the penis had continued to develop normally.

Agnes was also a psychological mystery. A total of approximately seventy hours of talk with the principal researchers and additional hours with various members of the urology and endocrinology departments had failed to elicit information about seven critical areas: "(1) the possibility of an exogenous source of hormones; (2) the nature and extent of collaboration between Agnes and her mother and other persons; (3) any usable evidence let alone detailed findings dealing with her male feelings and her male biography; (4) what her penis had been used for besides urination; (5) how she sexually satisfied herself and others . . . ; (6) the nature of any homosexual feelings, fears, thoughts, and activities; (7) her feelings about herself as a 'phony female.'"[22] Much, indeed, remained unexplained.

Two hypotheses competed. The first, accepted by Stoller, amounted to a diagnosis of "testicular feminization syndrome"[23] due to "a diffuse lesion of the testis."[24] The second, advanced by an unnamed resident, amounted to the charge of duplicity: Agnes, so this argument ran, "either alone or in league with others," had for years obtained estrogen "from an exogenous source."[25] The resident turned out to be on the mark. Eight years later Agnes revealed to Stoller that "she had never had a biological defect," that at the onset of puberty, as her voice was starting to lower and she was developing pubic hair, she stole Stilbestol from her mother, for whom it had been prescribed following a panhysterectomy.

> The child then began to fill the prescription on her own, telling the pharmacist that she was picking up the hormone for her mother and paying for it with money taken from her mother's purse. She did not know what the effects would be, only that this was a female substance; she had no idea how much to take, but more or less tried to follow the amounts her mother took. She kept this up continuously through adolescence, and because by chance she had picked just the right time to start taking the hormone, she was able to prevent the development of all secondary sex characteristics that might have been produced by androgens, and to substitute instead those produced by estrogens. Nonetheless, androgens continued to be produced, enough that a normal-sized adult penis developed with a capacity for erection and orgasm until sexual excitability was suppressed at age fifteen by the massive doses of estrogens. Thus she became a lovely-looking young "woman," though with a normal-sized penis.[26]

Long before the mystery was solved, Agnes had realized her hopes. In 1959, "a penectomy, bilateral orchiectomy and vaginoplasty were performed. The skin of the penis was preserved, inverted and utilized for the lining of the newly created vaginal opening in its anterior wall. The scrotal skin was fashioned into the labia-like folds on either side of the vaginal canal."[27] According to Stoller, the operation had been done primarily for psychological reasons: he had no doubt that Agnes's "identity was so strongly fixed in a female direction that no form of treatment could ever make her masculine" and that Agnes was right when she said that "if anybody attempted to make her a male, not only would the attempts be of no use but . . . they would drive her to despair if not suicide."[28]

What led Stoller and his colleagues to be so confident about their assessment? What led them to accede to their patient's wishes? Here the "latest" in scientific research—more precisely, the notion of gender—played a crucial role. When Agnes volunteered for the study on intersexuality—even though she was not intersexed—"gender" was in its infancy. The term had been deployed by John Money, who himself was conducting research on hermaphrodites at Johns Hopkins. In working with such patients he needed to talk about the mismatch between a person's social or legal status and his or her chromosomes, gonads, or genitals. To that end he borrowed the word "gender" from philology: it signified the social or legal without reference to the sex organs. Beyond that, he coined the term "gender role":

> By . . . gender role we mean all those things that a person says or does to disclose himself or herself as having the status of boy or man, girl or woman, respectively. It includes, but is not restricted to sexuality in the sense of eroticism. Gender role is appraised in relation to the following: general mannerisms, deportment and demeanor; play preferences and recreational interests; spontaneous topics of talk in unprompted conversation and casual comment; content of dreams, daydreams and fantasies; replies to oblique inquiries and projective tests; evidence of erotic practices and, finally, the person's own replies to direct inquiry.[29]

Was gender role something inherited or acquired? And once in place, how stable was it? In Money's view, it was "not determined in some automatic, innate, or instinctive fashion"; nor was it a matter solely of sex assignment and rearing. In a sample of 105 hermaphrodites, he found that in 100 cases, assigned sex and rearing proved more reliable prognosticators of a subject's gender role than any one aspect of biological sex; in five instances, however, the patient's gender role diverged from that of his or her assigned sex and rearing. These five kept Money from subscribing to a "simple-minded . . . environmental determinism."[30] At the same time, drawing on a study of eleven cases of sex reassignment, he reached the conclusion that gender role was established by roughly eighteen months of age and that by thirty months it had become well nigh ineradicable. Taken together, these two research projects prompted him to look for a concept that would capture the appearance of a function—gender role—post-natally and would also capture its enduring quality. "Imprinting" served his purpose. He saw no difficulty in moving from the experience of mallard ducks and Konrad Lorenz's experiment with them to human infants and left the concept unexplained and unelaborated in its human guise.

Did surgery do the trick in Agnes's case? After the lapse of nearly a decade, Stoller started seeing her again. (At this point he learned from her that she had not been intersexed; he now counted her a male transsexual.) She came to him seeking psychotherapy, her chief complaint being "boredom," even while having sexual relations. In the course of the treatment she found "that the boy lived deep within her. . . . [and] recognized that her boredom . . . was a state of dynamic equilibrium between the part of herself that felt female and the part that felt male. She experienced maleness as occupying only a small part of the total space of her sense of herself, but, since that small space was as integral as a vital organ, it was not possible to extirpate it. All that could be done was to encapsulate it and then maintain the capsule wall impervious against any psychological penetration. The result was that she could never be fully stirred, never abandon herself completely to any relationship (non-sexual as well as sexual), and never accept and give intimacy from any part of her depths for fear that this most private part would be entered. She was not trying to preserve it because it was precious; she would have preferred not to have it."[31]

Stoller set to work:

Stoller: What I am looking for: I am looking for *you*—a feeling that you have of being you. Now that's a very dangerous search for you, because you never know if you are going to run upon the boy you once were.
Agnes: That's what I'm afraid of.

So afraid that she broke off treatment, only to return months later in a despondent frame of mind:

Stoller: Are you fearful in some way that the masculine part of you is going to emerge?
Agnes: Uh huh. In fact last winter I got to the point where I would be uneasy when I would go into johns sometimes, like in theaters or in drive-ins, in some state of super-awareness that people would know what I am, everything about me. . . . I don't want to hide things and put up a wall against them. I want to understand them. I want to bring them out . . . and the personality that comes out of it still has to be a feminine personality. It cannot be duo this or something; I still have

to evolve out of it with a feminine personality. Otherwise then I am really totally screwed up.

Stoller: Right. You must not end up being a man *and* a woman. But we both agree about that.

Despite psychotherapy, Agnes was convinced that nothing would change:

Agnes: I'm not going to be around in a few more years. Everyone says that, or feels that, once in a while. Then you get to the other feeling; life seems complete and precious. But now it seems like it's merging.

Stoller: Closing in?

Agnes: Not closing in so much as just merging: all the diverse paths merging into something; you know; it is getting easier to prognosticate. . . .

Stoller: That you are going to die in a few years?

Agnes: I think so.[32]

On this note of hopelessness, Stoller concluded his report on Agnes. He never specified what became of her.

A decade later, Stoller reflected on Agnes's treatment and on that of patients like her. He expressed reservations: none of those whom he had followed, he wrote, felt she had used her "life well," though all were "happy" that they had had a "'sex change'" and said they preferred "their present problems and miseries" to what had come before. He placed quotation marks around "sex change." There could be sex reassignment, he pointed out, which was a social phenomenon; there could not be sex transformation, which "would require chromosomal and anatomic reversal." Guppies, he continued, could change sex; humans could not. "Cosmetic surgery and manipulating secondary sex characteristics with hormones and electrolysis" could create only "biologic facsimiles." After more than two decades, he was forced to conclude that the case for "'sex change'" was still unproven; "both the treatments and the patients (of both sexes) have been, at most, near misses."[33]

During that time Stoller had ample opportunity to reflect on the concept he had formulated in the course of Agnes's initial treatment: core gender identity—an unalterable sense of being male or female.[34] Here he expressed no reservations.

• • • • •

When Stoller published material on Agnes in 1964, when he still thought she figured as a case of intersexuality, he fell back on a "biological 'force'" to explain the fact—and he thought it was a fact—that her core gender identity was female. By "biological force" he meant "a sex-linked genetic biological tendency towards masculinity in males and femininity in females"; it worked "silently . . . from foetal existence on, being overlain after birth by the effects of environment."[35] In some, the "biological force" was stronger, in others weaker. In Agnes it had been so strong as to produce a need to belong to the gender other than the one to which she had been assigned and in which she had been raised. Four years later Stoller publicly acknowledged that Agnes had not been feminized as the result of a "biological force."[36] He did not, however, disavow the notion of such a force; rather, he considered it of secondary significance—and lost interest in it. He granted primary significance to "postnatal dynamic factors."[37] It was these that he was determined to pin down, and transsexuals—that is, persons who felt themselves to be members of the opposite sex—ranked as Stoller's favored research subjects.

But it was Lance, not Agnes, who figured as Stoller's paradigm case. When he first showed up in Stoller's office, the boy was five years old. The main reason his parents brought him, initially for an evaluation and then for treatment, was his compulsion to wear his mother's and his eleven-year-old sister's clothes. He had begun to crossdress as soon as he could walk. It had started with his wanting to put on his mother's and his sister's shoes; soon he preferred to walk around in his mother's high-heels. Later he managed "to run up and down stairs in those shoes, to climb trees in them, ride his bicycle, etc. He gradually put on other items of clothing: blouse, stockings, purse, hats, etc., until he began to insist on dressing as a girl." At nursery school, so the teacher informed the boy's parents, "he played with the girls and put on girls' clothes. . . . He often tried to get the [other] boys to put on girls' clothes as well. This was disturbing to the . . . boys' parents and they asked the teacher to keep Lance away from their offspring."[38] This, in turn, was disturbing to Lance's parents, who until then had taken the line that their son was merely going through a phase he would eventually outgrow. Stoller, in contrast, took the line that the boy was a transsexual, or a transsexual in the making.

Lance was treated not by Stoller but by his friend and fellow psychoanalyst Ralph Greenson. The boy was the first child Greenson attempted to work with psychoanalytically, and he wondered whether his unorthodox ways "would meet with the approval of child analysts." They certainly were unorthodox. The sessions took place at Greenson's home, and the boy seems to have been given free run of it, playing the piano, exploring the garden, and, above all, enjoying the swimming pool. During the first hour he asked Greenson to teach him how to swim, and Greenson impulsively promised to do so. He kept his promise. Other unorthodox proceedings: for Christmas, Greenson gave Lance a Marine uniform, and at the boy's request he taught him to box with boxing gloves. After a year's treatment, Greenson reported on his patient:

> Lance appears for his last hour before the summer break all dressed up and proud, in a cowboy suit, complete with cowboy hat and high cowboy boots, which he loved to stamp about in. We spend the hour practicing all our "special" water tricks. As he dresses, Lance asks me how many days there are in a month and will I write to him; and he bashfully gives me a photo of himself which I can keep. He says he hopes I shall not forget how to swim, and I tell him not to worry, that I will not change. We march out to the car together like Marine-Cowboys, and Lance stamps his cowboy boots much louder than I.[39]

Stoller treated the boy's mother. He hoped that by studying the mother of a transsexual he would be able to understand the genesis of transsexualism itself. In portraying his patient, he highlighted her "bisexuality." Here is his description:

> She wore only tailored blouses or shirts so that her slim body looked boyish in them. Her hair was tousled and kept fairly short, though in an appropriately smart style. Her voice was low and husky. . . .
>
> The over-all effect on her of this complex mixing of masculine and feminine qualities was a sense of having been essentially without gender since latency. She would take pride in photographs of herself in her early teens in which she appeared to be a boy. At every opportunity for masquerading (as at Halloween), she would dress-up and pass unrecognized as a boy. She was constantly getting groups of children together to put on little shows, in which she would take male or female parts with equal success. Of this she said, "When you take off your own clothes and put on different clothes, you can be anyone." . . .
>
> During these [latency] years, she competed with boys on equal terms in organized athletics, at school, and in games; she felt that the same standards in appearance and competitive performance should hold for her as for boys. Underlying this behavior were powerful wishes for her body to become male and, this not being likely, for it to be somehow neuter. The onset of her periods and the growth of breasts were very traumatic and ended her hopes for maleness.[40]

How did Stoller account for his patient's "bisexuality"? Here he pointed to her mother, father, and brothers. Mother, herself an empty woman, "not surprisingly gave the patient a profound sense of emptiness." A dream that she recalled from childhood, Stoller suggested, captured the patient's experience: " 'I had died and was now dead. But my mother kept sending me to the store on errands because she hadn't even paid enough attention to know it." Father filled the vacuum produced by the empty mother and took over much of her role in the patient's upbringing. "It was he who comforted the patient when she was sick and took her to the doctor, he who took her to sporting events (to which her brothers were not taken), and it was he who bought all her clothes." This was the affectionate father, "happy, humorous, singing"; there was also a drunken father, "a man of terrifying violence and scarcely veiled sexuality." A dream, Stoller wrote, exemplified how the daughter experienced the frightening father:

> "I am sitting with another girl younger than myself in an open field at night, when we suddenly see a wild, frenzied stallion charging down the road. As it approaches, I notice that instead of eyes, he has burning holes showing its red-hot interior. It is not running at us on purpose, but still it is coming directly at us. Just as it is about to trample us, it is turned aside by a fence railing, a railing which in fact had fronted our house in childhood.[41]

Despite her father's unpredictable moods, the patient felt she was his favorite—until a six-year-younger sister was born. Thereupon the relationship changed: from then to the age of sixteen, when she left home, the patient fought with her father continually.

The maleness of her brothers, Stoller argued, also contributed to the "masculine defect" in his patient's "gender identity." How? Two years older and three years younger than she, they were "vigorous boys, who, in the rather cramped living conditions of her childhood, gave her more than ample opportunity to compare differences in the anatomy of the sexes." Anatomical difference, Stoller continued, became male superiority, thanks to cultural traditions which clearly favored "penis-possessing brothers." Once again Stoller turned to the patient's dream material to illustrate his reconstruction: " 'I came out upon a parking lot looking for my car. There I saw my oldest brother in the center of a group of boys. He was the leader of this group and they were listening with fascination as he was telling dirty jokes. I looked and saw my car at the other end of the parking lot. The blue paint had been scraped off the side and the radiator in front had been smashed in.' "[42]

The childhood history in place, Stoller felt confident that he could now pinpoint the twin motives behind his patient's particular mothering behavior. The first derived from her experience with her own mother: "the main purpose," he wrote, "of her identification with her son (her inability to help him separate from her physically and to differentiate his own clear identity)" was "her need for him to 'cure' her of the emptiness" she had received "from her own mother." The second derived from the patient's intense and vengeful penis envy—itself "a result of the barren, frustrating, perfunctory care given by her mother," as well as of her damaging relations with father and brothers.[43] Curiously enough, "this depressed woman, with her rage against maleness," who had no difficulty expressing her hatred of her husband—a passive, withdrawn man and an absent father—managed to deflect her hostility from her son. His was the one penis she admired; all other penises she regarded as ugly. Perhaps, Stoller speculated, "the only penis such a woman" could stand was "a ruined one: beautiful, graceful, but without the 'masculine' attributes of dirty, brutal, penetrating sexuality."[44]

Her mothering, Stoller argued, was in fact ruining her son's penis—that is, robbing him of his masculinity. The process had begun with his birth. From the very first the "mother felt a supreme oneness with this boy," whose physical beauty unfolded and with it, "unfortunately," a grace of movement to match—"unfortunately," Stoller conjectured, for if he had "turned ugly or awkward, he . . . might have been spared the femininity." The mother did everything possible to preserve the blissful feeling created by her son's closeness. She had him with her constantly. He was in her arms "throughout a good part of the night because his sleep was broken. . . . He was with her as she did the household chores, in the first year or so on her hip and later at least in the same room so that he and she could constantly link with their eyes, and, after he began to talk, with continuous intimate, uninhibited conversation. He followed her as she went to the bathroom and was with her when she bathed or showered."

> Once, responding to my musing how the . . . mother . . . would quiet her crying son by placing him nude against her nude abdomen, . . . Greenson . . . said it sounded like a kangaroo infant in its mother's pouch, which is as intra-uterine as extrauterine existence can be. I see now that Greenson's imagery is even more apt, for this mother was in this way frequently (several times a day) placing the infant where she felt a penis should be. In addition she reported that she regularly sat with the baby in her lap (that is, not simply on her lap but between her spread-apart legs as she sat on the floor) for hours a day and for several years, this often occurring with both nude.[45]

What, Stoller asked, prevented the boy from remaining a "blob of grati-fied tissue"? The mother, he continued, did not stand in the way of Lance's "ego development." She encouraged him "to talk, to read, to become skilled in using his body, and in time she also rewarded his growing sensitivity for colors, textures, sounds, and smells that, already in the first few years of his life, showed as a keen, creative, artistic sensibility. . . . All of this was learned, as it were, in her lap." She thus had "ample opportunity to express by means of her body, the quality of her voice, the appearance of her face, and the other modes of communication between mother and infant" what she loved and what she hated in him.[46]

No wonder, then, that Greenson saw his task as one of helping Lance separate from his mother, of helping the boy, as Greenson put it, to "dis-identify" from her—an assignment that Lance's father had shirked.[47] It proved to be no easy undertaking. The report at the end of four years of treatment—Lawrence Newman took over from Greenson after about a year—was guarded. Once again an adult, this time more consciously, sought to manipulate the child: where Lance's mother had encouraged feminine traits and discouraged masculine ones, Newman, following Greenson's lead, did the reverse.

> Certain behaviors such as crossdressing were actively disapproved of and suppressed. The patient was told in no uncertain terms that such behavior was "no good for him" and after a continuous battle the mother began to adopt this attitude also, despite the temper tantrums which initially took place. . . .
>
> He [Lance] . . . renounced the wish to grow up to become a woman and when talking about the earlier years when he loved to crossdress said, "Oh, that was all baby stuff. I was just mixed up. I must have thought I was a girl or something. Now I don't.

Lance, Newman concluded, seemed to have "repressed" his active, con-scious feminine yearnings; the extent and intensity of his masculine striv-ings remained unclear. And efforts to induce the father to participate in his family's life had had to be abandoned.[48]

What lessons did Stoller draw from Lance and his mother? In the first instance, he felt confident that he had grasped the dynamic factors in transsexualism.

> One sees what happens if the loving, maternal preoccupation, the symbiosis, is too complete, too gratifying, too lengthy through the hours of the day and night and too extended as the months and then the years pass: neither mother nor infant will want to separate from each other—*and the principal effect is extreme*

femininity in the little boy. To the extent that a mother prolongs symbiosis, normal enough in the first weeks and months, and to the extent that she must at every moment gratify the infant, so will femininity creep into the core gender identity; at the extreme of such a continuum is transsexualism.[49]

In the second instance, Stoller felt equally confident that he had grasped the key factor in the development of core gender identity. Here he pointed to parental behaviors and attitudes. (He never claimed that such behaviors and attitudes constituted the sole factors, but he did grant them pride of place.) Encouragement and discouragement—a species of artificial selection—by the parents and learning by the child figured as central. So too did imprinting—a concept that Money had earlier taken over from ethology. Stoller thought of it as a "non-mental" mechanism that acted "directly on the brain and other parts of the nervous system . . . bypassing the nascent ego." Imprinted data, he continued, were not "of the mind," though they influenced it "as would, say, adrenal or thyroid activity." Whatever the exact mix of these two processes, Stoller was convinced "that the earliest and . . . unalterable part of gender identity—core gender identity"—developed "smoothly, silently, and without conflict." From birth on, then, Stoller argued, "non-traumatic and non-conflictual . . . experiences began creating masculinity in boys . . . and, unfortunately, femininity too, as in transsexuals."[50]

Only in transsexuals? Once Stoller had asserted that a kind of imprinting took place in the early, close relationship between mother and child, he was obliged to claim that femininity crept into the core gender identity of all males—or, as he put it, that there existed a "protofeminine core" in male core gender identity.[51] The "core" was simply not as stable as the word "core" suggested.

• • • • •

Stoller supplied an addendum to his account of Lance's mother. Early in her treatment she had mentioned in passing that she had a third brother, thirteen years her junior, and that this brother, like her son, had been a crossdresser. Many months later she talked of her sibling again and vouchsafed additional information. "*It was she, not her mother, who had brought the baby up,* their empty, withdrawn mother supplying only perfunctory nursing care." It was the patient, not her mother, who had produced the little boy's crossdressing. It was the patient who had damaged the male child. At the end of the session, she told Stoller "for the first time her brother's name: *Lance*."[52]

This woman, then, had a long history of nurturing femininity in males, of selecting traits and attitudes she regarded as feminine and encouraging their expression.

MRS. G'S PENIS

"What would convince a biologically normal woman that she had a penis?" With this question Stoller began his narrative of Mrs. G and his treatment of her. The book he wrote, entitled *Splitting: A Case of Female Masculinity*, recounts the protracted "process of finding out about her, about the development of masculinity and femininity, and about the role parents play in the creation of identity."[53] Stoller intended to use information he gathered about Mrs. G to continue his earlier work on core gender identity. As it turned out, he found himself prompted to reflect on questions of sexual object-choice as well.

Stoller met Mrs. G, a thirtyish, divorced housewife, in the late 1950s. He had gone to "the County Hospital to film a couple of interviews with typical psychiatric patients," to be used for final examinations testing medical students' skills in clinical evaluation. Mrs. G's name appeared on the list of paranoid schizophrenics. Stoller rapidly came to the conclusion that this label had been misapplied: "she was interested in talking" with him, "obviously enjoyed meeting somebody new, showed no disturbances in affect or thought processes, revealed no hallucinations or delusions, but rather was able to deal" with him warmly—all of which ruled out paranoid schizophrenia. Did it also rule her out of his filming project? Stoller quickly realized that she still might be of use: he was convinced that he had before him "a textbook psychopath (antisocial personality)."[54] And so he proceeded with the interview.

In retrospect it marked the beginning of treatment, though for a long time Stoller remained unaware that treatment had started. Just as he was about to leave, Mrs. G stopped him, "expressing diffidence and an uneasiness" that she was bothering him—"she did this genuinely without exaggeration or insincerity," and it was exactly the right approach to him. "She asked if she could be transferred to UCLA (in those days the County Hospital did not have a treatment program) so as not to be returned to the state hospital from which she had run away."

For the next seven years, Mrs. G was other people's patient. She was treated by many psychiatrists as both an inpatient and an outpatient; but I was always in the background of her mind. She would drop around to see me for a moment or write letters and Christmas cards [to me]. I enjoyed the few moments I spent with her; I especially enjoyed her not being my responsibility. I knew that as one's patient she would really be an unmitigated pain, with her teasing, manipulation, and true crises and false. She had to act on her impulses, and her repertoire of impulsive acts was just too dangerous for my liking: life is short, and there are too many other things to do to be forever involved with a dangerous, manipulative patient.[55]

A central feature of Mrs. G's treatment was the use of the UCLA hospital. Both before and after Stoller became her therapist, Mrs. G was a frequent inpatient. Before he officially took over "and for several hospitalizations thereafter, hospitalization was used only to patch over emergencies. When Mrs. G had been 'cooled,' by supportive means," Stoller and his colleagues considered it safe to "let her go home, assured that she would not kill herself or others." As the work with Stoller deepened, her hospital stays became longer.

> Being on the ward, Mrs. G could stand the intensity of the therapy I felt free to launch with twenty-four-hour control over her. It was when she was hospitalized that my own feeling of freedom from danger was sufficient to allow me to say anything that came to mind and say it right, without that special hesitation of searching for the politic phrase sometimes necessary with dangerous patients when they are to leave one's office and go out into the world. . . .
>
> Despite knowing that I would frequently make her psychotic and dangerous, I developed confidence that she could stand it and would survive it, that we would both learn more about her, and that a permanent, higher plateau of treatment would be reached after each such hospitalization.[56]

Another central feature of her treatment—and of "much clinical research" as well—was the personality of her therapist.

> In addition to the protection the hospital gave each of us, I could rely on Mrs. G being a woman and physically weaker than I. Naturally, I am less likely to say dreadful things to a patient who is physically capable of murdering me. Mrs. G could not have done so; and since we both knew this, the possibility could be ignored. No matter how infuriating I was, I never felt she could rise up and kill me with her bare hands, an experience that has threatened with male patients. It was fortunate that I had this sublime conviction and that it never occurred to me that she might want to kill me with an equalizer, like a gun. By the time she told

me she had once come in with a loaded gun in her bag prepared to shoot, the dangerous episode was only a report of what had happened several years before.[57]

Above all, there was nothing ambiguous about the therapist's gender identity. This threw the contrast with his patient into stark relief.

• • • • •

G: Did I tell you my dream about my penis?

S: No.

G: It was the other day. I woke up, and then I went back to sleep; and I dreamt I had a penis, a big penis. And everybody laughed at me; and I would walk down the street and show people, and they would laugh at me; so I decided to have it cut off. So I went to the doctor, and the doctor put me in the hospital; and they put me to sleep, and they cut it off. And when I woke up, I was still in pain. I had a pain right there just like they cut it off.

S: Who was the doctor who put you in the hospital?

G: You did.

S: And who was the one that cut it off?

G: I don't know. I was asleep when it was cut off.

S: Who was responsible for having it cut off?

G: You were.

S: Yeah, me. Isn't that really what's happened? Isn't it true that I have been trying to cut your penis off in this treatment?

G: Yeah.

S: There hasn't been any secret about it. I've told you I want you to be a woman.[58]

The person Stoller initially encountered looked like a boy. "Her hair was cut as a young man's. . . . All her movements were boyish: the way she sat in a chair, . . . lit up and smoked a cigarette. However, her appearance was not exaggerately masculine or tough; it was appropriate for a young man, inappropriate only in that one knew this was a woman being interviewed."[59] And from the outset Stoller took aim at her masculinity and at its embodiment, her hallucinated penis.

He insisted on making her describe in detail how her penis felt:

G: It's hard and it's average size. . . .

S: Is it erect?

G: Yeah.

S: Always?

G: Yeah.

S: Does it come when you have intercourse?

G: Yeah. . . .

S: Why does the penis stay erect after you ejaculate?

G: I don't know.

S: It never goes down. Have you ever known a penis that never went down? That's better than any man's. Do you believe that you could give a woman a baby?

G: No.

S: Why not?

G: Because I'm a female.

S: But you're a female with a penis that ejaculates. Why can't your penis that ejaculates make a woman pregnant?

G: Because I'm a female.

S: Not good enough. If you're a female, you can't even have a penis.

G: I don't want to make anybody pregnant. I never have put it into anybody. . . . Why should you want to take it away from me? I'm happy the way I am. . . . Why worry about this one little thing? It's not hurting anybody. . . . And it's not hurting me. . . . This is something I've always known, and I've always felt; and it's there, and it's real, and it's mine; and you can't take it away from me, and neither can anybody else, so you might as well kiss my ass.[60]

Stoller persevered:

S: When you masturbate, do you have a penis? . . .

G: It's in my vagina. What I mean is, I still rub my clitoris, but I feel my penis.

S: Is it inside in your vagina, or in your pelvis?

G: It depends on whether I'm having intercourse or I'm with a woman or I masturbate. If I masturbate, it's inside my vagina. During intercourse with a man, it's not in the vagina, but in my pelvic area. . . .

S: How about when you're with a woman?

G: Then it's outside.

S: And fills up the whole vagina? Right to where it would stick out, but it doesn't stick out? Have you ever put a finger in to feel if it's there?

G: I don't want to. If you have a vagina, you have a hole; but if you have a penis, you don't have a hole. . . .

S: Do you feel it fill it up, or is it one moment you've got a vagina and the next moment you've got a penis in a vagina?

G: I don't really know. It must move in because I wouldn't just one minute have a vagina and the next minute have a penis. It must move in. I didn't even think about it.[61]

Stoller summed up his understanding of Mrs. G's experiences. He distinguished three levels of awareness: "first, the penis as absent; second the penis as present but not felt, or if one asked about it, then noticed, but 'in its usual position'; and third, the penis at the forefront of consciousness" and taking part in an interpersonal encounter, such as sexual relations. These distinctions held up, he added, until Mrs. G's penis became involved in treatment. Stoller's concrete questioning, designed "to interrupt the hallucinatory process" and "to force reality" upon his patient, began to produce the results he desired. Mrs. G became accustomed to the penis's being gone much of the time and to its returning—all without fanfare. When it finally vanished altogether, during an LSD-induced psychosis—an experiment Mrs. G undertook without Stoller's knowledge—it did so in "a blaze of glory":

G: I found out I really don't have a penis. It just kind of blew up and exploded. I could see it and feel it and it just blew apart. I took the acid about 11:30 at night, and I was still hallucinating at six o'clock in the morning. And by that time I was getting to the point where I was tired of it. . . . So I laid [sic] down and I thought I was asleep, but I couldn't have been asleep. . . . I don't know if I was asleep or not. Anyway, I saw myself as a little child with an enormous penis. Standing there in the room. . . . I didn't have any clothes on. I was probably five or six. And I had a big penis. Like a man's penis on a child. Erect. I thought: How horrifying! What am I going to do with it? How am I going to hide it? And I thought: What are people going to think when they see it? . . . And then I looked inside myself, inside my stomach, inside my guts, and I saw this penis; and it was the same one I had when I was a child, but now it was hidden, so I knew what to do with it: just leave it hidden. And then I thought: I can't do that because I'm a woman; I can't have a penis. And suddenly it started to grow, and it came outside of me, the woman lying on the couch; and then it just exploded and went away. And I got up and went into the bathroom and took my pants down because I thought I must be bleeding. But I wasn't.[62]

How did Stoller understand Mrs. G's penis—an hallucinated yet "essential part of [her] body ego" that she had in place by the age of four?[63] Mrs. G, he learned, remembered as a "small child wanting desperately to be a boy." She remembered taping one of her younger brother's baby bottle nipples to her pubic area and pretending she had a penis. She behaved as much like a boy as she could: she often stood up to urinate; she "played with boys and worked hard to be the strongest, toughest, and to be the best in sports."[64] She thought that if she acted enough like a boy, she might grow up to be a man. And she did not abandon these wishes in adolescence.

In all of this, Stoller (once again) discerned parental influences at work. He elaborated: Mrs. G "felt that her mother was absolutely, totally, and desperately necessary for her existence—not only in infancy and childhood but right up to the time this feeling changed in treatment. . . . She also felt that her mother's benign attention was . . . precarious."

> *S:* A mistake was made . . . the two of you didn't really understand each other for many, many years. She suffered mildly that her daughter wasn't available to her, and you suffered terribly; I don't mean you felt the suffering; I mean you were damaged as a result of it. You got the wrong idea about her, not completely wrong. You felt that she wasn't interested, and apparently she wasn't; but she had always the capacity to have enjoyed you, and it was lost.

Part of the damage had to do with Mrs. G's femininity. Her mother made her believe that only boys were valuable.

> *G:* She wanted me to be as good as a boy. She always said, "See, your big brother can do this and he can do that. Why can't you do it? He gets good grades in school. Why don't you get good grades in school? He can hit a baseball this far. Why can't you do it? He can beat up all the boys in the neighborhood. Why can't you do that? So I did it. Maybe she didn't know what I was. I was a girl. . . . Why didn't . . . she know? I felt like a girl. . . . I was pleased that I was a girl. I don't know what more to tell you. I felt feminine, and I was cute when I was little, and I had long curly hair, and I wanted to be a woman; I wanted to be a mother, and I wanted all kinds of things that you can't have if you're not a girl. I was a girl. That was before I found out she didn't want a girl. She'll tell you. If she had it to do over again, she'd have . . . [only] boys.[65]

Until treatment, Stoller wrote, this mother had continued to exist within Mrs. G as a series of commands and disapprovals—a dictator of ideals beyond her daughter's ability to reach.

Mrs. G's mother allowed, indeed encouraged, her daughter's masculine behaviors. The father did not. Stoller commented that Mrs. G "almost had a good relationship" with him, and that was "perhaps the most optimistic statement" one could make about any of her childhood ties. On turning to her father for affection, Mrs. G found someone who knew she was a girl and wanted her to be one. On turning to him, she was not "encouraged . . . to be interested in and to spend time with him in masculine pursuits." This father, Mrs. G reported, was "very femi-nine. . . . He wore an apron, and he did the cooking and . . . the housework, and he bathed the babies."[66] Unfortunately, this father, who openly loved her, was scarcely ever at home.

How, then, did Stoller understand Mrs. G's penis?

> A little girl, tormented from birth on by hopes of closeness and love from each of her parents but forever repeating disappointments in this hope, either becomes unhinged or never quite has the hinges in place. . . . In addition, while knowing she is female, she observes her older brother's success because of his maleness. . . . So she creates masculinity by imitation and identification.

"A lonely and despairing child," Stoller wrote, "faced with the task of raising massive defenses," Mrs. G, by hallucination, had "invented . . . a penis."[67]

And in his view it had kept her from being a woman:

G: No, it doesn't. I can screw a man just the same as any other woman.

S: That's not all it takes to be a woman. And you don't screw a man like any other woman. You screw a man with a penis hidden up in your pelvis. Look, I don't think you're a freak, and I don't want you to think you're a freak, because any woman who has got a penis, in your book is a freak—even if you don't tell yourself you are. You know damn well that you would be different from every other woman in the world. Well—you always told yourself— that's marvelous. I'd rather you be a completely normal female because I think you would also.

Stoller was convinced that he had located remnants of femininity in Mrs. G, an "early femininity covered over by masculinity"—and, he added, by homosexuality as well.[68]

• • • • •

G: There's a nurse on the ward that I'm very fond of, and I've always been very uncomfortable talking to her; and when I would talk to her and she would sit in my room and talk to me, I would notice my penis was there. With the penis there [that is, before it departed in a "blaze of glory"], that makes it a healthier relationship. I can sit in my room with this nurse and know I'm not having homosexual feelings.[69]

After several years of treating Mrs. G, when he felt that his relationship with her was "strong enough" and that he "understood her well enough," Stoller "began charging in upon the subject of homosexuality." Initially, whenever it was merely implied, later when he stated "unequivocally that she was homosexual," he could "count on her becoming psychotic." Gradually she grew "'used' to this subject," whether because of increasing insight or because of increasing "familiarity with not being destroyed by the thought," he could not say.

S: Do you have a box?
G: Yeah.
S: She [a female lover] did too?
G: She sure did. . . .
S: Two homosexual women possessed of the same boxes would have said "Ha, homosexuality." Right? . . . The whole world would have said "Two boxes. Homosexuality." Right? But you didn't. Reason: she didn't touch yours, so she couldn't literally add it up although she knew damn well you had a box. And two: you had a penis; no box. So one plus one mustn't equal two. But you know, you are an intelligent woman and you're a logical woman . . ., and you *knew* that one plus one is two. You did know that. And to this day you hallucinate because of that, and to this day . . . that logic makes you sick.[70]

Treatment brought dramatic changes: Mrs. G finally came "to accept her homosexuality" and to "enjoy her body with another woman, free of guilt or psychosis."[71]

How did Stoller link his work on core gender identity with his discussion of Mrs. G's homosexuality? Here he made use of Mrs. G's penis. Transsexual wishes and homosexual object-choice went hand in hand: homosexuality, he wrote, could be "roughly quantified according to the intensity of transsexual wishes."[72] And although Mrs. G was not a transsexual—she did not "believe herself to be a member of the opposite sex (she only believed that she had one of the necessary anatomical features of the opposite sex)"; she did not ask or "expect to be transformed into a member of the opposite sex" (she only wished that "she had been born so"); she made "no effort to pass as a member of the opposite sex"—still, she had stronger masculine tendencies than almost any patient, other than female transsexuals, Stoller had ever seen. By the same token, heterosexuality and "normal" gender identity went hand in hand:

Heterosexuality is the expected as well as the normative state. This is not the case so much because it is biologically ordained (such a tendency is at best weakly sustained in humans) but rather because in all societies the styles of rearing encourage boys to be masculine and girls, feminine, making a person of the opposite sex more exciting and pleasurable.[73]

In this fashion Stoller harked back to artificial selection.

• • • • •

Stoller did not succeed in turning Mrs. G into a completely "normal" female. Contrary to what he had initally assumed, she did not wish to be one.

G: Remember when I was in the hospital last time? . . . I thought then that I would like to be a feminine female, so I kind of watched the nurses to see how they behaved, the ones that were feminine. I don't think I can do it. I think if I was to be like that, it would be an act. I don't think something like that could come naturally to me. . . . I was thinking about doing it [being feminine] . . . , not for me, because that's not what I want, but doing it for you; and I don't think I can do that.[74]

For her part, Mrs. G—or better, Stoller's experience with her—did not succeed in prompting him to question his basic concept. Stoller stuck to his notion of core gender identity.

BELLE'S "LOVELY"

If Belle says she is a delectable female and expresses pride in her female attributes; always looks feminine and never masculine; dreams incessantly of being pregnant and giving birth, of babies and children, of cupboards, cooking, and ovens, . . . of making, buying, and trying on clothes, of menstrual periods, vestibules, flowers, grassy lawns, mirrors, carpets, shops, curtains, kitchens, household appliances, lace, linen, silk, cotton, textures, . . . fields, earth, soil to be fertilized or planted: and if she is excited by men and not women, why not conclude that she believes herself to be a female and a woman, not just a castrated male?[75]

With this rhetorical question, Stoller announced, not for the first time, his dissent from his version of Freud. "In brief," he claimed, Freud considered maleness "superior . . . and masculinity the original and preferred state for both sexes"; consequently, "one's sense of femaleness and femininity" was "built on the pained awareness (with resultant humiliation, anger, denial, or resignation)" that one did not have—perhaps had even been robbed of—"a penis, that most ideal structure."[76] Were it not for Freud's theorizing, Stoller continued, would anyone have doubted the existence of what he proposed to call primary femininity?

Belle stood as Stoller's prime exhibit. She began treatment with him—psychoanalytic, as an outpatient—at the age of twenty-four. "A quiet, intelligent, attractive, well-groomed, feminine woman, white, American, Southern, middle-class, college-educated, single," Baptist fundamentalist, she "entered analysis with a sense of distress she could not clearly articulate, a feeling that she was wasting her life and would continue to do so forever, and especially that her wish to be a wife and mother would be thwarted by fate." Unlike most of Stoller's other patients, Belle did not seek treatment "because of a marked gender problem or as the parent of a child with a gender problem."[77]

What immediately caught Stoller's attention was a curious linguistic practice: Belle's use of the word "lovely." She did not use it simply as an adjective; she also used it as a noun. For "her 'lovely' was a commodity." Her mother had lots of it, "had had it since childhood, had never earned it, and could not lose it no matter what happened in the way of physical or mental deterioration." As her mother's daughter, Belle was entitled to "a certain amount of 'lovely'"; simultaneously mother made it clear that "Belle had not been assigned the same amount by fate, could never acquire it by effort," and would have a "lovely" that—at best—was precarious. "Mother and women like her might sweat, but their sweat was 'lovely'; such women, perhaps, had bowel movements, but of course their bowel movements were somehow 'lovely'; when 'lovely' women made love, every movement was lovely, while Belle was always in danger of fucking." Despite the chanciness of Belle's "lovely," Stoller insisted that she had gotten "a solid start in femininity."[78]

He did not want to be misunderstood: he was not implying that little girls, including Belle, did not experience penis envy. As for evidence, he expected the psychoanalysts in his audience to provide their own.

> What I am saying . . . is that penis envy may not be the earliest stage in the development of femininity, as Freud said, but may come after an unalterable sense of femaleness (core gender identity) has already been created.[79]

As for evidence, he admitted that he knew of no systematic reports and believed that none existed—because no one had bothered "to measure the obvious."

And it is obvious. Anyone who has observed little girls has seen that they can be feminine, as soon as any behavior appears that can be judged gender-related. . . . Little girls of two already show differences from little boys in style, inflections, carriage, and fantasy life.[80]

Once again Stoller set up a sharp contrast: little girls as castrated males or as the proud possessors of a primary, conflict-free femininity.

• • • • •

As a reason for entering analysis, Belle had mentioned that "her sexual pleasure was impaired but was not sure how." Here is her favorite masturbatory daydream:

A cruel man, the Director, a Nazi type, is directing the activity. It consists of Belle being raped by a stallion. . . . In a circle around the periphery stand vaguely perceived men, expressionless, masturbating while ignoring each other, the Director, and Belle. She is there for the delectation of these men, including the Director, who, although he has an erection, makes no contact with her: her function is to be forced to unbearable sexual excitement and pleasure, thereby making a fool of herself before these men. . . . And, behind the scenes, a part of herself permits the excitement because it (she) knows that she, who is masturbating in the real world, is not literally the same as "she" who is the suffering woman in the story. In the story, she is humiliated; in reality, she is safe.[81]

Belle first referred to her daydream a year or so into the analysis. She mentioned bits and pieces of it, prompted by associations to dreams, prompted by Stoller's request for details. Gradually she added more elements, often only a sentence at a time:

The men fasten her to . . . [the stallion] with rope or a leather device. He becomes wildly excited but not by her: the men have set a mare in heat off at a distance, at which, over Belle's nude body, as if she did not exist, the stallion stares. . . .

The man running the performance, called the Director, promises in his cruelty that at the right moment he will have intercourse with her or will arrange for another man—handsome, virile, heterosexual—to do so, the right moment being when the horse has gotten her so excited that she cannot bear it without now having a man. But the Director never grants her wish. Instead, the horse is removed and a disreputable-looking, old, lower-class, stocky and muscular, physically dirty, fumbling, incompetent man is substituted. . . . Up to that point, despite her mounting excitement, she has lain silently without moving, resisting the overwhelming pressure to humiliate herself by losing control. Finally, for all her reckless bravery in opposing the men and her struggle to keep her lady-like composure, she suffers the ultimate humiliation with the dirty-old-man. . . . Her orgasm occurs simultaneously in the daydream and in reality.[82]

Until late in treatment, Belle never reached orgasm in intercourse as a result of what her actual lover did. Instead, she managed it by "masturbating on his penis to the bidding of her fantasy, ignoring him as he pushed grimly on; or, after he was finished, she would take over and gratify herself by herself." Until late in treatment the daydream remained unchanged. Then it began to lose its rigid character: Belle introduced variants that "softened the hostility or even hinted at kindness"—among them, "normal intercourse with a potent, loving man." Only then did Belle have "orgasms during . . . intercourse and as a result of her lover's action."[83]

Stoller did not immediately appreciate the centrality of the daydream. By the time he wrote up the case, he saw it as "paradigmatic," by which he meant that it recapitulated or simulated (he used both words) "the primary relationships of infancy and childhood, trying to undo the frustrations, traumas, and conflicts that resulted therefrom."[84] Its chief function, he concluded, was to rewrite history.

Among the personae in the daydream Stoller considered the Director crucial. More feelings "attached to him than [to] any other figure, . . . more trauma and more hopeless hope." He was father, mother, and stepfather rolled into one. Father, hypochondriacal and unreliable, had run off with a teen-age girl when Belle was six. A year later he was dead. Mother, vain and tantalizing, had also run off, in pursuit of a career in the entertainment industry. Years later she returned for a public welcome that Belle had anticipated for months, with dreams of "being the center of her celebrated mother's attention." Instead she had not succeeded in catching her parent's eye: with a peck on Belle's cheek, mother had turned to more exciting people. Mother had also returned with a new husband, a retired European army officer. "Ramrod straight, inhibited, quiet, meticulous, and proper," he came closest to serving as a model for the Director. Above all, Stoller eventually realized and interpreted to Belle that the Director, no matter how frozen he might be, never wavered in his concentration on her. The daydream's action proved that she—who, from birth on, had "had to suffer and somehow cope with her parents' inconstancy"—was not abandoned.[85] In this fashion she undid the past.

Undoing the past was only one of the functions Stoller attributed to Belle's daydream. Preparing for the future was another. It had acquired this function when Belle was roughly nine. At that point, Stoller claimed, she "was filled with ideas of lovemaking, sex . . . as beautiful, pregnancy lovely, delivery an ecstasy, and motherhood a glory." Although it was clear that "she would never approach" her mother's "desirable womanliness nor be a marvel of the sex, she saw herself as able to get some leavings from the feast." Then "the news about the anatomy of intercourse shattered the all-too-susceptible child. . . . From that day on, she felt shame; not only did someone push that thing into you, you were supposed to enjoy it—be thrilled by it, as her mother had endlessly warbled." She "wondered how to come to terms with this dreadful news."[86] Daydreaming, Stoller argued, came to her rescue.

Once again Stoller was pointing to heterosexuality or wishes to be heterosexual as the normal accompaniment of primary femininity. In Belle's case a gap had opened, filled with shame and fear, between the wish and its fulfillment, which she had bridged with her erotic daydream. (How, Stoller never explained.) It would be difficult, he added parenthetically, to imagine a little girl, confronted with finding pleasure in intercourse, "who would not envy boys and their aggressive, penetrating, hedonistic, arrogant, unfettered, God-granted, antisocial, unsympathetic, humiliating, penis."[87] Still he insisted that primary, non-conflictual femininity, rather than penis envy, constituted bedrock. Still he insisted that these were the only alternatives.

• • • • •

> To repeat: a woman's sense of integrity (meaning completeness, intactness) is based on her parents' attitudes toward her anatomy, not just on penis envy or on the belief that she is castrated. . . . Then the girl must deal with . . . the discovery of male genitals, envy for the functions males enjoy, and the related but not identical powers and responsibilities males are granted by our society.[88]

By drawing, in this manner, a sharp distinction between an early phase of primary femininity and a later phase of oedipal struggle, Stoller defended his notion of core gender identity as conflict-free. In so doing, he, in effect, asked his readers to discount his experience with Agnes, Lance's mother, Mrs. G, and Belle. In so doing, he failed to reckon with his own rhetorical prowess; his very success in persuading his readers to trust his reports of his patients' gender perplexities made his hypothesis seem implausible.

THE REPRODUCTION OF (S)MOTHERING

> One of the things that people always ask me because, you know, I'm a product of this recent women's movement and a feminist, and yet obviously very committed to psychoanalytic theories and studies, how do you reconcile being, you know, a feminist and believing or thinking that this theory—which ranges from anywhere from, you know, it's male-centered or it's sexist or misogynist or phallocentric, I mean people use a lot of different terms—and I'm wondering whether in your history as an analyst or when you were in training—I don't mean the sort of accusations, although I'm interested in that too—but did that come up for you or for other women? Did you think of yourselves, I mean the issue of the theory of femininity in relation to yourselves, was that something you talked about or did it come up?[89]

In the early 1980s Nancy Chodorow asked this "extraordinarily convoluted and almost incomprehensible" question of pioneer women psychoanalysts. She was studying women trained in the 1920s, 1930s, and early 1940s and the question figured as part of the study. She wanted to know how her subjects, "idealized grand old women and foremothers," had reacted to the "sexist and misogynist views" prevalent in their profession: "that women must stay home full-time with their children during these children's early years or risk serious consequences, that women are naturally passive, that career achievement is a substitute for or expression of unresolved penis envy."[90] She wanted to know how they reconciled views that seemed to devalue them with the fact of their accomplishments. She wanted to know if, like women in the 1970s, they found such views offensive.

Chodorow reported that she had had difficulty making herself understood, and this was not simply because of her tangled phraseology. Her subjects seemed loath to make sweeping statements about their theory. Some demurred from Helene Deutsch's views on the ground that Deutsch "just wanted to please Freud or personally disliked women." One woman, trained in New York when Karen Horney was still a member of the New York Society, pointed out that "she and her friends held the 'secret theory' that penis envy was socially derived." Another interviewee argued that Melanie Klein's "'mammocentrism,'" her focus on the mother's breast, offered effective resistance to "Freud's phallocentrism." The early women psychoanalysts seemed equally reluctant to make sweeping statements about their female colleagues. Chodorow noted the response of one British analyst to her question of why there were so many women in the field:

Lots of men are too assertive and active. It is difficult for the *ordinary* sort of male to do a lot of sitting all day in a passive analysis, . . . that sort of experience is easier for women, don't you think? But then again one thinks of how bossy some of the women are; they're not very receptive. You know bisexuality is very real to me. I could never get 'round the fact that a lot of the women are very masculine. So how can you generalize?

Chodorow felt forced to conclude that her sense of the "pervasiveness of gender as a category" simply did not resonate with her subjects' "life experiences." She began to appreciate how much her "perceptual and analytic categories" had been shaped by her "coming of age in the women's movement."[91]

In writing about "Seventies Questions for Thirties Women," as she entitled her essay, Chodorow also felt a tension "between the feminist injunction to let women's voices be heard" and the feminist injunction to scrutinize "forms of consciousness" that served to maintain the existing social order.[92] There was a further tension—between the persona of the investigator, eager, respectful, and somewhat inarticulate, and the persona of the narrator, confident, assertive, and ready to pass judgment. In this essay the tension was maintained by the inclusion of interview materials, both the researcher's questions and the subjects' responses. In *The Reproduction of Mothering*, there was no comparable documentation, no textual challenge to the narrator's generalizations about women.

• • • • •

"Women mother. . . . Women's mothering is one of the few universal and enduring elements of the sexual division of labor." Like Marx at the start of the *Communist Manifesto* declaring that "the history of all hitherto existing society" was "the history of class struggles,"[93] Chodorow began with a sentence suggesting that the history of all hitherto existing society was the history of women's mothering—and wondered why no struggle had ensued. As she put it, her book analyzed what had rarely been analyzed before: the way women's mothering was "reproduced across generations."[94]

Chodorow set to work with the mother-infant relationship, drawing on a number of theorists. She led off with Anna Freud, quoting the following tortuous sentences:

At this early time of life the actions of the mother and her libidinal cathexis and involvement with the child exert a selective growth of some, and hold back, or fail to stimulate and libidinize, the growth of other potentialities. This determines certain basic trends in the child concerning his motility, the earliness or lateness of his verbalization, etc.[95]

Chodorow cited Michael Balint in a paragraph elaborating the infant's total dependence; she referred to W. R. D. Fairbairn for similar effect. She called upon Margaret Mahler to supply the notion of the infant's experiencing "itself as within a common boundary and fused, physically and psychologically, with its mother." Then she borrowed the term "good-enough mother" from D. W. Winnicott and applied it to a mother's feeling her "infant as continuous with the self and not separate." This, she claimed, echoing Winnicott, derived from the mother's having had such a relationship with her own mother "as a child and being able to regress—while remaining adult—to the psychological state of that experience."[96] From her psychoanalytic reading, Chodorow emerged with a critical question.

> On a theoretical level, then, *anyone*—boy or girl—who has participated in a "good-enough" mother-infant relationship has the relational basis of the capacity for parenting. . . . Yet in spite of this, women—and not men—continue to provide parental (we call it "maternal") care. What happens to the potential parenting capacities in males?"[97]

Chodorow's answer advanced in line with Stoller's narrative of artificial selection—or, rather, here her account evoked artificial selection and in so doing recalled the narrative that Stoller had already constructed. Her answer also advanced from his concept of core gender identity. She explicitly introduced it only in a late chapter, but by then the notion had performed its crucial task: it had allowed Chodorow to assume that mothering women had a gender identity that was both fixed and conflict-free.

> Because they are of the same gender as their daughters and have been girls, mothers of daughters tend not to experience these infant daughters as separate from them in the same way as do mothers of infant sons. . . . Symbiosis with daughters tend[s] to be stronger and cathexis of daughters is more likely to retain and emphasize narcissistic elements, that is, to be based on experiencing a daughter as an extension or double of a mother herself, with cathexis of the daughter as a sexual other usually remaining a weaker, less significant theme. . . .
>
> Because they are of different gender than their sons, by contrast, mothers experience their sons as a male opposite. Their cathexis of sons is more likely to consist from early on in an object cathexis of a sexual other, perhaps in addition

to narcissistic components. Sons tend to be experienced as differentiated from their mothers, and mothers push this differentiation (even while retaining, in some cases, a kind of intrusive controlling power over their sons). Maternal behavior, at the same time, tends to help propel sons into a sexualized, genitally toned relationship, which in its turn draws the son into triangular conflicts.[98]

To return to Chodorow's question: How did these differences in maternal treatment bear on "the potential parenting capacities in males"? To answer it, she turned from maternal behavior or manipulation to the child's response, meaning what was happening to the boy's psychic life. "When an omnipotent mother," she wrote, created "boundaries and a differentiated . . . love relation to her son," the boy reacted by relinquishing "the internal relationship" to his mother. When, subsequently, he was faced with the threat of castration—how parents conveyed that threat Chodorow did not say—he acted promptly and foreswore his internal relationships to his incestuous love objects. It was the boy's presumed renunciation of internal relationships that Chodorow regarded as decisive: his was an impoverished inner world, and as a result his "relational capacities" were "curtailed."[99]

What happened to "the potential parenting capacities in females"? According to Chodorow, where boys surrendered relationships, girls held fast. A girl, she argued, retained a "relation to her mother" that had "preoedipal, or early developmental, characteristics." She remained "preoccupied with issues of symbiosis . . . without sense of the other person's separateness." A girl, Chodorow continued, subsequently developed "important oedipal attachments to her mother *as well as* to her father." Her "internal oedipus situation" was "multilayered": her "relationship . . . of symbiosis to her mother" persisted, and "her oedipal (triangular, sexualized) attachments to her mother and then her father" were simply added. Finally, Chodorow claimed that a girl did not "need to repress her oedipal attachments" as thoroughly as a boy.[100] It was the girl's faithfulness to internal relationships that Chodorow emphasized: hers was a complex inner world, and that complexity seemed to enhance and encourage relational capacities.

Or did it? At this point Chodorow wavered:

> Those very capacities and needs which create women as mothers create potential contradictions in mothering. A mother's sense of continuity with her infant may shade into too much connection and not enough separateness. Empathy . . . , enabling anticipation of an infant's or child's needs, may become an unconscious labeling of what her child ought to need, or what she thinks it needs. The development of a sense of autonomous self becomes difficult for

children and leads to a mother's loss of sense of self as well. That women turn to children . . . to recreate a mother-child unity means that mothering is invested with a mother's often . . . powerful need for her own mother.[101]

From mother's smothering embrace, father held out the promise of liberation—more particularly, he held it out to his daughter. (As for a boy, Chodorow commented, "his penis and masculinity" encouraged his "independence and separateness from mother.") A daughter, she claimed, turned to her father as the person most likely to help her deal "with emotional issues of self and other." How he might actually assist her Chodorow did not specify; she stressed instead the father's function as a "symbol of freedom from dependence and merging"—and a symbol, she suggested, had a limited effect.[102]

How he might assist his daughter in the sexual realm Chodorow merely hinted at. Fulfilling that sketchy role, however, ranked as "crucial to his daughter's development" during "the oedipal period and early adolescence—both times when a girl" was "supposed to be negotiating her transition to heterosexuality." Both times it fell to him "to activate heterosexual genitality in his daughter" by interacting with her in ways that encouraged "her forming a heterosexual/feminine attachment to him." Chodorow was not impressed; she rendered a curt judgment on his performance:

> The father in most cases does not activate exclusive heterosexual love or exclusive generalized attachment. This "failure" is because of his own emotional qualities, because he is not her primary caretaker but comes on the scene after his daughter's relationship to this caretaker (her mother) is well established, and because he is not so involved with his children, however idealized and seductive he may be.[103]

The father thus proved unable to undo the processes set in motion by women's mothering, and these processes, according to Chodorow, were destined to cause a mismatch between men and women.

> As a result of being parented by a woman, both sexes look for a return to this emotional and physical union. A man achieves this directly through the heterosexual bond, which replicates the early mother-infant exclusivity. He is supported in this endeavor by women, who, through their own development, have remained open to relational needs. . . .
>
> As a result of being parented by a woman . . . , women have different and more complex relational needs in which an exclusive relationship to a man is not enough. . . . While they are likely to become and remain erotically heterosexual,

they are encouraged both by men's difficulties with love and by their own relational history with their mothers to look elsewhere for love and emotional gratification.

No wonder, then, that a woman turned "her marriage into a family" and became more involved with her children than with her husband.[104]

And so the cycle began afresh. What Chodorow had done was to graft onto Stoller's account of how a conflict-free, core gender identity came to be produced her own account of how gendered and conflict-causing mothering came to be reproduced.[105]

· · · · ·

The sexual division of labor and women's responsibility for child care are linked to and generate male dominance. Psychologists have demonstrated unequivocally that the very fact of being mothered by a woman generates in men conflicts over masculinity, a psychology of male dominance, and a need to be superior to women. Anthropologists argue . . . that women's continued relegation to the domestic, "natural" sphere, as an extension of their mothering functions, has ensured that they remain less social, less cultural, and also less powerful than men.[106]

"The philosophers," Marx had written, "have only *interpreted* the world . . . , the point is, to *change* it."[107] He had set out to do just that; so too did Chodorow.

My account points precisely to where intervention should take place. Any strategy for change whose goal includes liberation from the constraints of an unequal social organization of gender must take account of the need for a fundamental reorganization of parenting, so that primary parenting is shared between men and women.[108]

The utopia Chodorow envisaged was not a classless society; it was a genderless one.

My expectation is that equal parenting would leave people of both genders with the positive capacities each has, but without the destructive extremes these currently tend toward. Anyone who has good primary relationships has the foundation for nurturance and love, and women would be able to retain these even as men would gain them. Men would be able to retain the autonomy which comes from the differentiation without that differentiation being rigid and reactive, and women would have the opportunity to gain it.[109]

Marx had called upon working men of all countries; Chodorow called upon "all men and women" who recognized that their interests lay "in eliminating social inequality."[110]

• • • • •

> I suggest that gender difference is not absolute, abstract, or irreducible; it does not involve an essence of gender. Gender differences, and the experience of difference, like differences among women, are socially and psychologically created and situated. . . .
>
> My conclusions lead me to reject those currents of contemporary feminism that would found a politics on essentialist conceptions of the feminine.[111]

Here Chodorow positioned herself in feminist debates. She was insisting that she be counted among those who argued that one was not born but rather became a woman. What qualified her for membership in the constructivist camp—and would have qualified Stoller as well had he been interested in applying—was her rejection of biological determinism. To that end, each told a story that highlighted parental, largely maternal, manipulation and thus suggested artificial selection as the title for their tale.

What of cultural determinism? Were Stoller and Chodorow simply social engineers flying under psychoanalytic colors? The answer is no. Yet their accounts were curiously lopsided: in the parent-child relationship, they invariably located initiative on the side of the parent, with the child merely reacting. The child was in the course of being returned to a pre-Freudian innocence.

Chapter 5 Natural Selection: Melanie Klein and Judith M. Hughes

"Natural Selection; Or the Survival of the Fittest" is the title Darwin gave to the fourth chapter of his *On the Origin of Species* (1859). This, he wrote in his introduction, was "the doctrine of Malthus applied to the whole of the animal and vegetable kingdoms."

> As many more individuals of each species are born than can possibly survive; and as, consequently, there is a frequently recurring struggle for existence, it follows that any being, if it vary however slightly in any manner profitable to itself, under the complex and sometimes varying conditions of life, will have a better chance of surviving, and thus be *naturally selected*. From the strong principle of inheritance, any selected variety will tend to propagate its new and modified form.[1]

Darwin set out with two goals in mind: first, he sought to convince the scientific world that evolution, or descent with modification, had occurred; second, he proposed the theory of natural selection as its mechanism. The first won many followers; the second made little headway. Evolution could be readily conscripted into a Victorian campaign in favor of progress; natural selection proved more recalcitrant. It was a theory of "*local* adaptation to changing environments." It advanced "no perfecting principles, no guarantee of general improvement."[2] Not until the 1940s, not until the laws of inheritance were better understood, did the theory of natural selection gain widespread acceptance.

Melanie Klein, who began publishing two decades earlier, did not invoke the concept of natural selection. What justifies calling Klein's a story of natural selection is her emphasis on the issue the concept itself brings to the fore: the relation between the organism and its environment or, better, the fit between the two, with fitness or adaptedness a matter for the organism rather than the environment. (Here is how Klein put it: "After the termination of its analysis," she wrote, "the child cannot alter the circumstances of its life as the adult often can. But analysis will have helped it very greatly if it has enabled it to develop more freely and feel better in its actual environment.")[3] And thanks to her stress on the child's sadism and her adherence to Freud's notion of a death instinct, her account resembled Darwin's in all its goriness.

Like Deutsch and Horney, Klein appeared on the psychoanalytic scene in the 1920s.[4] Born in Vienna in 1882, which made her Deutsch's senior by two years and Horney's by three, she was the youngest of four children. Her father, who was over fifty when Melanie was born, had been raised in an orthodox Jewish milieu and had devoted his early adulthood to religious studies with the aim of becoming a rabbi. In his late thirties he broke with his origins and, without much success, began pursuing a medical career. Because of her husband's precarious financial circumstances, Melanie's mother was obliged to open a shop, and in so doing, to see her hopes for status disappear. As a breadwinner, the father proved a poor model; as a man of learning, however, he set his children a high standard—a standard that was impossible for his wife to reach, despite her energy and strength of will.

It was through two of Melanie's siblings that her father's intellectual aspirations reached her. Her sister, who died when Melanie was only four, taught Melanie the fundamentals of reading and arithmetic. Her brother, who died when she was twenty, shaped her interests from about the age of nine. She turned to him as "confidant," "friend," and "teacher"; he responded by coaching her in Greek and Latin and thus helping her pass the entrance examinations to the Gymnasium.[5] He expected great things of her, she felt, and her own expectations were equally high. She was to be disappointed: her dream, to enter medical school and to specialize in psychiatry remained just that—a dream. Unlike Deutsch and Horney, she was not among the few women who matriculated in German-speaking universities.

By the time she might have fought for admission to higher education, her father was dead, and the family's uncertain finances further hampered her. No doubt they also weighed heavily in her decision to marry Arthur Klein. An industrial chemist, in worldly terms, he was the most suitable of her admirers. They were married in 1903. Here too she was to be disappointed. Almost from the very beginning, Melanie's distress and dissatisfaction were evident. She found her life circumstances trying: in their first seven years together, Arthur's profession took him and his family to a series of small towns in Slovakia and Silesia. She found their children—Melitta, born in 1904, and Hans, born in 1907—also trying: in those years she regularly escaped to cures and seaside spots of one sort or another. And she found her mother trying: more and more the widowed woman took over the management of her daughter's household and the rearing of her children. In 1910 Arthur was transferred to Budapest, and it was there that Melanie freed herself from a depression that threatened to paralyze her.

That liberation was slow in coming. The earliest it can be dated is 1914, the year her third and last child, Erich, was born, her mother died, and Arthur was called for military service. During the war Melanie extricated herself unofficially from the marriage—it did not legally end until the mid-1920s. During the same period she became involved with the psychoanalytic movement, and here she was not to be disappointed. She attended the Fifth International Psycho-Analytical Congress in Budapest in 1918 and caught her first glimpse of Freud. The following July she read a paper to the Hungarian Psychoanalytic Society and was immediately made a member. Along the way she had an analysis with Sándor Ferenczi.

What went on in that analysis and in her subsequent analysis with Karl Abraham in 1924 and 1925? Klein did not say. Her scant comments about her two analysts pointed to their professional guidance rather than their therapeutic impact on her. These two men, intellectually and temperamentally very different from each other, agreed in encouraging Klein to work with children. It was Ferenczi, she claimed, who drew her attention to her great gift for understanding children and suggested that she devote herself to analyzing them.[6] Child patients—or perhaps any patients—were not, however, readily available to her; so she turned to her son Erich. The paper she presented to the Hungarian Society derived from work with him—she concealed his identity in later versions under the pseudonym "Fritz."[7] Just a few years later—political turmoil had forced her to leave Budapest, and in 1921 she had settled in Berlin—it was Abraham who defended her and her views in heated discussions within the Berlin Psychoanalytic Society.[8] By then she had become "absolutely firm" on "keeping parental influence . . . apart from analysis" and reducing it to "its minimum." That minimum, Alix Strachey quipped, was "to keep the child from absolutely poisoning itself on mushrooms, to keep it reasonably clean, and teach it its lessons."[9]

Klein met Strachey in 1924. (Together with Joan Riviere, Alix and her husband, James, were Freud's principal translators.) Alix had come to Berlin for an analysis with Abraham, and in her letters to James she reported on the German scene. Through the Stracheys, Klein's suggestion that she should give a series of lectures was passed on to Ernest Jones, president of the British Psycho-Analytical Society. He took her proposal to his colleagues, and James provided Alix with an account of what followed:

> Jones announced at the meeting that he'd had a letter from Frau Klein but that he hadn't answered it, so that he might first discover what the society thought about the matter. He then, very haltingly, read out her letter. When he got through her scenario, or whatever you call it, he muttered to himself "very interesting programme." . . . I had the impression, which afterwards turned out to be true, that he himself was very anxious that it should be put through but felt doubtful of what other people would think. Anyhow, after some talk, he said in dubious terms: "Well, as to the number that are likely to attend . . . I'm afraid it's much too early yet to ask people now if they'll be prepared to come . . . h'm? . . . well perhaps I might ask . . . h'm? . . . those who think they will to hold up their hands." It was a rather unusually small meeting: only 15 or 16 altogether. Without an instant's hesitation every single hand rose in the air. Jones's whole manner instantly changed. He became wreathed in smiles and exclaimed: "Oh, well! come! . . . "
>
> There couldn't be any question at all that there was a most unusual amount of interest at the prospect of her visit; quite a stir, in fact. So you can pile it on as thick as you please.[10]

And thus Klein went to London in the summer of 1925.[11] A year later, her position in Berlin having become quite uncomfortable after Abraham's premature death, she was ready to go permanently.

Klein had been "sniffed at" by people in Berlin[12]; she was fussed over in London. Within a year of her arrival, Ferenczi wrote to Freud, after visiting the British capital, of "the domineering influence" Klein exerted over "the whole group."[13] She attended her first meeting in October 1926 and presented her first paper the following month. After she became a member, in 1927, she played an equally active role in the educational and administrative life of the society; in 1929 she was named a training analyst, started work with her first candidate, and was elected a member of the Training Committee—a position she held for many years.[14] With the publication of *The Psycho-Analysis of Children* in 1932, she won her greatest acclaim within the British Society. Edward Glover, for example, had "no hesitation" in stating that her book was "of fundamental importance for the future of psychoanalysis"—indeed, that it constituted "a landmark in analytical literature worthy to rank with some of Freud's own classical contributions."[15]

In that book, dedicated in gratitude and admiration to the memory of Karl Abraham, Klein acknowledged her intellectual debt to both him and Ferenczi. She thanked Jones as well, not as someone who had mentored her, but as someone whose "studies" were "in close touch" with hers "in all essential points."[16] Klein was thus tightly linked with the three men who, after the First World War, ranked as Freud's chief lieutenants. She had no personal connection with Freud himself, and in the late 1920s there were already those who questioned her fidelity to him. Jones found such questions incomprehensible and said as much to Freud:

> Many thanks for your recent letter. I should like to return to one sentence in it of extreme importance, namely, where you say that you find Melanie Klein's views about the super-ego quite incompatible with your own. I would seem to be suffering from a scotoma, for I do not perceive this at all. The only difference I was aware of is that she dates both the Oedipus conflict and the genesis of the super-ego a year or two earlier than you have. As one of your chief discoveries has been the fact that young children are much more mature than had been generally supposed, both sexually and morally, I had regarded the conclusions reached by Frau Klein's experience as being simply a direct continuation of your own tendencies.[17]

Note what was at issue: the superego. This was Klein's starting point.

Ten years after the appearance of *The Psycho-Analysis of Children,* the question of Klein's loyalty to Freud, whether or not it was a fruitful one, could no longer be regarded as incomprehensible. In the intervening decade the founder of psychoanalysis had died, and his daughter Anna, having settled in London, had become the self-appointed guardian of her father's legacy. As James Strachey saw it, Anna considered psychoanalysis a "Game Reserve belonging to the F. Family" and viewed "Mrs. K's ideas" as "fatally subversive."[18] In the same decade Klein's originality and/or audacity had emerged with full force. And her earlier interest in female sexuality had waned.

• • • • •

I first happened upon *The Psycho-Analysis of Children* in the winter of 1974. My son, then aged five-and-a-half, had started to blink nervously, and I, like a typical intellectual, rushed to the library in search of information. There the title of Klein's book struck me, and I tried to distill from it lessons I could apply to my son. In this I failed—despite strenuous efforts. For whatever reason, the blinking disappeared in a few weeks.

By the time I came across Klein's work, I was an assistant professor at Harvard. Having graduated from Swarthmore, I had arrived in Cambridge in 1962 to pursue a doctorate in history. Eight years later, a Ph.D. in hand and a book in press, I decided to try something explicitly psychoanalytic or psychohistorical. Here Erikson's popularity acted as an inducement. In the course of that project—a study of late nineteenth-century British and German leaders—I developed preferences with regard to psychoanalytic theory: early on, thanks to a remark by a senior professor, I read the work of W. R. D. Fairbairn and was much impressed; a few years later I encountered that of D. W. Winnicott—and the two of them provided guidance. Behind their work, I noted, lay that of Melanie Klein, but I had not yet grappled with it.[19]

The years I spent in Cambridge witnessed the revival of feminism, and Gilligan and Chodorow soon became part of that revival. As a matter of practice, I did too.[20] It took me the better part of two decades, however, to see how my growing familiarity with psychoanalytic theory might equip me to say something about issues of concern to feminists. Along the way I had decided to become a psychoanalyst.

That decision came slowly. It began to take shape after 1975, when I joined the history department of the University of California, San Diego. With the completion of my psychohistorical project, I shifted to writing the history of psychoanalysis itself and embarked upon a book about Klein and the theorists I had been drawing on. I also began a personal analysis. The two went on simultaneously. A book on Freud followed,[21] and as I was nearing the end of it, I realized that I had reached the point where further work on the history/theory of psychoanalysis could not be done without clinical experience of my own. And so, in 1991 I started training at the San Diego Psychoanalytic Institute.

One reviewer of my book on Klein, Fairbairn, and Winnicott wondered how it came about that "a historian from this geopolitical outpost [San Diego], which is so remote from Great Britain in so many psychoanalytic ways," chanced upon my particular protagonists.[22] The query points to a disjunction between my intellectual and my guild affiliations. I reckon myself as part of an object-relations tradition, influenced more by Fairbairn than by Klein, and function in a psychoanalytic institute where she is little known or understood. There are interlocutors in my head I have never met and colleagues around a table I see weekly. Both constitute identifiable communities.

One might read my contribution as rounding out Klein's work. She wrote about sexuality; I am writing about gender. She told, and I am telling, the same evolutionary tale, a tale of natural selection.

MULTIPLE SEXUALITIES

The Psycho-Analysis of Children is not easy reading. Despite his "great admiration for the matter of the book," Glover felt compelled to "comment somewhat less favourably" on its "manner and arrangement."

> The author has been at considerable pains to weld together two sets of lectures. . . . but she has not succeeded altogether in hiding the joints. In spite of an admirable translation by Alix Strachey, it is difficult not to regret the amount of overlapping and cross-referencing.

Should Klein decide to bring out a second edition (as she subsequently did), Glover continued, he would recommend that she scrap the "existing mode of presentation in favour of a more systematic and coherent form."[23] She did not heed his advice; she was obviously satisfied with the manner and arrangement, as well as the matter, of her book.

Klein's work—and this is what makes it hard going—is several books at once, which co-exist, compete, sometimes mutually interfere. In the first place it is a book about her technique for treating children—that is, play analysis. Here Klein invited the reader to inspect her equipment:

> On a low table in my analytic room there are laid out a number of small and simple toys—little wooden men and women, carts, carriages, motor-cars, trains, animals, bricks and houses, as well as paper, scissor and pencils. Even a child that is usually inhibited in its play will at least glance at the toys or touch them, and will soon give me a first glimpse into its complexes by the way in which it begins to play with them or lays them aside, or by its general attitude towards them.

Second, the book is an ethnography—a description of "the mind of the young child" as Klein had learned to know it from the "early analyses" she had conducted. Here she showed her readers a world of serious distress. Take her patient Rita, who was two and three-quarters years old at the beginning of treatment:

> At that time she had a very marked obsessional neurosis. She exhibited obsessive ceremonials and alternated between "goody-goodiness" mixed with feelings of remorse, and uncontrollable "naughtiness." She had attacks of moodiness which showed all the signs of a melancholic depression; and in addition she suffered from severe anxiety, and extensive inhibition in play, a total inability to tolerate any kind of frustration, and an excessive woefulness.[24]

Third, Klein wrote a theoretical text. Here she assumed that her readers were already members of the psychoanalytic community, fully conversant with the writings of Freud, Abraham, and lesser lights. They were all insiders together, and there was no need to translate their common idiom into ordinary English (or German).

Among those insiders and one who doubted the feasibility of Klein's enterprise was Freud himself:

> An analysis which is conducted upon a neurotic child . . . cannot be very rich in material; too many words and thoughts have to be lent to the child and even so the deepest strata may turn out to be impenetrable. . . . An analysis of a child-hood disorder through the medium of recollection in an intellectually mature adult is free from these limitations, but it necessitates our taking into account the distortion and refurbishing to which a person's own past is subjected when it is looked back upon from a later period. The first alternative perhaps gives the more convincing results; the second is by far the more instructive.[25]

Now he had Klein's testimony to the contrary:

> If we approach the child patient with the technique of adult analysis it is quite certain that we shall not penetrate to the deepest levels. . . . But if we take into consideration how the child's psychology differs from that of the adult—the fact that its unconscious is as yet in close contact with its conscious and that its most primitive impulses are at work alongside of highly complicated mental pro-cesses—and if we correctly grasp the child's mode of expression, then all these drawbacks and disadvantages vanish and we find that we may expect to make as deep and extensive an analysis of the child as of the adult. More so in fact. In child-analysis we are able to get back to experiences . . . which, in the analysis of

adults can often only be reconstructed, whereas the child shows them to us as immediate representations.[26]

This passage is dotted with first person plural pronouns; elsewhere first person singular pronouns are freely sprinkled about. Their use points to the defining characteristic of Klein's book: a sense of the narrator's intense engagement. The tone is passionate without being polemical, ardent without being strident. The narrator is pleased with herself, pleased to be making a contribution, pleased with the contribution she is making—and she expects her audience to be appreciative as well as enlightened.

• • • • •

How the child adapted to its environment—that is, to the people in its environment—not how these people adapted to the child, this was the overarching question Klein posed:

> Neurotic children do not tolerate reality well. . . . They protect themselves from reality by denying it. . . . For this reason one of the results of early analysis should be to enable the child to adapt itself to reality.[27]

Erna was a case in point, and the one that Klein elaborated in greatest detail in *The Psycho-Analysis of Children*. What had brought this six-year-old to treatment?

> Erna . . . had a number of severe symptoms. She suffered from sleeplessness, which was caused partly by anxiety (in particular by a fear of robbers and burglars) and partly by a series of obsessional activities. These consisted in lying on her face and banging her head on the pillow, in making a rocking movement, during which she sat or lay on her back, in obsessional thumb-sucking and in excessive and compulsive masturbation. All these obsessional activities which prevented her from sleeping at night, were carried on in day-time as well. This was especially the case with masturbation which she practised even in the presence of strangers. . . . She suffered from severe depressions, which she would describe by saying "There's something about life I don't like." . . . A symptom which first became obvious during the analysis was that she had a very severe inhibition in learning. She was sent to school a few months after the analysis began, and it was soon evident that she was quite incapable of learning, nor could she adapt herself to her school-fellows. The fact that she herself felt she was ill—at the very beginning of her treatment she begged me to help her—was of great assistance to me in analyzing her.[28]

What came to the fore in Erna's analysis was her relationship to her mother. "In her numerous phantasies . . . about a mother and a child," Erna expressed "what she felt her own experience had been"; she also indicated "what she would like to do to her mother . . . if the mother-child relationship was reversed." In Klein's words:

> Erna played at being a child that had dirtied itself, and I, as the mother, had to scold her, whereupon she became scornful and out of defiance dirtied herself more and more. In order to annoy the mother still further she vomited up the bad food I had given her. The father was then called in by the mother, but he took the child's side. Next the mother was seized with an illness called "God has spoken to her"; then the child in turn got an illness called "mother's agitation" and died of it, and the mother was killed by the father as a punishment. The child then came to life again and was married to the father, who kept on praising it at the expense of the mother. The mother was brought to life again, too, but as a punishment, was turned into a child by the father's magic wand; and now she in turn had to suffer all the humiliation and ill-treatment to which the child herself had been subjected before.

"Every educational measure," Klein surmised, "every act of nursery discipline, every unavoidable frustration," was felt by Erna "as a purely sadistic act on the part of her mother."[29]

How had the mother actually behaved? In the early stages of the analysis, Klein wrote, she "had not succeeded in obtaining any detailed information" about Erna's real life:

> I never heard the least complaint or criticism from her about her *real* mother and what she actually did. Although Erna acknowledged that her phantasies were directed against her real mother—a fact which she had denied at an earlier stage of analysis—and although it became clearer and clearer that she copied her mother in an exaggerated and invidious manner, yet it was difficult to establish the connection between her phantasies and reality.

As the analysis progressed, Erna began to criticize her mother "as a real person with greater frankness." Her "unconscious grievances and adverse judgments," Klein maintained, could now "be tested against reality" and in this way "lose their . . . virulence." And so it happened that "Erna would often say with astonishment"—after having represented her ideas of persecution in play: " 'But mother can't *really* have meant to do that? She's very fond of me *really*.' "[30]

If the mother had not actually mistreated her, what had set Erna at odds with her environment and thus prompted her to take flight from reality in the first place? Here Klein found herself addressing the question of a punitive superego.

• • • • •

In *Beyond the Pleasure Principle* (1920) Freud introduced the notion of a death instinct; he continued to advance the notion until the end of his life. Alone among his descendants, Melanie Klein (and her followers) adopted it. She announced her adoption in *The Psycho-Analysis of Children*, where she deployed it to fashion an account of why Erna and other child patients felt so strong a sense of persecution.

It all began, so Klein explained, with a polarity of life and death instincts—putting the ego at immediate risk. In order to prevent the death instinct from destroying the ego, the ego deflected the death instinct outward on to its object. Now its fears had a focus: its external object, though grossly distorted. Against this danger, the infant sought to defend itself by destroying the object. Sadism, of all sorts, flourished:

> The idea of an infant of from six to twelve months trying to destroy its mother by every method at the disposal of its sadistic trends—with its teeth, nails and excreta and with the whole of its body, transformed in phantasy into all kinds of dangerous weapons—presents a horrifying, not to say an unbelievable picture to our minds. . . . But the abundance, force and multiplicity of the cruel phantasies . . . displayed before our eyes in early analyses so clearly and forcibly . . . leave no room for doubt.[31]

Both attack and deflection failed: the object was not destroyed; nor did it remain external.

What happened next was that the grossly distorted object was internalized. The ego then regarded "the internalized object," which, according to Klein, constituted "the beginnings of the early super-ego," as an enemy from which nothing but hostility could be expected:

> The threats of the early super-ego . . . contain in detail the whole range of sadistic phantasies that were directed to the object, which are now turned back against the ego item by item. Thus the pressure of anxiety exerted in this early stage will correspond in quantity to the extent of sadism originally present, and in quality to the variety and wealth of the accompanying sadistic phantasies.[32]

No wonder Erna and Klein's other child patients felt persecuted.

For Klein the superego's punitive harshness, readily apparent in clinical material, posed no problem, whereas for Freud it remained a puzzle. In his work he offered two different, though not mutually exclusive, explanations. As Klein summarized them, "According to one, the severity of the super-ego derived from the severity of the real father. . . . According to the other, . . . its severity . . . [was] an outcome of the destructive impulses of the subject."[33] Klein did more than endorse the second view. She had the right to claim priority in this matter, and Freud—who rarely referred to her work—granted her a measure of recognition, albeit only in a footnote.[34]

• • • • •

From a punitive superego, from internalized bad objects, how did the child find relief? Here Klein turned to libidinal drives:

> The vicious circle dominated by the death-instinct, in which aggression gives rise to anxiety and anxiety reinforces aggression can be broken by the libidinal forces when these have gained in strength; in the early stages of development, the life-instinct has to exert its power to the utmost in order to maintain itself against the death-instinct. But this very necessity stimulates sexual development.[35]

At this point Klein introduced the Oedipus complex. At this point she also differed with Freud. In "Female Sexuality" (1931) he had written:

> Where the woman's attachment to her father was particularly intense, analysis showed that it had been preceded by a phase of exclusive attachment to her mother which had been equally intense and passionate. . . . In several cases . . . [this attachment] had . . . lasted until well into the fourth year—in one case into the fifth year—so that it covered by far the longer part of the period of early sexual efflorescence.[36]

Not so, said Klein. Her "experience of analysis," she claimed, had convinced her that the "long-drawn-out and powerful attachment" of little girls to their mothers was "never exclusive" and was always "bound up with Oedipus impulses."[37] And this, she argued, was true of boys as well.

Note the two steps Klein had taken. First, she subsumed the Oedipus complex under the struggle between life and death instincts, thus emphasizing aggression and the intense anxiety it aroused. Second, she pushed the complex back in time, thus emphasizing the ways in which libidinal trends overlapped and coincided with oedipal dramas. Where Freud retained two separate developmental lines, libido and object love, whose convergence at a fairly late date produced the Oedipus complex, Klein assumed that so clear a delineation was misleading rather than helpful. In her account, oedipal dramas became less stories of a child's incestuous loves than stories of searches for new objects to combat the child's fear of his "terrifying introjected objects."[38]

One can find in Klein's writings, as in Freud's, four versions, two male and two female, of the Oedipus complex. For the boy the "normal" succession entailed a change of sexual aim but not of sexual object: when he abandoned "the oral and anal positions for the genital," he passed on "to the aim of *penetration* associated with possession of the penis"—all the while retaining his original love object. In contrast, for the girl the positive course involved carrying over the "*receptive* aim . . . from the oral to the genital position."[39] In so doing, she became receptive toward the penis and at the same time turned to her father as love object. From this outline the negatives were easy to infer: in the boy, retention of aim and change of object; in the girl, change of aim and retention of object. But just as Klein intermingled libidinal stages, so too she mixed together positive and inverted oedipal dramas. Rather than taking positive and negative elements and arranging them in a limited number of fixed patterns, she was intent on transforming the Oedipus complex into a constantly fluctuating configuration.

This work of transformation was already apparent in Klein's paper of 1928 entitled "Early Stages of the Oedipus Conflict." In that paper she had stressed the relationship among hating, fearing, and the projection of hostile impulses. By the time she published her book, four years later, she had fastened on the death instinct. The effect was to layer anxiety upon anxiety: on top of the initial anxiety engendered by the death instinct she saw piled the anxieties specific to the oedipal situation—and in her hands those anxieties had become quite specific.

The analyses of small children, Klein argued, showed that in its earliest stage the boy's sexual development ran along the same lines as the girl's. Boys and girls alike moved on "from an oral-sucking fixation upon the mother's breast to an oral-sucking fixation upon . . . father's penis."

> In the phantasy of the boy, his mother incorporates his father's penis, or rather a number of them, inside herself; side by side with his relations to his real father, or, to be more precise, his father's penis, he develops a relation in phantasy to his father's penis inside his mother's body. Since his oral desires for his father's penis are . . . [a motive] of his attacks on his mother's body—for he wants to take by

force the penis which he imagines as being *inside his mother* and to injure her in doing so—his attacks also represent . . . his earliest situations of rivalry with her.

She added:

> The anxiety-situations resulting from sadistic attacks made by children of both sexes on their mother's body fall into two categories. In the first, the mother's body becomes a place filled with dangers which give rise to all sorts of terrors. In the second, the child's own inside is turned into a place of a similar kind, by virtue of the child's introjection of its dangerous objects . . . and it becomes afraid of the perils and threats within itself.[40]

Very shortly, Klein maintained, genital impulses intervened, but the divergence they produced between boys and girls was far from absolute. To be sure, the boy might now desire to have sole possession of his mother "in an oral, anal and genital sense" and for that reason attacked "his father's penis within her with . . . the sadistic means at his disposal." This aroused in him "a proportionate fear," particularly a fear of "being castrated by his father's penis inside his mother." The girl for her part might now desire her father's penis, all the more so given that "the demands of her oral-sucking impulses, heightened by the frustration" she had suffered "from her mother's breast" created in her "a phantasy picture of her father's penis as an organ which, unlike the breast," could provide her with "a tremendous and never-ending gratification." But the girl did not escape fear of that organ.

> Since the small girl's phantasies about the enormous powers and huge size and strength of her father's penis arise from her own oral-, urethral- and anal-sadistic impulses, she will also attribute extremely dangerous properties to it. This aspect of it provides the substratum of her terror of the "bad" penis, which sets in as a reaction to the destructive impulses which, in combination with libidinal ones, are directed towards it. If her oral sadism is dominant, she will regard her father's penis within her mother principally as a thing to be hated, envied and destroyed; and the hate-filled phantasies which she centres upon her father's penis as something that is giving her mother satisfaction will in some cases be so intense that they will cause her to displace her deepest and most powerful anxiety—her fear of her mother—on to her father's penis as a hated appendage of her mother.[41]

The early oedipal wishes and anxieties, according to Klein, focused on the mother's body and the father's penis as part objects. When did the parents become whole persons? When did the father cease being perceived as a penis incorporated by the mother? Klein did not say. She simply moved on to the sadistic fantasies associated with parents as whole objects, more particularly combined in intercourse. In the most striking of these, children endowed the parents "with instruments of mutual destruction, transforming their teeth, nails, genitals, excrements and so on, *into* dangerous weapons and animals," and pictured them, in accord with the children's own desires, "as tormenting and destroying each other in the act of copulation."[42] No wonder boys and girls alike found the imagined primal scene terrifying.

How, in the face of the multiple anxieties Klein depicted, did children find their way to new objects? She discerned two strategies, the first magical, the second realistic. The first brought into view the anatomical differences between the sexes, or, more precisely, the elaboration in fantasy of those differences. The second pointed to the child's projecting his or her fears of internal dangers onto the external world and there finding evidence to disprove the fears. The neat distinction between the two existed in theory rather than in actuality.

In the boy's case, the magical route entailed pressing the penis into service. Physiology helped: it demonstrated that the penis really could change its appearance. Imagination did the rest: the boy took tumescence as proof of his penis's power and likened it to a "devouring and murderous" beast:

> This concentration of sadistic omnipotence in the penis is of fundamental importance for the masculine position of the boy. If he has a strong primary belief in the omnipotence of his penis he can pit it against the omnipotence of his father's penis and take up the struggle against that dreaded and admired organ.[43]

Magic thus equipped the boy with an all-powerful tool by means of which he might control internalized and real objects. But only in fantasy.

In the girl's case, magic played a lesser role. In her case, physiology did not help. As for the vagina, it was not undiscovered—on this point Klein cited Horney.[44] But the fact that "the structure of the body" did not permit the girl to know what was actually going on within aggravated her "deepest fear—namely that the inside of her body . . . [had] been damaged or destroyed."[45] As for the clitoris, it might assume the significance of a penis. Here reality dawned, and the girl came to appreciate—certainly not "in a flash," as Freud had suggested[46]—that her clitoris was no substitute for the penis she desired.

When did reality dawn? In fact, Klein remarked, it had been there all along. From the earliest stages of the child's existence, the behavior of his or her real objects contributed to intensifying or diminishing anxiety. From the very earliest stage the child needed a "helping" figure in the external world in order to disconfirm his or her fantastic fears.

> If, because . . . [the child's] anxiety is too great or for realistic reasons, its Oedipus objects have not become good imagos, other persons, such as a kindly nurse, brother or sister, a grandparent or an aunt or uncle can, in certain circumstances, take over the role of the "good" mother or the "good" father. In this way . . . [the child's] positive feelings, whose growth has been inhibited owing to its excessive fear of its Oedipus objects, can . . . attach themselves to a love-object.[47]

In subsequent years good objects were to come into their own in Klein's work. The result was a certain asymmetry: bad objects derived from a child's sadism, good objects from the external world; wicked mammas of whom "everything evil . . . was anticipated . . . differed fundamentally from the real objects";[48] fairy mammas—and good breasts—more closely approximated actual mothers who had been on hand in early infancy.

Love objects, Klein argued, offered a similar possibility; they too promised to disconfirm fantastic fears:

> If the [mature] girl . . . is supported by feelings of a confident and hopeful kind, she will be led to take as her object a person who represents the "good" penis. In this case, the relief of anxiety which is achieved by the sexual act will give her a strong enjoyment and considerably add to the purely libidinal satisfaction she experiences, and beyond this, it lays the foundations for lasting and satisfactory love relationships. But if . . . her fear of the introjected "bad" penis predominates, the necessary condition for her ability to love will be . . . that her partner in love shall be a sadistic person. . . . Even her anticipated injuries . . . serve to allay her anxiety.

This was so, she hastened to add, because "no suffering inflicted by outside sources" could be "as great as that inflicted in phantasy by continuous and overwhelming fear of internal injuries and dangers."[49]

Klein did not draw together the threads of the narrative she was telling. She conceived of sexuality as multiple and various. So too Freud had conceived of it as made up of components. Klein then added something. She took the multiplicity that was central to his conception and embedded it in a story of a child's elaboration of an inner world and his/her adaptation to an external one.

• • • • •

> I am of the opinion that your society followed Mrs. Klein on a wrong path, but I am unfamiliar with just that sphere of observations which she draws upon and hence have no right to a firm conviction.[50]

Thus Freud wrote to Jones in May 1935, a month after Jones visited the Austrian capital and delivered a lecture to the Vienna Psychoanalytic Society, the first in a series of four arranged to ensure that psychoanalysis in London and Vienna developed along similar lines.[51] For some years, Jones commented, it had been "apparent that many analysts in London" did not "see eye to eye with their colleagues in Vienna" and that there was "some danger of local views becoming unified to such an extent as to enable people to speak of a Vienna school or London school as if they represented different tendencies of a possibly divergent order." This was not so, he claimed: the differences were of "just that kind that go with imperfect contact." In the present case he pointed to geography and language, compounded by "political and economic disturbances," to account for the imperfect contact. At the same time he listed those topics on which analysts in London and Vienna were in the course of parting company: "the early development of sexuality, especially in the female, the genesis of the super-ego and its relation to the Oedipus complex, the technique of child analysis."[52] The list itself attested to the success Klein had had in London.

Jones took as his subject early female sexuality and located the "sharpest difference of opinion" between him and his audience in the "penis-clitoris question":

> If for brevity you will allow me purposely to exaggerate . . . , one might say that according to one view the girl hates her mother because she has disappointed her wish that her clitoris were a penis, whereas according to the other view the reason that the girl wishes that her clitoris were a penis is that she feels hatred for her mother which she cannot express. Similarly according to one view the girl comes to love her father because she is disappointed in her clitoris, whereas according to the other view she wishes to change her clitoris for a penis because of the obstacles in the way of loving her father.[53]

Jones did not pause to underline one of Klein's cardinal postulates: the primacy of object relations. Instead he moved quickly on to the sadism she considered characteristic of those relations—more specifically, on to what he, along with Klein, regarded as the fundamental expression of that sadism: the girl's wish (and the boy's for that matter) "to tear a way into the mother's body and devour the father's penis" believed "to be incorporated there." Almost in the same breath he moved on to "the girl's corresponding anxiety lest the inside of her own body be similarly robbed and destroyed."[54]

How did the notion of possessing a penis "allay this terrible sadism and its accompanying anxiety"? Jones couched his answer in terms of a "complex network of phantasies":

> The girl's idea of the penis is, of course, an ambivalent one. On the one hand, it is good, friendly, nourishing, and the fluid emanating from it is equated with milk. On the other hand, it is evil and destructive, its fluid having a corroding power. The use to which the girl puts her imaginary penis in her phantasies is therefore a double one. In so far as it is evil, sadistic and destructive it is a weapon that can be used to attack the mother in the way she fancies her father does, and thus obtain what she wants from the mother's body. In so far as it is good and beneficent it can be used to restore to the mother the penis the girl thinks she has robbed her of. . . . It can also be used to neutralise and thus make good again the bad internalised penis, the one the girl has swallowed and by her sadism turned into a harmful and self-destructive organ inside her own body; a visible and intact penis would be the best reassurance against the inaccessible internal anxieties.[55]

This "phallic phase," then, this phase in which the girl wished her clitoris were a penis, Jones reckoned as defensive. It followed that he was "sceptical about the existence of the phallic phase as a phase of development"; it also followed that he was "more sceptical than the Viennese . . . about its passing":

> It would seem to be more accurate to use the expression "phallic position" to describe the phenomena in question. We are concerned with an emotional attitude rather than a stage in libidinal development. This attitude is maintained by certain forces and needs, diminishes whenever these are weaker, but persists just so long as they persist—often throughout life. The "phallic position" is not seldom quite as pronounced at the age of six, ten or thirty as at the age of two or three.[56]

In his lecture Jones attempted both to sharpen the issues between him and his colleagues in Vienna and to indicate how specific items, such as penis envy, were embedded in a ramifying theoretical structure. He then implicitly left it to his audience to choose between competing hypotheses. At no point did he take the line, so common in psychoanalytic polemics, that his position ranked as psychoanalytic and his opponents' counted as something else—at no point, that is, until the final paragraph:

> Put more generally, I think the Viennese would reproach us with estimating the early phantasy life too highly at the expense of external reality. And we should answer that there is no serious danger of any analysts neglecting external reality, whereas it is always possible for them to underestimate Freud's doctrine of the importance of psychical reality.[57]

· · · · ·

> The depression, anger and anxiety which seized her during her play were due to a disturbance of her phantasies by some incursion of reality. She remembered, too, how greatly she was put out if anyone came near her in bed in the morning while she was thumb-sucking or masturbating. The reason for this was not only that she was afraid of being caught, but that she wanted to ward off reality.[58]

Here Klein was describing Erna and her vexed relationship to her environment. Klein considered anxiety a stimulus to knowledge-seeking; but if anxiety were too great, as in Erna's case, knowledge-seeking itself failed to thrive. (Erna's most resistant symptom, Klein noted, turned out to be her inhibition in learning. The treatment, which lasted for 575 hours and was terminated for external reasons, reduced it but did not remove it entirely.)[59] Ditto for sexuality: Klein thought anxiety stimulated it; but if anxiety were too great, a person's libido might "be unable to maintain any position whatever."[60] The nub of the matter was how an inner world defined a child's fitness and determined the environmental niche in which he or she might prosper.

Was a preference for Klein's conception of psychical reality dependent upon her notion (derived from Freud) of a death instinct? Jones did not think so (early on he had expressed his doubts about it).[61] Nor did Klein. During the "controversial discussions"—held by the British Psycho-Analytical Society in 1943 and 1944 to explore the divergence between Klein's approach to psychoanalysis and what her opponents, led by Anna Freud, referred to as Freudian psychoanalysis—Klein noted that "many colleagues had come to conclusions similar to hers without

believing in the death instinct," and she readily granted that those conclusions "did not stand or fall on that concept."[62] What ranked as crucial for her was anxiety, and the death instinct struck her as useful in
securing its status as unavoidable.

The question, then, could be displaced from the death instinct to anxiety. And the answer was clear: a preference for Klein's conception of psychical reality went hand in hand with an emphasis on anxiety. Or, to put it
another way: an emphasis on anxiety made compelling a notion of an inner
world that bore a family resemblance to Klein's formulation.

MULTIPLE GENDER IDENTITIES

Why have I put myself in a chapter with Klein? I do not share her views on
the death instinct, and I doubt that infants are capable of the complex
fantasies she attributed to them in their first year of life. (Her contemporaries' discourse on psychopathology, their attempt to explain "choice of
neurosis" by fixation at a point in a progression, may have influenced her.
The maxim, the sicker the patient, the earlier the fixation, may have encouraged her to stamp fantasy contents in her very disturbed patients with
an implausibly early date.) What I do share with Klein, and/or take from
her, is selecting punitive aspects of the superego as the point of departure
and, along with that, highlighting struggles to overcome anxieties generated
by relations with internalized bad objects. I also share her view that in those
struggles, external objects—for example, Klein's good breasts—figure as
psychologically significant from birth onwards. For external objects one can
read environment. And change that to the plural.

Internalized bad objects and multiple environments—these are elements for theory building that Klein provided. "Multiple environments"
means that there is more than one chance to find a place to fit; it also means
that initial fitness might prove maladaptive in a changed environment.
Klein told this story—a story that suggested natural selection as its title—
in terms of sexuality. I want to tell it in terms of gender identity.

Throughout this book and others as well, I have relied wherever possible
on clinical material to make concepts and conceptual development accessible. Once again I intend to use clinical material, this time taken from texts
by W. R. D. Fairbairn and by Freud. Here I am not trying to give an account
of their ideas but rather exploiting their material to elaborate ideas of my

own. My reading is aimed not at shedding light on their arguments but at making my own vivid and graphic.

• • • • •

The case that the Scottish psychoanalyst W. R. D. Fairbairn presented to the British Psycho-Analytical Society in 1931—and published more than two decades later—was one of a patient with a genital abnormality. In his account he included the description that her (the patient was presumed to be female) family doctor had provided: "She appeared to be a perfectly normal child until she reached the age of puberty. She began to grow unduly tall, did not menstruate, but kept perfectly well. When she was about twenty, I was consulted and made an examination. I found a complete absence of all genital organs with only a pinhead opening as a vagina which led nowhere. As she felt perfectly well, nothing further was done."[63]

After Fairbairn started treating the patient, he began to doubt the doctor's judgment. To put those doubts to rest, he induced the patient to consult two specialists, a gynecologist and an endocrinologist. They, however, reached contradictory conclusions. The gynecologist reported:

> The general development is strongly masculine, the chest is very broad but the mammary development is, if anything more suggestive of a female type in that the tissue is soft and slightly dependent. The pubic hair is normal in its distribution for the female and the more superficial external organs are quite definitely female, namely, labia, mons, clitoris, vestibule and urethra. The hymen is completely closed, and is represented by a series of small bands crossing the site of the normal depression. Rectal examination was not easy but I was able to determine quite definitely that the pelvis varies from the ordinary female pelvis in the fact that no cervix or uterine body was made out. . . . The general impression which I have formed is that we are dealing with a condition of essential masculinity with the presence of male gonads accompanied by secondary characters of a female type, that is, which usually goes by the name of "male pseudo-hermaphroditism."

The endocrinologist, who examined a specimen of the patient's urine, discovered estrogen in quantities "'similar to those found in a normal female subject,'" indicating "'the presence of female secretory gonads.'" Fairbairn himself concluded that the endocrinologist's testimony carried the greater weight. So "the original presumption that the patient was really female in sex" remained "undisturbed." That the patient was really a woman "psychosexually" Fairbairn had never doubted.[64]

What had induced her to seek psychoanalytic treatment? She was already well into middle age when she was referred to Fairbairn. Unmarried— "fortunately" (why fortunately?), Fairbairn remarked, "she had never taken advantage of any opportunity to marry"—by profession she was a teacher, but she "had been off work for more than a year on account of a nervous breakdown." The eldest of a large family, with many surviving sisters and one surviving brother, she was the only one to have developed "nervous symptoms." In this respect she was "less fortunate" than her sisters, more than one of whom shared her genital abnormality.[65]

The patient herself had shown no symptoms until adulthood. A "gay, irresponsible child," after puberty she had changed and devoted "every available moment to her studies," with the aim of a career in teaching. As things turned out, her hopes for finding satisfaction in that career were bitterly disappointed:

> In her very first post after qualification she began to find teaching a considerable strain. She was unduly conscientious about her duties and set herself a standard of perfection which it was impossible for her to realize in practice. The consequence was that from the outset she worried unduly about her work. The question of discipline occasioned her special anxiety. She could not tolerate the least inattention or insubordination on the part of the children in her class. In order to command the complete attention of the children, she taught with an intensity which left her limp at the end of the day; and after school hours she would wear herself out still further by endless preparation. The natural result of these misguided efforts after perfection was to impair her efficiency as a teacher and to antagonize the schoolchildren, who then became more difficult to teach. Thus, instead of rising, her standard of teaching fell. She was not slow to appreciate this fact herself; but the effect was to make her redouble her already over-strenuous efforts. The more she strove after efficiency, however, the less efficient she became; and the less efficient she became, the more she strove. A vicious circle was thus established; and during the passage of the school term her failure was progressive. This progressive failure was accompanied . . . by progressive feelings of self-reproach. And so by the end of each term she would find her powers of endurance almost at the breaking-point. The holidays, when they came round, provided a period of welcome recuperation; but at the beginning of each term the whirligig began again.[66]

It was some years before an actual breakdown occurred. "An individual of weaker character (i.e., an individual with a less firmly organized ego)," Fairbairn wrote, "would have given in more easily than she did."

> Once, indeed, she made an excursion outside the educational field; for at one stage she embarked upon a secretarial training under the impression that a change of occupation might mitigate her difficulties. This hope proved short-lived; and it was not long before she found the old anxieties attaching themselves to her secretarial work. Within two years, therefore, we find her teaching again—this time in sole charge of a small school in a remote country district. In such a sheltered environment, far from the usual beat of the dreaded inspector and with no supervision except that imposed by her own ego-ideal, she felt she could create educational paradise in which the lion of scholastic efficiency could lie down with the lamb of mental peace. Even in this Garden of Eden . . . the old anxieties returned. . . . She sought peace in a succession of posts in remote districts; but all in vain. So eventually she gave up teaching in despair and went home to try the effects of a prolonged period of rest.[67]

And to try the effects of psychoanalysis as well.

In all this Fairbairn saw the signs of superego pathology. A decade later, when he systematically set out to clarify and revise Freud's structural triad, he would stress, as Klein had already done, the axis running from ego to superego.[68] And when he set out, he would have in mind what he regarded as a remarkable feature of the case of the patient with a genital abnormality—that is, her tendency "to personify various aspects of her psyche."[69]

This tendency, Fairbairn claimed, first manifested itself in dreams. Aside from the "dreaming consciousness," which served as "an independent on-looker," Fairbairn mentioned four figures. Of the four, "the critic" assumed the most varied guises:

> Occasionally . . . a headmaster under whom she [the patient] had once worked or some other male figure of a similar character took over the role of "critic" in her dreams. When a male-figure played this part, he was invariably an authoritative father-figure whose good opinion she was anxious to secure. Nevertheless, "the critic" was characteristically represented by a serious, formidable, puritanical and aggressive woman of middle age. Sometimes this woman was a fanciful individual, who uttered public accusations against the dreamer; but more frequently she was represented by some actual female personage to whose authority the patient had been subject in the past, e.g. the matron of a students' hostel, or a senior teacher. At other times she was represented by the mother of a friend. Thus "the critic" was characteristically a figure endowed with maternal author-

ity; and not uncommonly the patient's own actual mother played the part without any disguise.[70]

The figure of "the critic," Fairbairn noted, was "obviously based . . . upon an identification with the dreamer's mother." The other figures, however, could not be explained in the same way. That of "the martyr" derived its name from a particularly vivid dream:

> In this dream the patient was visiting a college friend in prison. The friend was awaiting trial on an unspecified charge involving her brother as well as herself; and she was sitting in the prison cell on a kind of pedestal—a heroic figure, calm and majestic in demeanour. A small window behind her was so placed that the light entering the cell seemed to shed a halo round her head. . . . This figure . . . had been imprisoned by puritanical authorities for some daring, but not unnatural action committed in conjunction with her brother. In the dream she seemed to be a martyr about to suffer for her boldness in defying narrow and out of date conventions held to be almost sacred by a community soaked in . . . superstition. . . . Analysis showed that the college friend stood for the dreamer herself.

The figure of "the little girl" turned up repeatedly and always about five years old. "She was a charming . . . creature, full of the vivacity of childhood," whom the patient interpreted "as representing herself as she fain would have been . . . —a natural . . . self, to whom no exception could have been taken."[71] "Little girl" and "martyr" alike laid claim to innocence.

Not so the final figure, who along with "the critic" ranked as the "most persistent" personification: "the mischievous boy," a preadolescent, "completely irresponsible, and forever playing pranks and poking fun."

> This boy was frequently represented as annoying the dreamer by his tricks, or as being chased by more sedate figures, whom he mocked as he escaped. With him were identified certain other similar figures, usually of a facetious nature, such as clowns and music-hall comedians. "The mischievous boy" was regarded by the patient as representing her own childish self; and endless play seemed to constitute his sole object in life, as was actually the position in her own case during childhood.

His patient, Fairbairn claimed, considered the boy's penis "a magic talisman calculated . . . to open all the gates of laughter and to convert life into an endless jollification."[72]

Alone among the personifications, "the mischievous boy" invaded his patient's waking life—the others remained confined "to the realm of the unconscious as revealed in dreams." He behaved like a "mildly maniacal subject" and, in a prolonged phase of elation at the beginning of the analysis, "took almost complete possession" of the patient's conscious life. Looking back upon that phase, she later volunteered that she had been "a totally different person."[73] In this fashion "the mischievous boy" prompted Fairbairn to think about a "multiplicity of egos."[74]

More than a decade later that thinking resulted in a "revised conception of psychical structure."[75] Where earlier he had construed "the critic" and "the mischievous boy" as corresponding to the superego and the id, he now could have reckoned "the critic" an internalized object and "the mischievous boy" a split-off part of his patient's ego. Moreover, he now saw ego and object as invariably paired. In the case of "the critic," he could have wondered about the part of the ego that was attached to it; in the case of "the mischievous boy," he could have wondered about the object to which it was attached. And he could have continued to assume—thanks to the presence of "the martyr" and "the little girl"—that there were other structural units as well.

What do I want to take from Fairbairn? Three items stand out as worth exploiting. First, "the mischievous boy"—along with Fairbairn's notion of split-off parts of the ego—encourages me to expect gender identity to be multiple. Second, Fairbairn's stress on object relationships suggests that gender identity cannot be thought about in isolation. "The mischievous boy" represents a relationship between Fairbairn's patient and an unnamed (internal) object—a relationship that may be gratifying, but which may also serve to defend against something threatening. This brings me to my final point: the function of structural units—a gendered self-representation and an object-representation, linked by a particular affect—may itself be multiple.

What Fairbairn failed to do was to talk about the body. I want to avoid being misunderstood. Fairbairn did discuss physiology—but in order to dismiss it. In his view his patient's nervous symptoms could not be attributed to her physical abnormality—after all, her sisters who suffered from the same condition "were relatively free" of psychopathology. Her physical abnormality, Fairbairn concluded, "was only implicated in so far as its presence constituted a psychical trauma for her."[76] Fairbairn said nothing about that trauma nor about the meaning of bodily experiences. In his account "the mischievous boy" remained disembodied. How could a female subject regard a male personification as corporeal? At this point I turn to Freud.

• • • • •

"What can be more definite for a human being than what he has . . . felt on his own body?" It was Daniel Paul Schreber who posed this rhetorical question. Born in 1842, the second son of a well-known orthopedist and educational reformer, the younger Schreber had a long and distinguished judicial career, chiefly in Saxony. Then, in October 1884, after an unsuccessful campaign for the Reichstag, he suffered his first breakdown and had to be hospitalized. The following June he was pronounced cured. For the next eight years all seemed well; he made further professional advances, becoming in 1893 a presiding judge of Saxony's highest court. Those eight years, "rich" alike in the public and the private realm, were "marred only from time to time by the repeated disappointment" of his and his wife's hopes "of being blessed with children."[77] The period ended with a second breakdown.

In 1900 Schreber undertook legal steps for his release from tutelage (that is, guardianship by the courts), steps that in 1902 led to his discharge from an asylum. (In late 1907 he suffered a final breakdown and remained in a mental institution until his death three and a half years later.) For the court the decisive issue was not whether Schreber was mentally ill but whether he was capable of taking care of his own affairs. His insistence on publishing a volume of memoirs had not told against him; in the eyes of the court that wish stood not as proof of incapacity to look out for himself but rather as proof "of the strength of his belief in the truth of the revelations which had been granted him by God."[78] In 1903 his insistence bore fruit: Schreber saw his memoirs in print and brought "to the notice of a wider circle."[79] Within that circle was Freud.

In his preface Schreber explained why publication was so urgent: "I believe that expert examination of my body and observation of my personal fate during my lifetime would be of value both for science and the knowledge of religious truths." The medical examination that Schreber was eager to undergo would, he claimed, reveal a process of "unmanning" at work—a process "imperiously demanded" by the "Order of Things." In the event of a world catastrophe bringing about the destruction of humankind—and Schreber was convinced that such a catastrophe had occurred—the Order required the survival of a single human being. Schreber was the one chosen. (For a long time he thought that all the others were merely "fleeting-improvised-men.")[80] And once he was chosen, the rest followed: he would be transformed into a woman, impregnated by divine rays, and give birth to a new race of men. It also followed that whether or not he personally liked it, there was no reasonable course open to him but to reconcile himself to this transformation.

Schreber's shorthand for the work in progress was unmanning, and Freud echoed him in consistently referring to the delusion as one of emasculation—and a penis in retreat figured in the memoirs:

> Several times (particularly in bed) there were marked indications of an actual retraction of the male organ; . . . further the removal by miracles of single *hairs* from my *beard* and particularly my *moustache;* finally a *change in my whole stature* (diminution of body size)—probably due to a contraction of the vertebrae and possibly of my thigh bones.

The unmanning included swelling breasts:

> When the [divine] rays approach, my breast gives the impression of a pretty well-developed female bosom; this phenomenon can be *seen* by anybody who wants to observe me *with his own eyes.* . . . A brief glance however would not suffice, the observer would have to go to the trouble of spending 10 or 15 minutes near me. In that way anybody would notice the periodic swelling and diminution of my bosom. Naturally hairs remain under my arms and on my chest; these are by the way sparse in my case; my nipples also remain small as in the male sex. Notwithstanding, I venture to assert flatly that anybody who sees me standing in front of a mirror with the upper part of my body naked would get the undoubted *impression of a female trunk*—especially when the illusion is strengthened by some feminine adornments.

Schreber's femininity was more than a matter of a retreating penis and swelling breasts. His whole body, he claimed, was "filled with nerves of voluptuousness" from head to foot, such as was "the case only in the adult female."

> When I exert light pressure with my hand on any part of my body I can *feel* certain string or cord-like structures under the skin; these are particularly marked on my chest where the woman's bosom is, here they have the peculiarity that one can feel them ending in nodular thickenings. Through pressure on one such structure I can produce a feeling of female sensuous pleasure, particularly if I think of something feminine. I do this by the way, not for sensual lust, but I am

absolutely compelled to do so if I want to achieve sleep or protect myself against otherwise unbearable pain.[81]

Schreber never finished the transformation, which turned out to be far more complex than the shorthand metaphor of emasculation would suggest. "For several years . . . I lived in the certain expectation that one day my unmanning . . . would be completed . . . but whether . . . unmanning can really be completed I dare not predict. . . . It is therefore possible, indeed probable, that to the end of my days there will be strong indications of femaleness, but that I shall die a man." In the meantime Schreber had "wholeheartedly inscribed the cultivation of femininity" on his "banner."[82]

Schreber, of course, was insane. Freud, for one, was not prepared to dismiss his account on those grounds. A psychoanalyst, he wrote, should approach Schreber's delusional formations "with a suspicion that even thought-structures so extraordinary as these and so remote from our common modes of thinking" sprang from understandable "impulses of the human mind." The psychoanalyst would thus want to go thoroughly "into the details of the delusion and into the history of its development."[83]

I pause here to introduce a philosophical notion, or rather to allow Ian Hacking to introduce it for me—the notion of intentional action, things a person intends to do.

> Intentional actions are actions "under a description." The philosopher Elizabeth Anscombe gave this example. A man was moving a lever up and down. He was manually pumping water into the cistern of the house. He was pumping poisoned water into the country house where evil men met for planning sessions. He was poisoning the men who met in the house. Certainly there were not distinct physical sequences of activities, moving the lever, pumping the water, poisoning the men. Should we, however, say that there was a number of distinct actions, pumping water, on the one hand, and poisoning the men, on the other? Anscombe argued that there was just one action, under various descriptions. Each successive description of the action involves a larger range of circumstances, but only one intentional action is being described. . . .
>
> The thesis that action is action under a description has logical consequences for the future and for the past. When I decide to do something and do it, I am acting intentionally. There may be many kinds of actions with which I am unacquainted, and of which I have no description. It seems to follow from the thesis that I cannot intend to perform those actions. I cannot choose to do those things. I could of course choose to do something A, to which a subsequently constructed new description B applies; then by choosing to do A, and doing it, I did indeed do B, but I did not intend to do B. The limitation is not a physical

constraint or a moral prohibition. It is a trivial, logical fact that I cannot form those intentions.[84]

Note the soldering together (a favorite Freudian metaphor)[85] of an action and a description. Note as well the way in which description is elaborated: it is multiple and dependent on history. Here are components to be worked with; here also are hints for their extension. Gender identity, I suggest, can be likened to an intentional action—if both parts of the action/description schema are broadly construed.

Let's return to Schreber. Picture him standing "in front of the mirror with the upper part of his body naked"—except for "some feminine adornments" (jewelry?)—fondling his breasts and experiencing sensual pleasure.[86] I am reminded of (or associate to) Freud's discussion of masturbation and masturbation fantasies. The masturbatory act, he commented, is "compounded of two parts": one, "some active behaviour for obtaining self-gratification," the other, "the evocation of phantasy."[87] Here is an intentional action; here also is an extension of description to include fantasy—a promising extension indeed.

Recall Schreber again: he claimed that his body was "filled with nerves of voluptuousness,"[88] that it had acquired "the same susceptibility" as "the genitals . . . possessed." At this point the notion of erotogenic zones is relevant. An erotogenic zone, Freud made clear, is bound up with pleasurable sensations. It is also bound up with something somatic—as the mouth and the anus would indicate, with a vital bodily function—at least at the start. The crucial step, in fact, is the separation of a wish to repeat a pleasurable sensation from a somatic need. As an example, Freud pointed to a child's sucking on "part of his own skin" instead of on an "extraneous body" thereby turning the labial region into an erotogenic zone.[89] In Schreber's case the whole body had become erotogenic; it had also become increasingly female. Here what was being soldered together were bodily sensations and a delusion. Here were the components of intentional action—with action broadened to include bodily pleasure, and description to include delusion.

Schreber was psychotic. Fairbairn's patient was not. With her it was a matter of retrieving a personification that, one can readily infer, had been linked with bodily pleasures.

> The first feature of note in the analysis was the emergence of countless memories of childhood. . . . She [the patient] re-lived in memory endless days

of happy play. She re-entered the paradise of her childhood, which had become all the more elysian through the operation of unconscious phantasy during the intervening years. . . . This break-through of repressed emotional experiences was accompanied by the emergence of sexual sensations, which at first appeared to her entirely novel, but which eventually revived memories of sensations experienced on swings and see-saws in her early years.[90]

Fairbairn did not see the connection between erotogenic body and mischievous boy. He did not see that bodily pleasures had been soldered together with particular meanings and/or fantasies. And it was in his patient's history of pleasures, meanings, and their soldering together that gender identities had taken shape—the entire process amounting to an intentional action.

• • • • •

At this point it may be useful to review the argument I am advancing as a series of steps and to recall it in terms of particular concepts that figured, explicitly or by implication, earlier in the chapter.

It should be apparent that I am not a developmentalist; I am not concerned with ages and stages, with claims that specific psychic structures are formed at such and such a time in a person's life. (I have expressed my skepticism about Klein's early and precise dating of fantasy contents.) Nonetheless, I have implicitly committed myself to the position that the infant is separate and active: he/she is not, in the beginning, bound to mother in a symbiotic-like embrace; nor is he/she a blob to be molded by a parental object. So much constitutes a conceptual minimum.

I am an object-relations theorist—about that I have been explicit. I am thus committed to five propositions about objects. First, following Klein, I have taken the line that object relations begin at birth. (In the 1940s this was a controversial claim; it is no longer.) Second, again following Klein, I maintain that object relations are not simply to external objects; they are to internal ones as well. (Because the notion of internal objects obviously derived from the Freudian superego, this concept soon ceased to be a focus of contention.) Third, both Klein and Fairbairn emphasized the internalization of "bad" objects—and I share their emphasis. ("Internalization of objects," Fairbairn argued, "is essentially a measure of coercion and it is . . . the unsatisfying object that the infant seeks to coerce.")[91] Fourth, both Klein and Fairbairn talked about internal objects in the plural; both talked about splitting objects into bad and good. I agree. And finally, these internal objects form part of a world every bit as real as the world outside.

By virtue of my allegiance to object-relations theory, I am also committed to the notion of the ego as fissionable. Klein and Fairbairn both argued that when the ego splits the object, splitting takes place in the ego as well. Fairbairn further argued that the splits in the ego and the corresponding internal objects were entitled to structural status. That status allowed him to represent intrapsychic conflict as ongoing. And it was conflict that, as a psychoanalyst, concerned him.

The inner world, built up through a mix of real and fantasied relationships, is also a sexual and gendered world. I have construed both sexuality and gender identity as serving object ties; I have construed both as multiple. Fairbairn's patient, for example, the mischievous boy part of her, was attached to an object, and, given the history she reported, the most likely person was her grandfather. He took center stage in her "happy memories and phantasies of childhood. . . . In the background, however," Fairbairn noted, "there was always the menacing shadow of a mother-figure." As to the gratifying and defensive functions the mischievous boy performed, the answer lay in unknown details of the patient's personal history.

Early gender constructions (and sexual predilections), though they be considered fabrications, cannot be summarily unmade. They have enabled the subject to fit into his/her original environment(s), and their relative success has acted as reiteration and reinforcement. Environments, however, change. What worked earlier may no longer. What flourished in one environment—for example, Fairbairn's patient's mischievous boy-self—may wither in another. Natural selection, after all, is the story of imperfect fit.

Conclusion: The Narrative of Choice

In setting out to make a contribution to the debate about psycho-analysis and feminism, I announced my intention to exploit the notion of science as a selection process. I did not make a case for psychoanalysis as science. That vexed question would require a study in its own right, one that would at the same time address what ranks as a scientific endeavor. Nor did I make a case for the particular notion of science I planned to use. I simply adopted one, and, then, in accord with the model adopted, I wrote of the combination and recombination of ideas in conceptual lineages. Along the way I gave the protagonists of my study space enough to become presences in my text and invited my readers to participate in the selection process. At this point it may be useful for me to lay out not only the choice I have made—about that there is no surprise—but the reasons for so choosing as well. At this point it may also be useful for me to lay out my criteria for selection.

I have two criteria in mind, one Freudian, the other feminist—both are criteria my protagonists would have recognized as relevant.

• • • • •

What does "Freudian" as a criterion mean? It does not mean loyalty to Freud's precepts on women. One of the points of this study, after all, has been to show how in the hands of his descendants, his tenets could be and were modified. By "Freudian" I mean the fundamentals he postulated. Elsewhere I have traced the emergence of psychoanalysis as an autonomous discipline dedicated to the exploration of unconscious meaning. More specifically, I have charted that exploration along twin philosophical axes: the ontological problem of mind and body and the epistemological problem of subject and object.[1] I have argued that it was Freud's view of sexuality as psychosexuality, as a linkage between somatic sexual excitation and psychical sexual ideas, that made possible his conceptualization of an erotogenic body; it also encouraged him to construe objects, primarily oedipal objects, as soldered together with sexual fantasy. In this fashion, I have further argued, Freud pushed aside intractable problems and put in their place new formulations that became central preoccupations within psychoanalysis. By choosing "Freudian" as a criterion I aim to assess how my protagonists pursued the exploration he had begun.

Deutsch and Erikson took off from a similar point of departure, from what Erikson referred to as "the Freudian laws of psychosexual growth."[2] Starting where they did, they focused on the mind-body problem and bracketed the question of how the subject comes to know the object world. Oral, anal, and phallic dominated their thinking; sexual object-choice was ignored, as in the case of Erikson, or, as in the case of Deutsch, was fitted into a narrative framework of progression and retrogression that proceeded along a libidinal track.

Having decided to concentrate on one philosophical axis, how did they handle the hindrance it presented to psychological inquiry? To put matters simply, what did they say about the connection between soma and psyche? Of the two, Erikson's seems the more straightforward account—but seeming can be deceptive. The relation between physiology and psychology, he argued, was one of correspondence: both fetal and psychic development adhered to the same epigenetic principle. The epigenetic principle had (and still has) scientific credentials, and thus Erikson was not obliged to make a case for it. Not so correspondence. It harked back to the *Naturphilosophie* of late eighteenth- and early nineteenth-century Germany, with its "uncompromising . . . belief in the unity of nature and its laws."[3] It did not hark back to Freud. Freud had come to appreciate that he possessed no tools to sort out the relationship between the physiological and the psychological; Erikson showed no similar appreciation.

Of the two, Deutsch's joining of soma and psyche seems the more ambiguous. She used biology as a crutch: she leaned on an analogy between "actual phylogenetic forms of development . . . and pregenital phases of the libido" to justify her symbolic trading in body parts.[4] Take the crutch away, and the symbolic trading could continue all the same. One could reformulate that trading in terms of fantasies about bodily pleasures. This was the move Freud had made, and in so doing he had abandoned whatever dreams he had had of finding physiological grounding for his psychology. So long as she remained in Europe, Deutsch dreamed on.

On the Freudian criterion I would argue that Deutsch's early work ranks as superior—not because she was closer to Freud's view on women, but because she came closer to his concept of an erotogenic body, a concept that paved the way for exploring the unconscious meaning of bodily experiences.

I have coupled Deutsch and Erikson; I can similarly couple Horney and Stoller. Both took off from the Oedipus complex, Horney from the complex as Freud initially presented it, with the boy's sexual wishes directed toward mother and the girl's toward father, Stoller from Freud's revised account, with mother figuring as the original love object of the girl as well as of the boy. Starting where they did, they granted the subject-object problem priority. The problem of mind and body lost its prominence.

Still, it had a place. On this question Horney remained close to Freud. As long as she used the instinctual idiom of her early psychoanalytic training, it was the psychical meaning of physical sensations rather than the sensations themselves that concerned her. Like Freud she worked back to bodily experiences from the psychical elaboration of them. She, however, worked back to a female as well as a male body. At least initially, Stoller referred to the physiological and the erotogenic body (each of which, for him, came in female and male versions). When he first wrote of core gender identity, he invoked a "biological force" to account for it, by which he meant something genetic that operated throughout fetal existence. He never disavowed that force; he simply lost interest in it. The body as a source of pleasure and meaning, conspicuous in his accounts of his clinical work, was curiously absent from his theoretical discussions of gender.

Having given preference to the philosophical axis of subject and object, how did Stoller and Horney manage the epistemological issues it raised?

How did they handle the relation between a person's remembered past and his/her historical past? Stoller addressed the question specifically, albeit fleetingly. (In writing of Belle, he professed to feeling "shy" about reconstructing a patient's past, finding it "unsafe for research.")[5] Yet his study of gender crucially depended on such reconstruction. From patients' reports he reconstructed parental behaviors and attitudes and then pointed to them as the key factor in the development of core gender identity. If encouragement and discouragement by the parents and learning by the child figured as central, so too did imprinting. Stoller thought of it as a "non-mental" mechanism that acted "directly on the brain and other parts of the nervous system."[6] In his theoretical as opposed to his clinical writing, he dealt with the subject-object problem by minimizing the subjective and the fantastic—when he turned to imprinting, he dealt with it by simply eliminating subjective experience.

Horney did not grapple explicitly with the difficulties of recovering the historical past. She was, however, very clear that the past she considered relevant for understanding a patient's "mental sexual character" was not confined to parental behaviors and attitudes. The child's fantasies—for example, a girl's fantasy of being sexually appropriated by father and its disappointment—loomed large in her account of the masculinity complex in women. With psychical elaboration of childhood events and not the events themselves as her quarry, Horney continued on the track of subjective experience.

So too, of course, did Freud. His understanding of the Oedipus complex as a work of thought and fantasy amounted to redefining the object, a redefinition that contributed to the emergence of psychoanalysis as an autonomous discipline. Horney readily adopted this redefinition. On the Freudian criterion, then, her work passes muster better than Stoller's.

Does a choice between Deutsch and Horney boil down to a choice between a girl ignorant of her vagina and one possessing knowledge of that organ? Certainly this ranks as a salient difference between them. Here the Freudian criterion will not help. I now turn to my second criterion—the feminist. Here also I bring Gilligan and Chodorow into the discussion.

• • • • •

What does "feminist" as a criterion mean? It is not a matter of ideology or political program. By "feminist" I mean capable of capturing the experiences of women—potentially of all women.

In turning to this criterion I see two couples—Deutsch and Gilligan, Horney and Chodorow. Within each pair there is a similarity of tone: the dogmatic tone of the late Deutsch, the post-emigration Deutsch, finds an echo in Gilligan; the combative tone of the early Horney, the pre-emigration Horney, finds an echo in Chodorow. Within each pair there is an implicit agreement on essentialism as well.

Both Deutsch and Gilligan can be read as subscribing to an essentialist conception of the feminine—and a very flattering one to boot. Deutsch's belief that women started out as little men, that one was not born a woman but rather became one, did not prevent her from charting a normative course for women and from suspecting pathology in those who did not follow it. With Gilligan the presumption of a normative course obscured differences among women; it created a divide between women and men. Variety among women had no place in her account—thus hers is less inclusive than Deutsch's.

In contrast, Chodorow and Horney distanced themselves from essentialism. Chodorow did so explicitly. She thought she could avoid what she regarded as pernicious by eschewing biological determinism. She thought she was protected by her claim that difference was constructed, created by relations with parents. She was mistaken. By confidently assuming that girls internalized one set of relations and boys another—and that thanks to this process they came out behaving differently—Chodorow seemed to be suggesting that she had captured, if not the eternal feminine, at least the feminine under the prevailing sexual division of labor. Horney, with her emphasis on rivalry among women, implicitly acknowledged variety and rejected essentialism. She would have regarded with incredulity Gilligan's idealization of women—and her homogenization of them as well. On the same grounds she might have been suspicious of Chodorow. On the feminist criterion, then, Horney's theory shows to advantage.

• • • • •

So far I have said nothing about Klein. With regard to the Freudian criterion, she followed Freud's double lead. The erotogenic body, a body of pleasures, pains, and above all fantasy was certainly a presence in her texts. Her conceptualization of fantasy as "the mental corollary, the psychic representative of instinct," and, along with it, her belief that every impulse, every instinctual urge or response was "experienced as unconscious phantasy," fit

Freud's strategy of foregrounding the question of how the mind perceives the body.[7] Oedipal objects also figured centrally in her work, with fantasy again playing a crucial role. In her view, unconscious fantasy not only transcribed instinctual drives but recorded external reality as well, albeit in potentially distorted form. Once again, Klein adopted Freud's strategy of foregrounding subjective experience. Here she went beyond the question of how the mind perceived body or object; she explored how experiences with already distorted objects altered the ego or self. In this fashion she avoided what Jones regarded as a constant threat to psychoanalysts—the danger of underestimating "Freud's doctrine of psychical reality."[8]

What about the feminist criterion? Some preliminaries are in order. The majority of my study's protagonists felt obliged to decide which came first, sexuality or gender. Erikson and Gilligan did not address the question; they did not address sexuality. Stoller and Chodorow tied sexual object-choice to gender, with heterosexuality (frequently conflictual) figuring as the normal accompaniment to a core gender identity that at least in girls was conflict-free. For both of them erotic desire appeared as something added on, not as something to be reckoned with from the very beginning. In contrast, Deutsch and Horney adhered more closely to Freud's notion of infantile sexuality. For Deutsch sexuality, though not of the genital variety, was part of the equipment with which a child entered the world. In her account a woman's heterosexual object-choice went along with her identification with mother, and a homosexual object-choice followed from a failed attempt at heterosexuality—that is, from retrogression from a positive Oedipus complex. Heterosexuality thus derived from gender; homosexuality, however, did not. Horney took the opposite tack: according to her, heterosexuality preceded gender; homosexuality, however, succeeded it. She started by assuming heterosexuality, with a girl's experience of her father shaping her "mental sexual character"; should that experience produce a masculinity complex, homosexuality came as a likely sequel. At first glance Klein seemed close to Horney's presumption of heterosexual preference. On further inspection she turns out to have recast the problem in such a way as to avoid the chicken-and-egg quality that characterized much of the discussion.

Klein did so by taking the superego as her point of departure and transforming it. Stressing its punitive aspect, she reconceptualized it in terms of internalized bad objects. Sexuality, in her account, was there from the beginning, and it was quickly pressed into service to aid the ego in its internal struggles. Oedipal dramas, in her account, became less a matter of a child's incestuous loves than of searches for new objects to combat fears of "terrifying introjected objects."[9] It would have been a logical next step for Klein to have suggested that "mental sexual characters" or gender identity played a role in that search as well, and an independent one. Sexual object-choice and gender identity, she might have argued, were not derived one from the other; instead they both figured in a story of internal object relations. She might have argued thus, but she did not. This is an argument that I have been advancing.

At the same time I have adopted Freud's strategy of pursuing the psychical elaboration of bodily experiences. Here I have introduced the notion of gender identity as intentional action. I have suggested that the elements of an intentional action—the soldering together of action and description, with action extended to include bodily sensation and description to include fantasy—resonate with how gender identity becomes embodied through a person's history of physical pleasures, meanings, and their soldering together. In any individual case, I have argued, gender identity and sexuality as well depend upon the peculiarities of a person's past and the particularities of his/her object ties.

From the outset Klein stressed the multiplicity and variety of sexuality. In so doing she remained faithful to Freud's conception of sexuality as made up of components and of the complete Oedipus complex as made up of both positive and negative aspects. I have continued in similar vein and have pointed to the possibility of multiple gender identities—a possibility that follows from the notion of the ego as fissionable. The mere possibility, I would claim, encourages one to talk about differences among women. It represents a move clearly away from essentialism: it is diametrically opposite. None of my protagonists has gone that far.

• • • • •

Feminism, it seems, has always been divided. On the one hand, many women are attracted to it by its promise of solidarity, by its determination to extol an identity that has been denigrated, by its commitment to reclaim a past that has been forgotten. On the other hand, there are many women who rebel against having to be "women" at all. They argue that whenever women uncritically accept the monolith "woman," they run a risk of donning once again the straitjacket of unchanging feminine nature. A preference for one or the other of these two positions—and there appears to be no middle ground—may very well arise apart from conscious choice. Making conscious what has been unconscious is thus crucial for evaluating past allegiances and future affiliations as well. It is, of course, similarly crucial for psychoanalysis.

Abbreviations

IJP   *The International Journal of Psycho-Analysis*
JAPA   *Journal of the American Psychoanalytic Association*
SE   Sigmund Freud, *The Standard Edition of the Complete Psychological Works of Sigmund Freud,* translated under the general editorship of James Strachey (London: Hogarth Press, 1953–1974).

Notes

INTRODUCTION

1. Freud, *The Question of Lay Analysis: Conversations with an Impartial Person* (1926), in *SE* 20: 212.

2. On science as a selection process, see Karl R. Popper, *Conjectures and Refutations: The Growth of Scientific Knowledge,* 2d ed. (London: Routledge and Kegan Paul, 1965); Stephen Toulmin, *Human Understanding,* vol. 1, *General Introduction and Part I* (Princeton, N.J.: Princeton University Press, 1972); Donald T. Campbell, "Evolutionary Epistemology," in Paul Arthur Schilpp, ed., *The Philosophy of Karl Popper* (LaSalle, Ill.: Open Court, 1974), pp. 413–463; Robert J. Richards, *Darwin and the Emergence of Evolutionary Theories of Mind and Behavior* (Chicago: University of Chicago Press, 1987), pp. 559–593; David L. Hull, *Science as a Process: An Evolutionary Account of the Social and Conceptual Development of Science* (Chicago: University of Chicago Press, 1988).

3. Not so Carl Gustav Jung and Jacques Lacan. Both had a patrimony of philosophical attitudes and problems that was far more crucial for their projects than their ambivalent allegiances to Freud.

CHAPTER 1   RETROGRESSION: HELENE DEUTSCH

1. See Peter Weingart, "Biology as Social Theory: The Bifurcation of Social Biology and Sociology in Germany, circa 1900," in Dorothy Ross, ed., *Modern*

Impulses in the Human Sciences 1870–1930 (Baltimore: Johns Hopkins University Press, 1994), pp. 255–271. Freud encountered the concept of retrogression in the work of his Darwinian professor, Carl Claus: see Lucille B. Ritvo, *Darwin's Influence on Freud: A Tale of Two Sciences* (New Haven: Yale University Press, 1990), pp. 156–158.

2. See Richard F. Sterba, *Reminiscences of a Viennese Psychoanalyst* (Detroit: Wayne State University Press, 1982), p. 29. For biographical information I have drawn on Helene Deutsch, *Confrontations with Myself: An Epilogue* (New York: Norton, 1973), and Paul Roazen, *Helene Deutsch: A Psychoanalyst's Life* (Garden City, N.Y.: Doubleday, 1985; reprint, New Brunswick, N.J.: Transaction, 1992). See also Marie H. Briehl, "Helene Deutsch," in Franz Alexander, Samuel Eisenstein, and Martin Grotjahn, eds., *Psychoanalytic Pioneers* (New York: Basic Books, 1966), pp. 282–298. For useful commentary, see Brenda S. Webster, "Helene Deutsch: A New Look," *Signs* 10 (1985): 553–571; Nellie L. Thompson, "Helene Deutsch: A Life in Theory," *The Psychoanalytic Quarterly* 56 (1987): 317–353; Janet Sayers, *Mothers of Psychoanalysis: Helene Deutsch, Karen Horney, Anna Freud, Melanie Klein* (New York: Norton, 1991), pp. 25–81.

3. Deutsch, *Confrontations with Myself*, p. 133.

4. Roazen, *Helene Deutsch*, p. 156.

5. Deutsch, *Confrontations with Myself*, p. 134.

6. "In fact," Deutsch wrote, "the whole transference situation could have come out of a textbook on psychoanalysis. (By a remarkable coincidence, my father left Vienna to go home to Poland at the end of the war on the very same day in August 1918 that I began analysis with Freud.)" Ibid., p. 132.

7. Ibid., p. 131.

8. Freud, *New Introductory Lectures on Psycho-Analysis* (1933), in *SE* 22: 116–117.

9. Freud, *Civilization and Its Discontents* (1930), in *SE* 21: 106*n*.

10. Helene Deutsch, *Psychoanalysis of the Sexual Functions of Women* (1925), ed. Paul Roazen, trans. Eric Mosbacher (London: Karnac, 1991), p. 3.

11. Ibid., p. 2.

12. In her otherwise favorable review of Deutsch's book, Karen Horney expressed the hope that the clinical material on which it was based would soon be published: see Karen Horney, review of *Zur Psychologie der weiblichen Sexualfunktionen*, by Helene Deutsch, *IJP* 7 (1926): 92–100.

13. Freud, *Three Essays on the Theory of Sexuality* (1905), in *SE* 7: 197–198.

14. Freud, "The Infantile Genital Organization (An Interpolation into the Theory of Sexuality)" (1923), in *SE* 19: 142.

15. Karl Abraham, "A Short History of the Development of the Libido, Viewed in the Light of Mental Disorders" (1924), in *Selected Papers of Karl Abraham*, trans. Douglas Bryan and Alix Strachey (London: Hogarth Press, 1927; reprint, London: H. Karnac, Maresfield Reprints, 1979), pp. 424, 482.

16. Ibid., pp. 498, 500. Freud picked up Abraham's comments about the embryonic blastopore: see Freud, *Three Essays*, p. 199*n*. For the most extravagant biogenetic fantasy in the psychoanalytic literature, see Sándor Ferenczi, *Thalassa: A Theory of Genitality* (1924), trans. Henry Alden Bunker (London: Karnac, Maresfield Library, 1989).

17. Deutsch, *Psychoanalysis of the Sexual Functions of Women*, p. 15.

18. Ibid., p. 11.

19. See Freud, *Group Psychology and the Analysis of the Ego* (1921), in *SE* 18: 105–106, and Freud, *The Ego and the Id* (1923), in *SE* 19: 31. Freud objected to Deutsch's account of the little girl's identification with her father: see Freud, "Female Sexuality" (1931), in *SE* 21: 242.

20. Freud, *New Introductory Lectures*, p. 125; see also Freud, *Three Essays*, p. 195.

21. Freud, "Some Psychical Consequences of the Anatomical Distinction between the Sexes" (1925), in *SE* 19: 252.

22. Freud, *New Introductory Lectures*, p. 125.

23. Deutsch, *Psychoanalysis of the Sexual Functions of Women*, pp. 25, 27.

24. Ibid., pp. 20, 24.

25. Ibid., p. 27.

26. For Deutsch's use of this word, see ibid., p. 106; see also Helene Deutsch, "Homosexuality in Women" (1932), in Helene Deutsch, *Neuroses and Character Types: Clinical Psychoanalytic Studies* (New York: International Universities Press, 1965), pp. 184, 185, 187.

27. Deutsch, *Psychoanalysis of the Sexual Functions of Women*, p. 13.

28. Ibid., pp. 12, 14.

29. See Freud, *The Ego and the Id*, p. 29. Deutsch's notion of the superego echoes Freud's discussion of the ego-ideal in his *Group Psychology and the Analysis of the Ego*, pp. 111–116.

30. Deutsch, "Homosexuality in Women," p. 165. For an illuminating discussion of this paper, see Teresa de Lauretis, *The Practice of Love: Lesbian Sexuality and Perverse Desire* (Bloomington: Indiana University Press, 1994), pp. 58–65.

31. Freud subsequently acknowledged Deutsch's contribution: see Freud, *New Introductory Lectures*, p. 131.

32. Freud, "Female Sexuality," pp. 226, 227.

33. See Deutsch, "Homosexuality in Women," p. 185.

34. Ibid., pp. 167, 168. Deutsch had reported on this patient in an earlier paper: see Helene Deutsch, "On the Psychology of Mistrust" (1921), in Helene Deutsch, *The Therapeutic Process, the Self, and Female Psychology: Collected Psychoanalytic Papers*, ed. Paul Roazen, trans. Eric Mosbacher (New Brunswick, N.J.: Transaction, 1992), pp. 137–139. She subsequently reused this material in *The Psychology of Women: A Psychoanalytic Interpretation*, vol. 1 (New York: Grune and Stratton, 1944), pp. 341–346.

35. Deutsch, "Homosexuality in Women," p. 166.

36. Ibid., pp. 166, 171.

37. Ibid., pp. 168, 169.

38. Ibid., p. 169.

39. Ibid., pp. 169–170.

40. Ibid., p. 171.

41. Ibid., pp. 171, 181.

42. Freud, "Female Sexuality," pp. 229–230.

43. Deutsch, "Homosexuality in Women," p. 170.

44. Ibid., pp. 171, 172–173, 188.

45. Ibid., pp. 181, 184, 187.

46. Freud, "Female Sexuality," p. 234.

47. Helene Deutsch, "Hysterical Conversion Symptoms: Fits, Trance States" (1930), in Deutsch, *Neuroses and Character Types,* pp. 70–71, 62, 69.

48. Freud, "Hysterical Phantasies and Their Relation to Bisexuality" (1908), in *SE* 9: 163–164.

49. Deutsch, "Hysterical Conversion Symptoms," pp. 68, 70.

50. Ibid., pp. 67, 70.

51. Ibid., p. 70.

52. Freud, *Three Essays,* p. 221.

53. Deutsch, *Psychoanalysis of the Sexual Functions of Women,* p. 61.

54. Freud, *Three Essays,* pp. 220-221.

55. Deutsch, *Psychoanalysis of the Sexual Functions of Women,* p. 67.

56. Ibid., p. 65.

57. Ibid., pp. 65, 66, 87.

58. Ibid., pp. 83,87, 88. See also Freud, "On Transformations of Instinct as Exemplified in Anal Erotism" (1917), in *SE* 17: 127–133.

59. Deutsch, *Psychoanalysis of the Sexual Functions of Woman,* pp. 88, 92, 84.

60. Ibid., pp. 65, 81, 92–93.

61. Ibid., pp. 100–101.

62. Ibid., pp. 106, 109, 117.

63. Helene Deutsch, "The Psychology of Women in Relation to the Functions of Reproduction" (1925), in Deutsch, *The Therapeutic Process, the Self, and Female Psychology,* p. 8.

64. Deutsch, *Psychoanalysis of the Sexual Functions of Women,* p. 84.

65. Stanley Cobb, foreword to Deutsch, *Psychology of Women,* 1: viii.

66. Cobb, foreword to Deutsch, *Psychology of Women,* 1: viii. On the matter of Deutsch's audience, see Marjorie Brierley, review of *The Psychology of Women:* Vol. 1, *Girlhood;* Vol. 2, *Motherhood,* by Helene Deutsch, *IJP* 29 (1948): 251–254.

67. Cobb, foreword to Deutsch, *Psychology of Women,* 1: vii.

68. Deutsch, *Psychology of Women,* 1: xii.

69. Ibid., p. xii.

70. Ibid., p. x.

71. Ibid., pp. 212, 217.

72. Ibid., pp. 289, 290, 291.

73. Ibid., p. 217.

74. Ibid., p. x.

75. Helene Deutsch, "The Significance of Masochism in the Mental Life of Women" (1930), in Deutsch, *The Therapeutic Process, the Self, and Female Psychology,* p. 58.

76. Deutsch, *Psychology of Women,* 1: 252–253, 277, 278.

77. Ibid., pp. 187, 188, 278.

78. Helene Deutsch, *The Psychology of Women: A Psychoanalytic Interpretation,* vol. 2, *Motherhood* (New York: Grune and Stratton, 1945), pp. 24–25.

79. Deutsch, *Psychology of Women,* 1: 214.

80. Ibid., p. 279.

CHAPTER 2   EPIGENESIS: ERIK H. ERIKSON AND CAROL GILLIGAN

1. Charles R. Stockard, *The Physical Basis of Personality* (New York: Norton, 1931), pp. 48–49, 50–51. See also Stephen Jay Gould, *Ontogeny and Phylogeny* (Cambridge, Mass.: Harvard University Press, 1977), pp. 17–28, and Stephen Jay Gould, *Ever Since Darwin: Reflections on Natural History* (New York: Norton, 1977), pp. 201–206.

2. Erik H. Erikson, *Childhood and Society,* 2d, revised and enlarged ed. (New York: Norton, 1963), p. 65.

3. Erik H. Erikson, "Problems of Infancy and Early Childhood" (1940), in Stephen Schlein, ed., *A Way of Looking at Things: Selected Papers from* 1930–1980 *Erik H. Erikson* (New York: Norton, 1987), pp. 548–549.

4. See Erik H. Erikson, "Autobiographic Notes on the Identity Crisis," *Daedalus* 99 (1970): 730–759, and Erik H. Erikson, *Life History and the Historical Moment* (New York: Norton, 1975), pp. 17–47. On this point, see also Paul Roazen, *Erik H. Erikson: The Power and Limits of a Vision* (New York: Free Press, 1976), pp. 86–106. For a useful biography, see Robert Coles, *Erik H. Erikson: The Growth of His Work* (Boston: Little, Brown, 1970). For useful commentary, see H. Stuart Hughes, *The Sea Change: The Migration of Social Thought,* 1930–1965 (New York: Harper and Row, 1975), pp. 217–232.

5. See Howard I. Kushner, "Taking Erikson's Identity Seriously: Psychoanalyzing the Psychohistorian," *The Psychohistory Review* 22 (1993): 21.

6. See Paul Roazen, "Erik Erikson as a Teacher," *The Psychohistory Review* 22 (1993): 112–113.

7. Erikson, "Autobiographic Notes," pp. 742, 743.

8. Erikson to Robert Coles (n.d.), quoted in Coles, *Erik H. Erikson,* p. 181.

9. Erikson, "Autobiographic Notes," p. 743.

10. Fritz K. Ringer, *The Decline of the German Mandarins: The German Academic Community,* 1890–1933 (Cambridge, Mass.: Harvard University Press, 1969), pp. 87, 108.

11. Erikson, "Autobiographic Notes," p. 744.

12. Coles, *Erik H. Erikson,* p. 20.

13. Erikson, *Life History,* p. 24.

14. Erikson, "Autobiographic Notes," pp. 744–745.

15. Erikson, *Life History,* p. 38.

16. Erikson, *Childhood and Society,* p. 11.

17. H. S. Hughes, *The Sea Change,* p. 227.

18. Roazen, "Erik H. Erikson as a Teacher," p. 116. According to Erikson's current biographer, Gilligan served as Erikson's teaching assistant in 1968–1969: Lawrence J. Friedman to Judith M. Hughes, June 2, 1995.

19. See Carol Gilligan, "In a Different Voice: Women's Conceptions of Self and Morality," *Harvard Educational Review* 47 (1977): 481, 509, 514, 515.

20. Ibid., p. 509.

21. Freud, *The Interpretation of Dreams* (1900), in *SE* 4: 107, 118–120.

22. See Roazen, *Erik H. Erikson,* p. 7.

23. Erik Homburger Erikson, "The Dream Specimen of Psychoanalysis," *JAPA* 2 (1954): 27,

31, 32, 37. For recent commentary on this paper, see Stanley J. Coen, "The Passions and Perils of Interpretation: An Appreciation of Erik Erikson's Dream Specimen Paper," *IJP* 77 (1996): 537–548.

24. Erikson, "The Dream Specimen of Psychoanalysis," p. 33. I have quoted, above, Strachey's translation in the *Standard Edition* of the Irma Dream. Erikson used the only then available and defective Brill translation—a curious slip on the part of someone who was critical of it and elsewhere did his own translating. Where Strachey translated the German word *spüren* as notice, Brill translated it as feel.

25. Ibid., pp. 33, 37, 48.

26. Ibid., p. 49.

27. Erikson, *Childhood and Society,* p. 70.

28. Erik Homburger, "Configurations in Play—Clinical Notes" (1937), in Schlein, ed., *A Way of Looking at Things,* p. 106.

29. Ibid., p. 106.

30. Erikson, *Childhood and Society,* p. 82.

31. Ibid., pp. 66, 78, 88.

32. Ibid., pp. 91–92.

33. Ibid., p. 224.

34. Erik H. Erikson, "Studies in the Interpretation of Play: Clinical Observation of Play Disruption in Young Children" (1940), in Schlein, ed., *A Way of Looking at Things,* p. 184.

35. Ibid., pp. 172–173.

36. Ibid., pp. 173–174.

37. Ibid., p. 158.

38. Erikson, *Childhood and Society,* p. 228.

39. Erikson, "Studies in the Interpretation of Play," p. 175.

40. Ibid., p. 175.

41. Ibid., p. 175.

42. Compare Homburger, "Configurations in Play," p. 113.

43. Erikson, "Studies in the Interpretation of Play," p. 154.

44. Erikson, *Childhood and Society,* pp. 229–230.

45. Erikson, "Studies in the Interpretation of Play," p. 177.

46. Erikson, *Childhood and Society,* pp. 230–231.

47. Erikson, "Studies in the Interpretation of Play," pp. 177–178.

48. Ibid., p. 178.

49. Ibid., p. 154.

50. Ibid., p. 179.

51. Erikson, *Childhood and Society,* p. 232.

52. Ibid., p. 97.

53. Coles, *Erik H. Erikson,* p. 43.

54. Erik. H. Erikson, "Sex Differences in the Play Configurations of American Preadolescents" (1955), in Schlein, ed., *A Way of Looking at Things,* pp. 281–282.

55. Ibid., p. 282.

56. Erikson, *Childhood and Society,* pp. 99–100.

57. Ibid., p. 101.

58. Ibid., p. 102.

59. Erikson, "Sex Differences in . . . Preadolescents," p. 293.

60. Ibid., pp. 293–294.

61. Ibid., pp. 294, 295.

62. Ibid., p. 294.

63. Ibid., p. 295.

64. Erikson, *Childhood and Society,* p. 108.

65. Stephen R. Graubard, "Preface to 'The Woman in America,'" *Daedalus* 93 (1964): 579.

66. Erik H. Erikson, "Inner and Outer Space: Reflections on Womanhood," *Daedalus* 93 (1964): 584–585, 599.

67. Ibid., p. 587.

68. Ibid. pp. 593–594.

69. Ibid., p. 605.

70. Erik H. Erikson, "Once More the Inner Space: Letter to a Former Student," in Jean Strouse, ed. *Women and Analysis: Dialogues on Psychoanalytic Views of Femininity* (New York: Grossman, 1974), p. 320. For another version of this paper, see Erik H. Erikson, *Life History and the Historical Moment* (New York: Norton, 1975), pp. 225–247. The two books critical of him that Erikson cited are: Kate Millett, *Sexual Politics* (New York: Doubleday, 1970), and Elizabeth Janeway, *Man's World, Woman's Place: A Study in Social Mythology* (New York: Morrow, 1971).

71. Erikson, "Once More the Inner Space," p. 327.

72. Erikson, "Inner and Outer Space," p. 599.

73. Erikson, "Once More the Inner Space," pp. 339, 340.

74. Freud, *Three Essays on the Theory of Sexuality* (1905), in *SE* 7: 151.

75. Carol Gilligan, "The Conquistador and the Dark Continent: Reflections on the Psychology of Love," *Daedalus* 113 (1984): 87.

76. Josef Breuer and Sigmund Freud, *Studies on Hysteria* (1893–1895), in *SE* 2: 28–29.

77. Ibid., p. 273.

78. Freud, "Fragment of an Analysis of a Case of Hysteria" (1905), in *SE* 7: 19.

79. Gilligan, "The Conquistador and the Dark Continent," p. 82.

80. Freud to Fliess, January 25, 1901, *The Complete Letters of Sigmund Freud to Wilhelm Fliess 1887–1904,* trans. and ed. Jeffrey Moussaieff Masson (Cambridge, Mass.: Harvard University Press, 1985), p. 433.

81. Gilligan, "The Conquistador and the Dark Continent," p. 84.

82. Freud, "Fragment of an Analysis," p. 120n.

83. Ibid., p. 120n.

84. Gilligan, "The Conquistador and the Dark Continent," p. 84.

85. Ibid., pp. 84, 90.

86. Carol Gilligan, *In a Different Voice: Psychological Theory and Women's Development* (Cambridge, Mass.: Harvard University Press, 1982) p. 25. For useful commentary on Gilligan's book, see Judy Auerbach, Linda Blum, Vicki Smith, and Christine Williams, "Commentary: On Gilligan's *In a Different Voice,*" *Feminist Studies* 11 (1985): 149–161, and Linda K. Kerber, Catherine G. Greeno and Eleanor E. Maccoby, Zella Luria, Carol

B. Stack, and Carol Gilligan, "On *In a Different Voice:* An Interdisciplinary Forum," *Signs* 11 (1986): 304–333.

87. Gilligan, *In a Different Voice,* p. 26.

88. Ibid., pp. 26–27, 32, 62.

89. Ibid., p. 28.

90. Ibid., pp. 28–29.

91. Ibid., pp. 28–29.

92. Ibid., pp. 31, 32.

93. Ibid., pp. 39, 33.

94. Ibid. p. 2.

95. Ibid., pp. 6, 70.

96. Ibid., pp. 71–72.

97. See Carol Gilligan and Mary Field Belenky, "A Naturalistic Study of Abortion Decisions," in Robert L. Selman and Regina Yando, eds., *Clinical-Developmental Psychology,* New Directions for Child Development, no. 7 (San Francisco: Jossey-Bass, 1980), pp. 69–90.

98. Gilligan, *In a Different Voice,* pp. 72, 73.

99. Ibid., pp. 110, 109.

100. Ibid., pp. 111, 112.

101. Ibid., pp. 78–79.

102. Ibid., pp. 79, 81, 82.

103. Ibid., pp. 83, 84, 85.

104. Ibid., pp. 116, 91.

105. Ibid., pp. 91–92, 94.

106. Ibid., p. 94.

107. Gilligan, "In a Different Voice: Women's Conception of Self and Morality," p. 507.

108. Gilligan, *In a Different Voice,* p. 12. Erikson, in contrast to Gilligan, frequently cited Deutsch: see, for example, Erikson, "Inner and Outer Space," p. 594.

109. Gilligan, *In a Different Voice,* p. 173.

CHAPTER 3   SEXUAL SELECTION: KAREN HORNEY

1. Ernst Mayr, *The Growth of Biological Thought: Diversity, Evolution, and Inheritance* (Cambridge, Mass.: Harvard University Press, 1982), p. 597.

2. For the centrality of female competition in sexual selection, see Sarah Blaffer Hrdy, *The Woman That Never Evolved* (Cambridge, Mass.: Harvard University Press, 1981).

3. Karen Horney, "The problem of the Monogamous Ideal" (1928), in Karen Horney, *Feminine Psychology* (New York: Norton, 1967), p. 95.

4. Karen Horney, *The Adolescent Diaries of Karen Horney* (New York: Basic Books, 1980), January 13, 1907, p. 184. For biographical information I have drawn on Jack L. Rubins, *Karen Horney: Gentle Rebel of Psychoanalysis* (New York: Dial Press, 1978), and Susan Quinn, *A Mind of Her Own: The Life of Karen Horney* (New York: Summit Books, 1987). Rubins and Quinn differ on the age difference between Horney's parents: Rubins says 18 years (p. 9); Quinn says 16 (p. 20). For useful commentary, in addition to

the two biographies, see Dee Garrison, "Karen Horney and Feminism," *Signs* 6 (1981): 672–691; Nellie Louise Buckley, "Women Psychoanalysts and the Theory of Feminine Development: A Study of Karen Horney, Helene Deutsch, and Marie Bonaparte" (Ph.D. Diss., University of California, Los Angeles, 1982), pp. 4–46; Marcia Westkott, *The Feminist Legacy of Karen Horney* (New Haven: Yale University Press, 1986); Janet Sayers, *Mothers of Psychoanalysis: Helene Deutsch, Karen Horney, Anna Freud, Melanie Klein* (New York: Norton, 1991), pp. 85–141; Marianne Horney Eckardt, "Feminine Psychology Revisited: A Historical Perspective," *The American Journal of Pychoanalysis* 51 (1991): 235–243; Alexandra Symonds, "Gender Issues and Karen Horney," *The American Journal of Psychoanalysis* 51 (1991): 301–312; Bernard J. Paris, *Karen Horney: A 'Psychoanalyst's Search for Self-Understanding* (New Haven: Yale University Press, 1994).

5. Karen Horney, *Self-Analysis* (New York: Norton, 1942), p. 51.

6. Quinn, *A Mind of Her Own*, p. 138.

7. Abraham to Freud, April 28, 1910, *A Psycho-Analytic Dialogue: The Letters of Sigmund Freud and Karl Abraham 1907–1926*, ed. Hilda C. Abraham and Ernst L. Freud, trans. Bernard Marsh and Hilda C. Abraham (New York: Basic Books, 1965), pp. 88–89.

8. Horney, *The Adolescent Diaries*, April 18, 1910, p. 238, and July 15, 1910, p. 247. See also Horney to Abraham, July 9, 1911, in ibid., pp. 270–271.

9. On the question of how long Horney's analysis with Abraham lasted, see Paris, *Karen Horney*, p. 57n2.

10. Abraham to Freud, February 25, 1912, *A Psycho-Analytic Dialogue*, p. 114.

11. Freud, "The Dissolution of the Oedipus Complex" (1924), in *SE* 19: 178.

12. The actual institutional rupture took place in 1941, when Horney resigned from the New York Psychoanalytic Society and founded her own, the Association for the Advancement of Psychoanalysis.

13. Karen Horney, "The Flight from Womanhood: The Masculinity Complex in Women as Viewed by Men and by Women" (1926), in *Feminine Psychology*, p. 56. Horney repeated herself and mentioned, for good measure, the Jewish morning prayer in which the man gives thanks that he has been born a man, whereas the woman given thanks that she has been born a human being: see Karen Horney, "Der Männlichkeitskomplex der Frau," *Archiv für Frauenkunde* 13 (1927): 152–153.

14. Horney to Groddeck (n.d.), quoted in Rubins, *Karen Horney*, p. 112.

15. Freud, *New Introductory Lectures on Psycho-Analysis* (1933), in *SE* 22: 116–117.

16. Horney, "The Flight from Womanhood," pp. 57–58.

17. See Karen Horney, "On the Genesis of the Castration Complex in Women" (1923), in *Feminine Psychology*, p. 52; Karen Horney, "The Problem of the Monogamous Ideal," in ibid., p. 95; Karen Horney, "The Dread of Woman: Observations on a Specific Difference in the Dread Felt by Men and by Women Respectively for the Opposite Sex" (1932), in ibid., p. 135.

18. Freud, "The Taboo of Virginity (Contributions to the Psychology of Love III)" (1918), in *SE* 11: 193, 194.

19. Ibid., p. 198.

20. Ibid., pp. 199, 201.

21. Ibid., p. 201.

22. Ibid., pp. 204, 205.

23. Ibid., p. 207.

24. Horney, "The Dread of Woman," pp. 135–136.

25. Ibid., p. 136.

26. Ibid., p. 137.

27. Ibid., pp. 137–138.

28. Freud, "The Infantile Genital Organization (An Interpolation into the Theory of Sexuality)" (1923), in *SE* 19: 142.

29. Freud, *New Introductory Lectures,* p. 118.

30. Horney, "The Dread of Woman," p. 144.

31. Freud, "Analysis of a Phobia in a Five-Year-Old Boy" (1909), in *SE* 10: 134–135.

32. Horney, "The Dread of Woman," p. 140. Compare Josine Müller, "A Contribution to the Problem of the Libidinal Development of the Genital Phase in Girls," *IJP* 13 (1932): 362–368, and Karen Horney, "The Denial of the Vagina: A Contribution to the Problem of the Genital Anxieties Specific to Women" (1933), in *Feminine Psychology,* pp. 147–161.

33. Horney, "The Dread of Woman," p. 142.

34. Freud, "Analysis of a Phobia," p. 134; see also Freud, "The Infantile Genital Organization," p. 143.

35. Horney, "The Dread of Woman," p. 142.

36. Ibid., pp. 142, 143, 144.

37. Freud, "The Infantile Genital Organization," p. 142.

38. Horney, "The Dread of Woman," p. 144.

39. Freud, "Analysis of a Phobia," p. 95.

40. Horney, "The Flight from Womanhood," pp. 60–61.

41. Karen Horney, "The Distrust Between the Sexes" (1931), in *Feminine Psychology,* p. 115.

42. Ibid. See also Karen Horney, "Inhibited Femininity: Psychoanalytical Contributions to the Problem of Frigidity" (1926–1927), in *Feminine Psychology,* p. 77.

43. Horney, "The Distrust Between the Sexes," p. 116.

44. Horney, "Genesis of the Castration Complex in Women," p. 49.

45. See Zenia Odes Fliegel, "Feminine Psychosexual Development in Freudian Theory: A Historical Reconstruction," *The Psychoanalytic Quarterly* 42 (1973): 385–408.

46. Freud, "The Psychogenesis of a Case of Homosexuality in a Woman" (1920), in *SE* 18: 164.

47. Ibid., p. 147.

48. Ibid., p. 155.

49. Ibid., pp. 150–151.

50. Ibid., pp. 155, 156, 158.

51. Ibid., p. 157.

52. Ibid., p. 157.

53. Ibid., pp. 158, 156.

54. Ibid., pp. 160–161.

55. Ibid., p. 169.

56. Ibid., p. 170. About his use of the terms "masculine" and "feminine," Freud commented, "psycho-analysis cannot elucidate the intrinsic nature of what in conventional or in

biological phraseology is termed 'masculine' and 'feminine': it simply takes over the two concepts and makes them the foundation of its work." Ibid., p. 171.

57. Freud, "Some Psychical Consequences of the Anatomical Distinction between the Sexes" (1925), in *SE* 19: 252.

58. See Freud, "Female Sexuality" (1931), in *SE* 21: 229–230.

59. Freud cited Horney's paper along with Karl Abraham, "Manifestations of the Female Castration Complex" (1921), and Helene Deutsch, *Psychoanalysis and the Sexual Functions of Women* (1925): ibid., p. 258.

60. Horney, "Genesis of the Castration Complex in Women," pp. 37, 38. In this essay Horney diverged from Abraham in characterizing the castration complex and the masculinity complex as "practically synonymous": see ibid., p. 38.

61. Freud, "Analysis Terminable and Interminable" (1937), in *SE* 23: 252.

62. Horney, "Genesis of the Castration Complex in Women," p. 38.

63. Ibid., pp. 38, 39, 40, 41.

64. Horney, "The Flight from Womanhood," p. 65.

65. See Freud, "On the Sexual Theories of Children" (1908), in *SE* 9: 215.

66. Horney, "The Denial of the Vagina," p. 155.

67. Horney, "Genesis of the Castration Complex in Women," p. 43. On the girl's identification with her mother, see also Horney, "Inhibited Femininity," p. 79.

68. Horney, "Genesis of the Castration Complex in Women," p. 44.

69. Horney, "The Dread of Woman," p. 142.

70. Horney, "Genesis of the Castration Complex in Women," pp. 44, 45–46 (emphasis in the original).

71. See Freud, "On Transformations of Instinct as Exemplified in Anal Erotism" (1917), in *SE* 17: 127–133.

72. Horney, "The Genesis of the Castration Complex in Women," p. 48.

73. Ibid., p. 51.

74. Ibid., p. 49. Freud came close to Horney's view when he wrote that the "'masculinity complex' in women can . . . result in a manifest homosexual choice of object." See Freud, "Female Sexuality," p. 230.

75. Horney, "Genesis of the Castration Complex in Women," p. 52.

76. Horney, "The Distrust Between the Sexes," p. 111.

77. Karen Horney, "The Overvaluation of Love: A Study of a Common Present-Day Feminine Type" (1934), in *Feminine Psychology*, pp. 184, 185, 186–187.

78. Ibid., pp. 188.

79. Ibid., pp. 189, 190.

80. Ibid., p. 191.

81. Ibid., p. 192.

82. Ibid., p. 193.

83. Ibid., p. 192.

84. Ibid., pp. 194–195.

85. Ibid., pp. 195–196.

86. Ibid., p. 182.

87. See Karen Horney, "Culture and Neurosis," *American Sociological Review* 1 (1936): 221–235.

88. Ruth Benedict, review of *The Neurotic Personality of Our Time*, by Karen Horney, *Journal of Abnormal and Social Psychology* 33 (1938): 135.

89. Ernest Jones, review of *The Neurotic Personality of Our Time*, by Karen Horney, *IJP* 21 (1940): 240, 241.

90. Karen Horney, *The Neurotic Personality of Our Time* (New York: Norton, 1937), pp. xi, x.

91. Ibid., p. xi.

92. See Quinn, *A Mind of Her Own*, p. 285.

93. Karen Horney, "The Problem of Feminine Masochism" (1935), in *Feminine Psychology*, p. 223.

94. Horney, *The Neurotic Personality*, pp. 160–161.

95. Ibid., pp. 157, 159–160.

96. See ibid., p. 148.

97. Ibid., pp. 79, 80–81 (emphasis omitted).

98. Ibid., pp. 96, 103.

99. Ibid., p. 107.

100. Ibid., pp. 150–151.

101. Ibid., pp. 163, 166, 173, 176–177.

102. Ibid., pp. 208, 211, 214, 216.

103. Ibid., p. 287.

104. Harry Guntrip, *Personality Structure and Human Interaction: The Developing Synthesis of Psychodynamic Theory* (London: Hogarth Press, 1961), p. 163.

CHAPTER 4   ARTIFICIAL SELECTION: ROBERT J. STOLLER AND NANCY CHODOROW

1. Nora Barlow, ed. *The Autobiography of Charles Darwin* 1809–1882 (New York: Norton, 1969), pp. 119, 120.

2. See Michael Ruse, "Charles Darwin and Artificial Selection," *Journal of the History of Ideas* 36 (1975): 339–350.

3. See Freud, "Some Psychical Consequences of the Anatomical Distinction between the Sexes" (1925), in *SE* 19: 248–258; "Female Sexuality" (1931), in *SE* 21: 225–243; *New Introductory Lectures on Psycho-Analysis* (1933), in *SE* 22: 112–135.

4. Robert J. Stoller, *Presentations of Gender* (New Haven: Yale University Press, 1985), p. 44.

5. Sybil Stoller, interview with the author, May 3, 1996; see also Morton and Estelle Shane, "Obituary: Robert Stoller," *IJP* 73 (1992): 773–774, and David James Fisher, "Remembering Robert J. Stoller (1924–1991)," *Psychoanalytic Review* 83 (1996): 1–9.

6. Stoller, *Presentations of Gender*, pp. 3–4.

7. Ibid., pp. 4, 5, 6, 8.

8. Robert J. Stoller, *Pain and Passion: A Psychoanalyst Explores the World of S&M* (New York: Plenum, 1991), pp. 51, 53, 54. See also Stoller's co-authored account of doing "clinical ethnography" in New Guinea: Gilbert Herdt and Robert J. Stoller, *Intimate Communications: Erotics and the Study of Culture* (New York: Columbia University Press, 1990).

9. Donna J. Haraway, *Simians, Cyborgs, and Women: The Reinvention of Nature* (New York: Routledge, 1991), p. 136.

10. Stoller had read Chodorow's *The Reproduction of Mothering*, and when he met her at the San Francisco Psychoanalytic Institute a decade after its publication, he expressed his pleasure that she had acknowledged his work: Stoller to Chodorow, October 20, 1988, Robert J. Stoller Papers, Department of Special Collections—University Research Library, UCLA.

11. Nancy J. Chodorow, *Feminism and Psychoanalytic Theory* (New Haven: Yale University Press, 1989), pp. 1, 8.

12. Nancy Chodorow, *The Reproduction of Mothering: Psychoanalysis and the Sociology of Gender* (Berkeley: University of California Press, 1978), p. 214.

13. Robert J. Stoller, *Observing the Erotic Imagination* (New Haven: Yale University Press, 1985), pp. 168–169.

14. Stoller, *Presentations of Gender*, p. 206.

15. Robert J. Stoller, *Sex and Gender*, vol. 1, *The Development of Masculinity and Femininity* (New York: Science House, 1968; reprint, London: Karnac, Maresfield Library, 1984), pp. ix–x.

16. Sybil Stoller, interview with the author, May 3, 1996.

17. Stoller, *Pain and Passion*, p. 52.

18. Robert J. Stoller, Harold Garfinkel, and Alexander Rosen, "Passing and the Maintenance of Sexual Identification in an Intersexed Patient," *Archives of General Psychiatry* 2 (1960): 379–380. See also Harold Garfinkel, *Studies in Ethnomethodology* (Englewood Cliffs, N.J.: Prentice-Hall, 1967), pp. 116–185, and Arthur D. Schwabe, David H. Solomon, Robert J. Stoller, and John Burnham, "Pubertal Feminization in a Genetic Male with Testicular Atrophy and Normal Urinary Gonadotropin," *Journal of Clinical Endocrinology and Metabolism* 22 (1962): 839–845.

19. Stoller et al., "Passing and the Maintenance of Sexual Identification," p. 380.

20. Ibid., pp. 380–381.

21. Endocrinological report, quoted in Garfinkel, *Studies in Ethnomethodology*, p. 152n6.

22. Garfinkel, *Studies in Ethnomethodology*, p. 163.

23. Robert J. Stoller, "A Further Contribution to the Study of Gender Identity," *IJP* 49 (1968): 365.

24. Schwabe et al., "Pubertal Feminization," p. 844.

25. Garfinkel, *Studies in Ethnomethodology*, p. 160.

26. Stoller, *Sex and Gender*, pp. 135–136.

27. Schwabe et al., "Pubertal Feminization," p. 842.

28. Robert J. Stoller, description of Agnes following her operation, quoted in Garfinkel, *Studies in Ethnomethodology*, p. 152n6.

29. John Money, Joan G. Hampson, and John L. Hampson, "An Examination of Some Basic Sexual Concepts: The Evidence of Human Hermaphroditism," *Bulletin of Johns Hopkins Hospital* 97 (1955): 302n; see also John Money, "Hermaphroditism, Gender and Precocity in Hyperadrenocorticism: Psychologic Findings," *Bulletin of Johns Hopkins Hospital* 96 (1955): 253–264, and John Money, Joan G. Hampson, and John L. Hampson, "Hermaphroditism: Recommendations Concerning Assignment of Sex, Change of Sex, and Psychologic Management," *Bulletin of Johns Hopkins Hospital* 97

(1955): 284–300. For useful commentary, see Suzanne J. Kessler, "The Medical Construction of Gender: Case Management of Intersexed Infants," *Signs* 16 (1990): 3–26, and Bernice L. Hausman, *Changing Sex: Transsexualism, Technology, and the Idea of Gender* (Durham, N.C.: Duke University Press, 1995), ch. 3.

30. John Money, Joan G. Hampson, and John L. Hampson, "Imprinting and the Establishment of Gender Role," *American Medical Association: Archives of Neurology and Psychiatry* 77 (1957): 334, 335.

31. Robert J. Stoller, *Sex and Gender,* vol. 2, *The Transsexual Experiment* (London: Hogarth Press, 1975), pp. 81, 83.

32. Ibid., pp. 84, 87, 264.

33. Stoller, *Presentations of Gender,* pp. 163, 167, 170.

34. See Robert J. Stoller, "A Contribution to the Study of Gender Identity," *IJP* 45 (1964): 223. See also Robert J. Stoller, "Gender Role Change in Intersexed Patients," *Journal of the American Medical Association* 188 (1964): 684–685.

35. Stoller, "A Contribution to the Study of Gender Identity," p. 225.

36. Stoller, "A Further Contribution to the Study of Gender Identity," p. 365; see also Howard J. Baker and Robert J. Stoller, "Can a Biological Force Contribute to Gender Identity?" *American Journal of Psychiatry* 124 (1968): 1653–1658.

37. Stoller, *Sex and Gender,* p. 83.

38. Ralph R. Greenson, "A Transvestite Boy and a Hypothesis," *IJP* 47 (1966): 396.

39. Ibid., pp. 396, 401–402.

40. Stoller, *Sex and Gender,* pp. 112–113.

41. Ibid., pp. 113–114.

42. Ibid., p. 114.

43. Ibid., pp. 125, 115.

44. Stoller, *The Transsexual Experiment,* pp. 31, 50.

45. Ibid., pp. 21, 26, 41.

46. Ibid., pp. 25, 44.

47. See Ralph R. Greenson, "Dis-identifying from Mother: Its Special Importance for the Boy," *IJP* 49 (1968): 370–373.

48. Richard Green, Lawrence E. Newman, and Robert J. Stoller, "Treatment of Boyhood 'Transsexualism': An Interim Report of Four Years' Experience," *Archives of General Psychiatry* 26 (1972): 214. For an account of a psychoanalytic treatment of a transsexual child, see Loretta Loeb and Morton Shane, "The Resolution of a Transsexual Wish in a Five-Year-Old Boy," *JAPA* 30 (1982): 419–434.

49. Stoller, *The Transsexual Experiment,* p. 293. For challenges to Stoller's views, see Adam Limentani, "The Significance of Transsexualism in Relation to Some Basic Psychoanalytic Concepts," *The International Review of Psycho-Analysis* 6 (1979): 139–153, and Susan Coates, Richard C. Friedman, and Sabina Wolfe, "The Etiology of Boyhood Gender Identity Disorder: A Model for Integrating Treatment, Development, and Psychodynamics," *Psychoanalytic Dialogues* 1 (1991): 481–523.

50. Stoller, *The Transsexual Experiment,* pp. 289, 33, 35. For a useful critique, see Juliet Mitchell, review of *The Transsexual Experiment,* Vol. 2 of *Sex and Gender,* by Robert Stoller, *IJP* 57 (1976): 357–360.

51. Robert J. Stoller, "Femininity," in Martha Kirkpatrick, ed., *Women's Sexual Development: Explorations of Inner Space* (New York: Plenum, 1980), p. 143; see also Robert J. Stoller, "Symbiosis Anxiety and the Development of Masculinity," *Archives of General Psychiatry* 30 (1974): 164–172. For criticism of Stoller's notion of a protofeminine core, see Ethel S. Person and Lionel Oversey, "Psychoanalytic Theories of Gender Identity," *Journal of the American Academy of Psychoanalysis* 11 (1983): 214–215.

52. Stoller, *Sex and Gender*, p. 125 (emphasis in the original).

53. Robert J. Stoller, *Splitting: A Case of Female Masculinity* (London: Hogarth Press, 1974; reprint, New Haven: Yale University Press, 1997), p. ix. For a feminist critique of this case, see Patricia Elliot, *From Mastery to Analysis: Theories of Gender in Psychoanalytic Feminism* (Ithaca, N.Y.: Cornell University Press, 1991), pp. 26–51.

54. Stoller, *Splitting*, p. 1.

55. Ibid., p. 304.

56. Ibid., pp. 307, 308.

57. Ibid., pp. 305, 309.

58. Ibid., pp. 183–184.

59. Ibid., p. 11.

60. Ibid., pp. 14–15.

61. Ibid., pp. 16–17.

62. Ibid., pp. 23, 21, 27–28. "What I do not know," Stoller wrote, "and I feel I cannot know, is how she was able to create a penis that she felt was really there. We are familiar with women who (consciously) daydream of having a penis or who (unconsciously) have such fantasies; but Mrs. G was not one of these. She did not just imagine having a penis, but actually had one, insofar as subjective experience was concerned. What is different in her that lifted fantasy to hallucinated reality? Our work never revealed the answer." Ibid., p. 371*n*4.

63. Ibid., p. 24.

64. Stoller, *Sex and Gender*, p. 173.

65. Stoller, *Splitting*, pp. 249, 264, 260.

66. Ibid., pp. 234, 391, 245.

67. Ibid., pp. 196, 186.

68. Ibid., pp. 17, 197.

69. Ibid., p. 25.

70. Ibid., pp. 290, 286–287.

71. Ibid., pp. 291, 301.

72. Ibid., p. 282. Elsewhere he seemed less certain and spoke of "feminine homosexual women" and "masculine heterosexual women": Stoller, *The Transsexual Experiment*, p. 239*n*.

73. Stoller, *Splitting*, pp. 283, 272.

74. Ibid., p. 295.

75. Robert J. Stoller, *Sexual Excitement: Dynamics of Erotic Life* (New York: Pantheon, 1979; reprint, London: Karnac, Maresfield Library, 1986), p. 161.

76. Robert J. Stoller, "Femininity," p. 131.

77. Stoller, *Sexual Excitement*, p. 59.

78. Ibid., pp. 149, 152.

79. Ibid., p. 150.

80. Robert J. Stoller, "Primary Femininity," *JAPA* 24 (Supplement) (1976): 66.

81. Stoller, *Sexual Excitement,* p. 68.

82. Ibid., pp. 72, 71.

83. Ibid., p. 85.

84. Ibid., p. 77; see also p. 82.

85. Ibid., pp.. 77, 82, 78, 61.

86. Ibid., pp. 73, 74.

87. Ibid., p. 74.

88. Ibid., p. 157.

89. Chodorow, *Feminism and Psychoanalytic Theory,* p. 206.

90. Ibid., pp. 206, 200, 201.

91. Ibid., pp. 205, 204, 203, 216, 217.

92. Ibid., p. 200.

93. Karl Marx and Frederick Engels, *Manifesto of the Communist Party* (1848), in *Karl Marx and Frederick Engels: Selected Works* (Moscow: Progress Publishers, 1968), p. 35.

94. Chodorow, *The Reproduction of Mothering,* p. 3. For useful commentary on Chodorow's book, see Judith Lorber, Rose Laub Coser, Alice S. Rossi, and Nancy Chodorow, "On *The Reproduction of Mothering:* A Methodological Debate," *Signs* 6 (1981): 482–514; Parveen Adams, "Mothering," *m/f* 8 (1983): 41–52; Iris Marion Young, "Is Male Gender Identity the Cause of Male Domination?" in Joyce Trebilcot, ed., *Mothering: Essays in Feminist Theory* (Totawa, N.J.: Rowman and Allanheld, 1983), pp. 129–146; Pauline Bart, "Review of Chodorow's *The Reproduction of Mothering,*" in Trebilcot, ed., *Mothering,* pp. 147–152; Paul Robinson, "Freud and the Feminists," *Raritan* 6 (1987): 43–61; Marcia C. Westkott, "On the New Psychology of Women: A Cautionary View," *Feminist Issues* 10 (1990): 3–18; Elliot, *From Mastery to Analysis,* pp. 122–146.

95. Anna Freud, "Contribution to Discussion, 'The Theory of the Parent-Infant Relationship,'" *IJP* 43 (1962): 241, quoted in Chodorow, *The Reproduction of Mothering,* p. 58.

96. Chodorow, The Reproduction of Mothering, pp. 60, 62, 87.

97. Ibid., pp. 87–88.

98. Ibid., pp. 109, 110.

99. Ibid., pp. 121, 127, 93.

100. Ibid., pp. 115, 127, 129, 133.

101. Ibid., pp. 211–212.

102. Ibid., pp. 122, 121.

103. Ibid., pp. 139, 126, 128.

104. Ibid., pp. 199–200, 202.

105. In her more recent work, Chodorow has moved away from the notion of core gender identity: see Nancy J. Chodorow, *Femininities, Masculinities, Sexualities: Freud and Beyond* (Lexington: University of Kentucky Press, 1994); "Gender As a Personal and Cultural Construction" *Signs* 20 (1995): 516–544; "Theoretical Gender and Clinical

Gender: Epistemological Reflections on the Psychology of Women," *JAPA* 44 (Supplement) (1997): 215–238.

106. Chodorow, *The Reproduction of Mothering* p. 214.

107. Karl Marx, "Theses on Feuerbach," (1888), in *Marx and Engels: Selected Works,* p. 30.

108. Chodorow, *The Reproduction of Mothering,* p. 215.

109. Ibid., p. 218.

110. Ibid., p. 219.

111. Chodorow, *Feminism and Psychoanalytic Theory,* p. 100.

CHAPTER 5   NATURAL SELECTION: MELANIE KLEIN AND JUDITH M. HUGHES

1. Charles Darwin, *On the Origin of Species* (1859), in *The Works of Charles Darwin,* ed. Paul H. Barrett and R. B. Freeman (London: William Pickering, 1988), 15: 3–4.

2. Stephen Jay Gould, *Ever Since Darwin: Reflections in Natural History* (New York: Norton, 1977), p. 45; see also Elliott Sober, *The Nature of Selection: Evolutionary Theory in Philosophical Focus* (Cambridge, Mass.: MIT Press, 1984), pt. 1, and Robert M. Young, *Darwin's Metaphor: Nature's Place in Victorian Culture* (Cambridge: Cambridge University Press, 1985), pp. 79–125.

3. *The Writings of Melanie Klein,* under the general editorship of Roger Money-Kyrle, in collaboration with Betty Joseph, Edna O'Shaughnessy, and Hanna Segal (London: Hogarth Press, 1975), vol. 2, *The Psycho-Analysis of Children,* trans. Alix Strachey, p. 12*n*.

4. For biographical information I have drawn on Phyllis Grosskurth, *Melanie Klein: Her World and Her Work* (New York: Knopf, 1986). For useful commentary, see Judith M. Hughes, *Reshaping the Psychoanalytic Domain: The Work of Melanie Klein, W. R. D. Fairbairn, and D. W. Winnicott* (Berkeley: University of California Press, 1989), ch. 3. See also Hanna Segal, *Introduction to the Work of Melanie Klein,* enl. ed. (London: Hogarth Press, 1978); Hanna Segal, *Melanie Klein* (New York: Viking, 1980); Jean-Michel Petot, *Melanie Klein,* vol. 1, *First Discoveries and First System* 1919–1932, trans. Christine Trollope (Madison, Conn.: International Universities Press, 1990); Jean-Michel Petot, *Melanie Klein,* vol. 2, *The Ego and the Good Object* 1932–1960, trans. Christine Trollope (Madison, Conn.: International Universities Press, 1991).

5. Melanie Klein, "Autobiography," quoted in Grosskurth, *Melanie Klein,* p.16.

6. See Klein, *The Psycho-Analysis of Children,* pp. x–xi. For Ferenczi's appraisal of Klein, see Ferenczi to Freud, June 29, 1919, *The Correspondence of Sigmund Freud and Sándor Ferenczi,* vol. 2, 1914–1919, ed. Ernst Falzader and Eva Brabant, trans. Peter T. Hoffer (Cambridge, Mass.: Harvard University Press, 1996), p. 361.

7. Petot, *Melanie Klein, I:* 14–22.

8. See Alix to James Strachey, December 14, 1924, *Bloomsbury/Freud: The Letters of James and Alix Strachey* 1924–1925, ed. Perry Meisel and Walter Kendrick (New York: Basic Books, 1985), p. 145. For Klein's acknowledgment of Abraham's help, see Klein, *The Psycho-Analysis of Children,* p. xi. For Abraham's appraisal of Klein, see Abraham to Freud, October 7, 1923, *A Psycho-Analytic Dialogue: The Letters of Sigmund Freud and Karl Abraham* 1907–1926, ed. Hilda C. Abraham and Ernst L. Freud, trans. Bernard Marsh and Hilda C. Abraham (New York: Basic Books, 1965), p. 339.

9. Alix to James Strachey, February 11, 1925, *Bloomsbury/Freud,* p. 201.

10. James to Alix Strachey, May 7, 1925, ibid., pp. 258–259.

11. For Jones's report to Freud on Klein's lectures, see Jones to Freud, July 17, 1925, *The Complete Correspondence of Sigmund Freud and Ernest Jones 1908–1939,* ed. R. Andrew Paskaukas (Cambridge, Mass.: Harvard University Press, 1993), pp. 577–578.

12. Alix to James Strachey, January 12, 1925, *Bloomsbury/Freud,* p. 182.

13. Ferenczi to Freud, n.d., quoted in Grosskurth, *Melanie Klein,* p. 162. See also Jones to Freud, September 30, 1927, *Complete Correspondence of Freud and Jones,* pp. 627–628.

14. Pearl H. M. King, "The Life and Work of Melanie Klein in the British Psycho-Analytical Society," *IJP* 64 (1983): 252.

15. Edward Glover, review of *The Psycho-Analysis of Children,* by Melanie Klein, *IJP* 14 (1933): 119.

16. Klein, *The Psycho-Analysis of Children,* p. xi.

17. Jones to Freud, June 20, 1927, *Complete Correspondence of Freud and Jones,* pp. 619–620.

18. Strachey to Glover, April 1940, quoted in Grosskurth, *Melanie Klein,* p. 257. On the series of meetings that took place to examine theoretical differences,—a series that came to be known as the "controversial discussions"—see Pearl King and Riccardo Steiner, eds., *The Freud-Klein Controversies 1941–45* (London: Routledge, 1991), and Riccardo Steiner, "Some Thoughts about Tradition and Change Arising from an Examination of the British Psycho-Analytical Society's Controversial Discussions (1943–1944)," *The International Review of Psycho-Analysis* 12 (1985): 27–71.

19. See Judith M. Hughes, *Emotion and High Politics: Personal Relations at the Summit in Late Nineteenth-Century Britain and Germany* (Berkeley: University of California Press, 1983), p.6n5.

20. For an account of that practice, see H. Stuart Hughes, *Gentleman Rebel: The Memoirs of H. Stuart Hughes* (New York: Ticknor and Fields, 1990), ch. 33.

21. See Judith M. Hughes, *From Freud's Consulting Room: The Unconscious in a Scientific Age* (Cambridge, Mass.: Harvard University Press, 1994). For reflections on writing that book, see Judith M. Hughes. "Another 'Impossible' Profession?" *The Psychohistory Review* 25 (1997): 119–126.

22. James S. Grotstein, review of *Reshaping the Psychoanalytic Domain: The Work of Melanie Klein, W. R. D. Fairbairn, and D. W. Winnicott,* by Judith M. Hughes, *The Psychoanalytic Quarterly* 60 (1991): 136.

23. Glover, review of *The Psycho-Analysis of Children,* p. 128.

24. Klein, *The Psycho-Analysis of Children,* pp. 16, 3.

25. Freud, "From the History of an Infantile Neurosis" (1918), in *SE* 17: 8–9. Klein herself quoted parts of this passage: see Klein, *The Psycho-Analysis of Children,* p. 9.

26. Klein, *The Psycho-Analysis of Children,* p. 9.

27. Ibid., pp. 11–12.

28. Ibid., pp. 35–36. For a discussion of Erna's importance to Klein's theorizing, see Claudia Frank and Heinz Weiß, "The Origins of Disquieting Discoveries by Melanie Klein: The Possible Significance of the Case of 'Erna,'" *IJP* 77 (1996): 1101–1126.

29. Klein, *The Psycho-Analysis of Children,* pp. 41, 40. Throughout I have spelled "fantasy"

with an "f." According to the Oxford English Dictionary, fantasy means "caprice, whim, fanciful invention"; phantasy means "imagination, visionary notion." The psychoanalytic concept is closer to imagination than to whimsy, and thus British writers use the "ph" spelling. American authors, however, have not followed suit.

30. Ibid., pp. 43, 47, 53.

31. Ibid., p. 130.

32. Ibid., pp. 137, 136, 140.

33. Ibid., p. 138.

34. See Freud, *Civilization and Its Discontents* (1930), in *SE* 21: 130*n*.

35. Klein, *The Psycho-Analysis of Children,* p. 150. In 1935, in her paper "A Contribution to the Psychogenesis of Manic-Depressive States," Klein elaborated the notion of the depressive position and therewith provided a different answer.

36. Freud, "Female Sexuality" (1931), in *SE* 21: 225–226.

37. Klein, *The Psycho-Analysis of Children,* p. 239.

38. Ibid., p. 179. By 1932 Klein had come to see the superego "as a forbear rather than as an heir to the Oedipal complex, since the early introjections . . . which enter into the composition of the superego precede the Oedipus complex": Segal, *Melanie Klein,* p. 55.

39. Melanie Klein, "Early Stages of the Oedipus Complex" (1928), in *The Writings of Melanie Klein,* vol. 1, *Love, Guilt and Reparation and Other Works* 1921–1945 (London: Hogarth Press, 1975), p. 186.

40. Klein, *The Psycho-Analysis of Children,* pp. 240–241, 242.

41. Ibid., pp. 241, 242, 197–198.

42. Ibid., p. 200.

43. Ibid., pp. 243, 244.

44. See ibid., p. 217.

45. Ibid., pp. 209–210.

46. Freud, "Some Psychical Consequences of the Anatomical Distinction between the Sexes" (1925), in *SE* 19: 252.

47. Klein, *The Psycho-Analysis of Children,* pp. 222–223.

48. Melanie Klein, contribution to "Symposium on Child Analysis" (1927), in *Love, Guilt and Reparation,* p. 157.

49. Klein, *The Psycho-Analysis of Children,* pp. 201–202, 202*m*.

50. Freud to Jones, May 26, 1935, *Complete Correspondence of Freud and Jones,* p. 743.

51. "The first return paper was given by Robert Wälder (Vienna) on 'Problems of Ego Psychology.' . . . The next paper was given by Joan Riviere (London) on 'The Genesis of Psychical Conflict in Early Infancy.' . . . The return paper was again given by Robert Wälder on 'The Problem of the Genesis of Psychical Conflict in Early Infancy', in which he carefully discusses the points raised in Joan Riviere's paper." Pearl King, "Background and Development of the Freud-Klein Controversies in the British Psycho-Analytical Society," in King and Steiner, eds., *The Freud-Klein Controversies,* p. 23.

52. Ernest Jones, "Early Female Sexuality" (1935), in Ernest Jones, *Papers on Psycho-Analysis,*

5th ed. (London: Ballière, Tindall and Cox, 1948; reprint, London: Karnac, Maresfield Reprints, 1977), p. 485.

53. Ibid., pp. 489–490.

54. Ibid., p. 490.

55. Ibid., pp. 490, 491.

56. Ibid., pp. 492, 493. See also Ernest Jones, "The Phallic Phase" (1933), in Jones, *Papers on Psycho-Analysis,* pp. 452–484.

57. Jones, "Early Female Sexuality," p. 495.

58. Klein, *The Psycho-Analysis of Children,* p. 44.

59. Ibid., pp. 51–52.

60. Ibid., p. 255*n*.

61. See Ernest Jones, *The Life and Work of Sigmund Freud,* vol. 3, *The Last Phase* 1919–1939 (New York: Basic Books, 1957), p. 196.

62. "Eighth Discussion of Scientific Differences," February 16, 1944, in King and Steiner, eds., *The Freud-Klein Controversies,* pp. 747–748.

63. W. Ronald D. Fairbairn, "Features in the Analysis of a Patient with a Physical Genital Abnormality" (1931), in W. Ronald D. Fairbairn, *Psychoanalytic Studies of the Personality* (London: Tavistock and Routledge and Kegan Paul, 1952), p. 197.

64. Ibid., pp. 198, 199.

65. Ibid., p. 200.

66. Ibid., pp. 200–201.

67. Ibid., pp. 201, 202–203.

68. In the late 1920s Fairbairn was already thinking hard about the superego, but he was not publishing his thoughts: see W. Ronald D. Fairbairn, "What Is the Superego?" and "Is the Superego Repressed?" in Ellinor Fairbairn Birtles and David E. Scharff, eds., *From Instinct to Self: Selected Papers of W. R. D. Fairbairn,* vol. 2, *Applications and Early Contributions* (Northvale, N.J.: Jason Aronson, 1994), pp. 80–114.

69. Fairbairn, "Analysis of a Patient with a Physical Genital Abnormality," p. 216.

70. Ibid., pp. 216–217.

71. Ibid., pp. 219, 215, 217.

72. Ibid., pp. 216.

73. Ibid., pp. 216, 219.

74. W. Ronald D. Fairbairn, "Endopsychic Structure Considered in Terms of Object-Relationships" (1944), in Fairbairn, *Psychoanalytic Studies of the Personality,* p. 90.

75. Ibid., p. 95.

76. Fairbairn, "Analysis of a Patient with a Physical Genital Abnormality," p. 220.

77. Daniel Paul Schreber, *Memoirs of My Nervous Illness,* ed. and trans. Ida Macalpine and Richard A. Hunter (Cambridge, Mass.: Harvard University Press, 1988), pp. 132*n*, 63. For biographical information on Schreber, see Franz Baumeyer, "The Schreber Case," *IJP* 37 (1956): 61–74; William G. Niederland, *The Schreber Case: Psychoanalytic Profile of a Paranoid Personality* (New York: Quadrangle/New York Times, 1974); Han Israëls, *Schreber: Father and Son,* trans. H. J. Lake (Madison, Conn.: International Universities Press, 1989); Zvi Lothane, *In Defense of Schreber: Soul Murder and Psychiatry* (Hillsdale, N.J.: Analytic Press, 1992).

78. "Judgment of the Royal Superior Country Court Dresden of 14th July, 1902," in Schreber, *Memoirs*, p. 354.

79. Daniel Paul Schreber, "Grounds of Appeal" (July 23, 1901), in Schreber, *Memoirs*, p. 307.

80. Ibid., pp. 31, 148, 85.

81. Ibid., pp. 132, 207, 204, 205.

82. Ibid., pp. 149, 212.

83. Freud, "Psycho-Analytic Notes on an Autobiographical Account of a Case of Paranoia (Dementia Paranoides)" (1911), in *SE* 12: 18.

84. Ian Hacking, *Rewriting the Soul: Multiple Personality and the Sciences of Memory*, (Princeton, N.J.: Princeton University Press, 1995), pp. 234–236. See also G. E. M. Anscombe, *Intention* (Ithaca, N.Y.: Cornell University Press, 1963), pp. 37–44.

85. See J. M. Hughes, *From Freud's Consulting Room*, p. 82.

86. Schreber, *Memoirs*, p. 207.

87. Freud, "Hysterical Phantasies and Their Relation to Bisexuality" (1908), in *SE* 9: 161.

88. Schreber, *Memoirs*, p. 204.

89. Freud, *Three Essays in the Theory of Sexuality* (1905), in *SE* 7: 184, 182.

90. Fairbairn, "Analysis of a Patient with a Physical Genital Abnormality," pp. 204–205.

91. Fairbairn, "Endopsychic Structure," p. 111.

CONCLUSION: THE NARRATIVE OF CHOICE

1. See Judith M. Hughes, *From Freud's Consulting Room: The Unconscious in a Scientific Age* (Cambridge, Mass.: Harvard University Press, 1994).

2. Erik H. Erikson, *Childhood and Society*, 2d, revised and enlarged ed. (New York: Norton, 1963), p. 65.

3. Stephen Jay Gould, *Ontogeny and Phylogeny* (Cambridge, Mass.: Harvard University Press, 1977), p. 35.

4. Helene Deutsch, *Psychoanalysis of the Sexual Functions of Women* (1925), ed. Paul Roazen, trans. Eric Mosbacher (London: Karnac, 1991), p. 84.

5. Robert J. Stoller, *Sexual Excitement: Dynamics of Erotic Life* (New York: Pantheon, 1979; reprint, London: Karnac, Maresfield Library, 1986), p. 118.

6. Robert J. Stoller, *Sex and Gender*, vol. 2, *The Transsexual Experiment* (London: Hogarth Press, 1975), p. 289.

7. Susan Isaacs, "The Nature and Function of Phantasy," in Pearl King and Riccardo Steiner, eds., *The Freud-Klein Controversies 1941–45* (London: Routledge, 1991), p. 277.

8. Ernest Jones, "Early Female Sexuality" (1935), in Ernest Jones, *Papers of Psycho-Analysis*, 5th ed. (London: Ballière, Tindall and Cox, 1948; reprint, London: Karnac, Maresfield Reprints, 1977), p. 495.

9. *The Writings of Melanie Klein*, under the general editorship of Roger Money-Kyrle, in collaboration with Betty Joseph, Edna O'Shaughnessy, and Hanna Segal (London: Hogarth Press, 1975), vol. 2, *The Psycho-Analysis of Children*, trans. Alix Strachey, p. 179.

Selected Bibliography

Abel, Elizabeth. *Virginia Woolf and the Fictions of Psychoanalysis.* Chicago: University of Chicago Press, 1989.

Abel, Elizabeth, Marianne Hirsch, and Elizabeth Langland, eds. *The Voyage In: Fictions of Female Development.* Hanover, N.H.: University Press of New England, 1983.

Abraham, Karl. *Selected Papers of Karl Abraham.* Translated by Douglas Bryan and Alix Strachey. London: Hogarth Press, 1927. Reprint, London: H. Karnac, Maresfield Reprints, 1979.

Achinstein, Peter, and Stephen F. Barker, eds. *The Legacy of Logical Positivism: Studies in the Philosophy of Science.* Baltimore: Johns Hopkins University Press, 1969.

Adams, Parveen. "Mothering." *m/f* 8 (1983): 41–52.

Alexander, Franz. Review of *The Neurotic Personality of Our Time,* by Karen Horney. *The Psychoanalytic Quarterly* 6 (1937): 536–540.

———. "Psychoanalysis Revised." *The Psychoanalytic Quarterly* 9 (1940): 1–38.

Anderson, Robin, ed. *Clinical Lectures on Klein and Bion.* London Tavistock/Routledge, 1992.

Andersson, Malte. *Sexual Selection.* Princeton, N.J.: Princeton University Press, 1994.

Andreas-Salomé, Lou. *The Freud Journal of Lou Andreas-Salomé.* Translated by Stanley A. Leavy. New York: Basic Books, 1964.

Anscombe, G. E. M. *Intention*. Ithaca, N.Y.: Cornell University Press, 1963.

Anzieu, Didier. "Comment devient-on Melanie Klein?" *Nouvelle Revue de Psychanalyse* 26 (1982): 235–251.

———. *Freud's Self-Analysis*. Translated by Peter Graham. London: Hogarth Press, 1986.

Appignanesi, Lisa, and John Forrester. *Freud's Women*. New York: Basic Books, 1992.

Aron, Lewis. "The Internalized Primal Scene." *Psychoanalytic Dialogues* 5 (1995): 195–237.

Auerbach, Judy, Linda Blum, Vicki Smith, and Christine Williams. "Commentary: On Gilligan's *In a Different Voice*." *Feminist Studies* 11 (1985): 149–161.

Ayala, Francisco Jose, and Theodosius Dobzhansky, eds. *Studies in the Philosophy of Biology: Reduction and Related Problems*. Berkeley: University of California Press, 1974.

Baker, Howard J., and Robert J. Stoller. "Can a Biological Force Contribute to Gender Identity?" *American Journal of Psychiatry* 124 (1968): 1653–1658.

Balint, Michael. *Primary Love and Psycho-Analytic Technique*. London: Hogarth Press, 1952. Reprint, London: Karnac, Maresfield Library, 1985.

———. "Pleasure, Object and Libido: Some Reflections on Fairbairn's Modification of Psychoanalytic Theory." *The British Journal of Medical Psychology* 29 (1956): 162–167.

———. "The Concepts of Subject and Object in Psychoanalysis." *The British Journal of Medical Psychology* 31 (1958): 83–91.

———. *Thrills and Regressions*. London: Hogarth Press; New York: International Universities Press, 1959.

———. *The Basic Fault: Therapeutic Aspects of Regression*. London: Tavistock Publications, 1968.

Barnett, Marjorie. "Vaginal Awareness in the Infancy and Childhood of Girls." *JAPA* 14 (1966): 129–140.

Barr, Marleen S., and Richard Feldstein, eds. *Discontented Discourses: Feminism/Textual Intervention/Psychoanalysis*. Urbana: University of Illinois Press, 1989.

Bart, Pauline. "Review of Chodorow's *The Reproduction of Mothering*." In *Mothering: Essays in Feminist Theory*, edited by Joyce Trebilcot. Totawa, N.J.: Rowman and Allanheld, 1983.

Baruch, Elaine Hoffman, and Lucienne J. Serrano. *Women Analyze Women: In France, England, and the United States*. New York: New York University Press, 1988.

Bassin, Donna. "Beyond the He and the She: Toward the Reconciliation of Masculinity and Femininity in the Postoedipal Female Mind." *JAPA* 44 (Supplement) (1997): 191–214.

Baumeyer, Franz. "The Schreber Case." *IJP* 37 (1956): 61–74.

Beauvoir, Simone de. *The Second Sex*. Translated and edited by H. M. Parshley. New York: Knopf, 1952. Reprint, New York: Knopf, Vintage Edition, 1989.

Beckner, Morton. *The Biological Way of Thought*. Berkeley : University of California Press, 1968.

Beer, Gavin de. *Charles Darwin: A Scientific Biography*. London: Thomas Nelson and Sons, 1963.

Beer, Gillian. *Darwin's Plots: Evolutionary Narrative in Darwin, George Eliot and Nineteenth-Century Fiction*. London: Routledge and Kegan Paul, 1983.

Benedict, Ruth. Review of *The Neurotic Personality of Our Time*, by Karen Horney. *Journal of Abnormal and Social Psychology* 33 (1938): 133–135.

Benjamin, Jessica. *The Bonds of Love: Psychoanalysis, Feminism, and the Problem of Domination.* New York: Pantheon, 1988.

———. "Father and Daughter: Identification with Difference—A Contribution to Gender Heterodoxy." *Psychoanalytic Dialogues* 1 (1991): 277–299.

———. *Like Subjects, Love Objects: Essays on Recognition and Sexual Difference.* New Haven: Yale University Press, 1995.

———. "In Defense of Gender Ambiguity." *Gender and Psychoanalysis* 1 (1996): 27–43.

Berger, Milton, M., ed. *Women beyond Freud: New Concepts of Feminine Psychology.* New York: Brunner/Mazel, 1994.

Bernheimer, Charles, and Claire Kahane, eds. *In Dora's Case: Freud-Hysteria-Feminism.* New York: Columbia University Press, 1985.

Bernstein, Doris. "The Female Superego: A Different Perspective." *IJP* 64 (1983): 187–202.

———. "Female Genital Anxieties, Conflicts and Typical Mastery Modes." *IJP* 71 (1990): 151–165.

Bertin, Celia. *Marie Bonaparte: A Life.* New York: Harcourt Brace Jovanovich, 1982.

Bettelheim, Bruno. *Symbolic Wounds: Puberty Rites and the Envious Male.* Glencoe, Ill.: Free Press, 1954.

Bibring, Edward. "The So-Called English School of Psychoanalysis." *The Psychoanalytic Quarterly* 16 (1947): 69–93.

Binion, Rudolph. *Frau Lou: Neitzsche's Wayward Disciple.* Princeton, N.J.: Princeton University Press, 1968.

Birksted-Breen, Dana. "Unconscious Representation of Femininity." *JAPA* 44 (Supplement) (1997): 119–132.

Blum, Harold T. "Masochism, the Ego Ideal, and the Psychology of Women." *JAPA* 24 (Supplement) (1976): 157–191.

Bonaparte, Marie. *Female Sexuality.* New York: International Universities Press, 1953.

Borch-Jacobsen, Mikkel. *The Freudian Subject.* Translated by Catherine Porter. Stanford, Calif.: Stanford University Press, 1988.

Bowler, Peter J. *The Eclipse of Darwinism: Anti-Darwinian Evolution Theories in the Decades around 1900.* Baltimore: Johns Hopkins University Press, 1983.

———. *Evolution: The History of an Idea.* Berkeley: University of California Press, 1984.

———. *Theories of Human Evolution: A Century of Debate, 1844–1944.* Baltimore: Johns Hopkins University Press, 1986.

———. *The Non-Darwinian Revolution: Reinterpreting a Historical Myth.* Baltimore: Johns Hopkins University Press, 1988.

Breen, Dana, ed. *The Gender Conundrum: Contemporary Psychoanalytic Perspectives on Femininity and Masculinity.* London: Routledge, 1993.

Brennan, Teresa. "Controversial Discussions and Feminist Debate." In *Freud in Exile: Psychoanalysis and Its Vicissitudes,* edited by Edward Timms and Naomi Segal. New Haven: Yale University Press, 1988.

———. *The Interpretation of the Flesh: Freud and Femininity.* New York: Routledge, 1992.

———, ed. *Between Feminism and Psychoanalysis.* New York: Routledge, 1989.

Breuer, Josef, and Sigmund Freud. *Studies on Hysteria* (1893–1895). In *SE,* vol.2.

Briehl, Marie H. "Helene Deutsch." In *Psychoanalytic Pioneers,* edited by Franz Alexander, Samuel Eisenstein, and Martin Grotjahn. New York: Basic Books, 1966.

Brierley, Marjorie. "Some Problems of Integration in Women." *IJP* 13 (1932): 433–448.

———. "Specific Determinants in Feminine Development." *IJP* 17 (1936): 163–180.

———. Review of *The Psychology of Women:* Vol. 1, *Girlhood;* Vol. 2, *Motherhood,* by Helene Deutsch, *IJP* 29 (1948): 251–254.

———. *Trends in Psycho-Analysis.* London: Hogarth Press, 1951.

Brome, Vincent. *Freud and His Early Circle: The Struggles of Psycho-Analysis.* London: Heinemann, 1967.

———. *Ernest Jones: Freud's Alter Ego.* New York and London: Norton, 1983.

Brooks, Peter. *Reading for the Plot: Design and Intention in Narrative.* New York: Knopf, 1984.

———. *Psychoanalysis and Storytelling.* Oxford: Blackwell, 1994.

Broughton, John M. "Women's Rationality and Men's Virtues: A Critique of Gender Dualism in Gilligan's Theory of Moral Development." *Social Research* 50 (1983): 597–642.

Brown, J. A. C. *Freud and the Post-Freudians.* Harmondsworth: Penguin Books, 1961.

Brown, Lyn Mikel, and Carol Gilligan. *Meeting and the Crossroads: Women's Psychology and Girl's Development.* Cambridge, Mass.: Harvard University Press, 1992.

Brunswick, Ruth Mack. "The Preoedipal Phase of the Libido Development." In *The Psychoanalytic Reader: An Anthology of Essential Papers with Critical Introductions,* edited by Robert Fliess. New York: International Universities Press, 1948.

Buckley, Nellie Louise. "Women Psychoanalysts and the Theory of Feminine Development: A Study of Karen Horney, Helene Deutsch, and Marie Bonaparte." Ph.D. dissertation, University of California, Los Angeles, 1982.

Burach, Cynthia. *The Problem of the Passions: Feminism, Psychoanalysis, and Social Theory.* New York: New York University Press, 1994.

Burlingham, Michael John. *The Last Tiffany: A Biography of Dorothy Tiffany Burlingham.* New York: Atheneum, 1989.

Burston, Daniel. *The Legacy of Erich Fromm.* Cambridge, Mass.: Harvard University Press, 1991.

Butler, Judith. *Gender Trouble: Feminism and the Subversion of Identity.* New York: Routledge, 1990.

———. *Bodies That Matter: On the Discursive Limits of "Sex".* New York: Routledge, 1993.

———. "Melancholy Gender—Refused Identification." *Psychonalytic Dialogues* 5 (1995): 165–180.

Campbell, Bernard, ed. *Sexual Selection and the Descent of Man, 1871–1971.* Chicago: Aldine, 1972.

Campbell, Donald T. "Evolutionary Epistemology." In *The Philosophy of Karl Popper,* edited by Arthur Schilpp. LaSalle, Ill.: Open Court, 1974.

Chabot, C. Barry. *Freud on Schreber: Psychoanalytic Theory and Critical Act.* Amherst: University of Massachusetts Press, 1982.

Chasseguet-Smirgel, Janine. "Freud and Female Sexuality: The Consideration of Some Blind Spots in the Exploration of the 'Dark Continent.'" *IJP* 57 (1976): 275–286.

———. *Creativity and Perversion.* New York: Norton, 1984.

———. *Sexuality and Mind: The Role of the Father and Mother in the Psyche.* New York: New York University Press, 1986.

Chasseguet-Smirgel, Janine, C.-S.Luquet-Paret, Béla Grunberger, Joyce McDougall, Maria Torok, and Christian David. *Female Sexuality: New Psychoanalytic Views.* Ann Arbor: University of Michigan Press, 1970. Reprint, London: Karnac, Maresfield Reprints, 1985.

Chodorow, Nancy. "Mothering, Object-Relations, and the Female Oedipal Configuration." *Feminist Studies* 4 (1978): 137–158.

———. *The Reproduction of Mothering: Psychoanalysis and the Sociology of Gender.* Berkeley: University of California Press, 1978.

———. *Feminism and Psychoanalytic Theory.* New Haven: Yale University Press, 1989.

———. "Where Have All the Eminent Women Psychoanalysts Gone? Like the Bubbles in Champagne, They Rose to the Top and Disappeared." In *Social Roles and Social Institutions: Essays in Honor of Rose Laub Coser,* edited by Judith R. Blau and Norman Goodman. Boulder, Colo.: Westview Press, 1991.

———. *Femininities, Masculinities, Sexualities: Freud and Beyond.* Lexington: University of Kentucky Press, 1994.

———. "Gender as a Personal and Cultural Construction." *Signs* 20 (1995): 516–544.

———. "Reflections on the Authority of the Past in Psychoanalytic Thinking." *The Psychoanalytic Quarterly* 65 (1996): 32–51.

———. "Theoretical Gender and Clinical Gender: Epistemological Reflections on the Psychology of Women." *JAPA* 44 (Supplement) (1997): 215–238.

Clifford, James. "On Ethnographic Authority." *Representations* 1 (1983): 118–146.

———. "On Ethnographic Self-Fashioning: Conrad and Malinowski." In *Reconstructing Individualism: Autonomy, Individuality, and the Self in Western Thought,* edited by Thomas C. Heller, Morton Sosna, and David E. Wellbery. Stanford, Calif.: Stanford University Press, 1986.

Clifford, James, and George E. Marcus, eds. *Writing Culture: The Poetics and Politics of Ethnography.* Berkeley University of California Press, 1986.

Coates, Susan, Richard C. Friedman, and Sabina Wolfe. "The Etiology of Boyhood Gender Identity Disorder: A Model for Integrating Treatment, Development, and Psychodynamics." *Psychoanalytic Dialogues* 1 (1991): 481–523.

Coen, Stanley J. "The Passions and Perils of Interpretation: An Appreciation of Erik Erikson's Dream Specimen Paper." *IJP* 77 (1996): 537–548.

Coles, Robert. *Erik H. Erikson: The Growth of His Work.* Boston: Little, Brown, 1970.

Connell, Robert W. *Gender and Power.* Stanford, Calif.: Stanford University Press, 1987.

———. "Bodies and Genders." *Agenda: A Journal About Women and Gender* No. 23 (1994): 7–18.

Crane, Diana. *Invisible Colleges: Diffusion of Knowledge in Scientific Communities.* Chicago: University of Chicago Press, 1972.

Crews, Frederick. *Skeptical Engagements.* New York: Oxford University Press, 1986.

Cronin, Helena. *The Ant and the Peacock: Altruism and Sexual Selection from Darwin to Today.* Cambridge University Press, 1991.

Darwin, Charles. *The Works of Charles Darwin,* edited by Paul H. Barrett and R. B. Freeman.

Vol. 15 *On the Origin of Species* (1859); vol. 23 *The Descent of Man, and Selection in Relation to Sex* (1871). London: William Pickering, 1986–1989.

———. *The Autobiography of Charles Darwin.* Edited by Nora Barlow. New York: Norton, 1969.

David-Ménard, Monique. *Hysteria from Freud to Lacan: Body and Language in Psychoanalysis.* Translated by Catherine Porter. Ithaca, N.Y.: Cornell University Press, 1989.

De Lauretis, Teresa. *Technologies of Gender: Feminism, Film, and Fiction.* Bloomington: Indiana University Press, 1987.

———. *The Practice of Love: Lesbian Sexuality and Perverse Desire.* Bloomington: Indiana University Press, 1994.

Decker, Hannah. *Freud, Dora, and Vienna 1900.* New York: Free Press, 1990.

Degler, Carl N. *In Search of Human Nature: The Decline and Revival of Darwinism in American Social Thought.* New York: Oxford University Press, 1991.

Deutsch, Helene. *Psychoanalysis of the Sexual Functions of Women* (1925). Edited by Paul Roazen. Translated by Eric Mosbacher. London: Karnac, 1991.

———. *The Psychology of Women: A Psychoanalytic Interpretation,* 2 vols. New York: Grune and Stratton, 1944–1945.

———. *Neuroses and Character Types: Clinical Psychoanalytic Studies.* New York: International Universities Press, 1965.

———. *Selected Problems of Adolescence: With Special Emphasis on Group Formation.* The Psychoanalytic Study of the Child, Monograph no. 3. Madison, Conn.: International Universities Press, 1967.

———. *Confrontations with Myself: An Epilogue.* New York: Norton, 1973.

———. *The Therapeutic Process, the Self, and Female Psychology: Collected Psychoanalytic Papers.* Edited by Paul Roazen. Translated by Eric Mosbacher. New Brunswick, N.J.: Transaction, 1992.

Dimen, Muriel. "Deconstructing Difference: Gender, Splitting, and Transitional Space." *Psychoanalytic Dialogues* 1 (1991): 335–352.

Dinnerstein, Dorothy. *The Mermaid and the Minotaur: Sexual Arrangements and Human Malaise.* New York: Harper and Row, 1976.

Eckardt, Marianne Horney. "Feminine Psychology Revisited: A Historical Perspective." *The American Journal of Psychoanalysis* 51 (1991): 235–243.

Edgcumbe, Rose, and Marion Burgner. "The Phallic-Narcissistic Phase: A Differentiation between Preoedipal and Oedipal Aspects of Phallic Development." *The Psychoanalytic Study of the Child* 30 (1975): 161–180.

Eiseley, Loren. *Darwin's Century: Evolution and the Men Who Discovered It.* New York: Doubleday, 1958.

Eisenstein, Hester, and Alice Jardine, eds. *The Future of Difference.* Boston: G. K. Hall, 1980.

Elliot, Patricia. *From Mastery to Analysis: Theories of Gender in Psychoanalytic Feminism.* Ithaca, N.Y.: Cornell University Press, 1991.

Elmhirst, Susanna Isaacs. "The Early Stages of Female Psychosexual Development: A Kleinian View." In *Women's Sexual Development: Explorations of Inner Space,* edited by Martha Kirkpatrick. New York: Plenum, 1980.

Erikson, Erik H. *Childhood and Society.* New York: Norton, 1950. 2d, revised and enlarged ed. New York: Norton, 1963.

———. "The Dream Specimen of Psychoanalysis." *JAPA* 2 (1954): 5–56.

———. *Young Man Luther: A Study in Psychoanalysis and History.* New York: Norton, 1958.

———. *Identity and the Life Cycle.* Psychological Issues Monograph, no. 1. New York: International Universities Press, 1959. Reprint, New York: Norton, 1980.

———. "Inner and Outer Space: Reflections on Womanhood." *Daedalus* 93 (1964): 582–606.

———. *Insight and Responsibility: Lectures on the Ethical Implications of Psychoanalytic Insight.* New York: Norton, 1964.

———. *Identity: Youth and Crisis.* New York: Norton, 1968.

———. *Gandhi's Truth: On the Origins of Militant Nonviolence.* New York: Norton, 1969.

———. "Autobiographic Notes on the Identity Crisis." *Daedalus* 99 (1970): 730–759.

———. *Dimensions of a New Identity: The 1973 Jefferson Lectures in the Humanities.* New York: Norton, 1974.

———. "Once More the Inner Space: Letter to a Former Student." In *Women and Analysis: Dialogues on Psychoanalytic Views of Femininity,* edited by Jean Strouse. New York: Grossman, 1974.

———. *Life History and the Historical Moment.* New York: Norton, 1975.

———. *Toys and Reasons: Stages in the Ritualization of Experience.* New York: Norton, 1977.

———. "On the Generational Cycle." *IJP* 61 (1980): 213–223.

———. *The Life Cycle Complete: A Review.* New York: Norton, 1982.

———. *A Way of Looking at Things: Selected Papers from 1930–1980 Erik H. Erikson.* Edited by Stephen Schlein. New York: Norton, 1987.

Evans, Richard I. *Dialogue with Erik Erikson.* New York: Harper and Row, 1967.

Fairbairn, W. Ronald D. *Psychoanalytic Studies of the Personality.* London: Tavistock Publications and Routledge and Kegan Paul, 1952.

———. *From Instinct to Self: Selected Papers of W. R. D. Fairbairn.* Vol. 1, *Clinical and Theoretical Papers.* Edited by David E. Scharff and Ellinor Fairbairn Birtles. Vol. 2, *Applications and Early Contributions.* Edited by Ellinor Fairbairn Birtles and David E. Scharff. Northvale, N.J.: Jason Aronson, 1994.

Fast, Irene. *Gender Identity: A Differentiation Model.* Hillsdale, N.J.: Analytic Press, 1984.

Fausto-Sterling, Anne. *Myths of Gender: Biological Theories about Women and Men.* 2d ed. New York: Basic Books, 1992.

Feldstein, Richard, and Judith Roof, eds. *Feminism and Psychoanalysis.* Ithaca, N.Y.: Cornell University Press, 1989.

Ferenczi, Sándor. *Thalassa: A Theory of Genitality* (1924). Translated by Henry Alden Bunker. London: Karnac, Maresfield Library, 1989.

———. *First Contributions to Psycho-Analysis.* 2d ed. Translated by Ernest Jones. London: Hogarth 1950.

———. *Further Contributions to Psycho-Analysis.* 2d ed. Compiled by John Rickman. Translated by Jane Isabel Suttie. London: Hogarth, 1950.

———. *The Clinical Diary of Sándor Ferenczi.* Edited by Judith Dupont. Translated by

Michael Balint and Nicola Zarday Jackson. Cambridge, Mass.: Harvard University Press, 1988.

Fisher, David James. "Remembering Robert J. Stoller (1924–1991)." *Psychoanalytic Review* 83 (1996): 1–9.

Flax, Jane. *Thinking Fragments: Psychoanalysis, Feminism, and Postmodernism in the Contemporary West.* Berkeley : University of California Press, 1990.

Fleck, Ludwig. *Genesis and Development of a Scientific Fact.* Edited by Thaddeus J. Trenn and Robert K. Merton. Translated by Fred Bradley and Thaddeus J. Trenn. Chicago: University of Chicago Press, 1979.

Fliegel, Zenia Odes. "Feminine Psychosexual Development in Freudian Theory: A Historical Reconstruction." *The Psychoanalytic Quarterly* 42 (1973): 385–408.

———. "Half a Century Later: Current Status of Freud's Controversial Views On Women." *Psychoanalytic Review* 69 (1982): 7–28.

———. "Women's Development in Analytic Theory: Six Decades of Controversy." In *Psychoanalysis and Women: Contemporary Reappraisals,* edited by Judith L. Alpert. Hillsdale, N.J.: Analytic Press, 1986.

Frank, Claudia, and Heinz Weiß. "The Origins of Disquieting Discoveries by Melanie Klein: The Possible Significance of the Case of 'Erna.'" *IJP* 77 (1996): 1101–1126.

Freeman, Lucy, and Herbert S. Strean. *Freud and Women.* New York: Ungar, 1981.

Freud, Anna. *The Writings of Anna Freud.* Vol. 1, *Introduction to Psychoanalysis: Lectures for Child Analysts and Teachers* 1922–1935. New York: International Universities Press, 1974.

———. "Personal Memories of Ernest Jones." *IJP* 60 (1979): 285–290.

Freud, Sigmund. *Gesammelte Werke, Chronologisch Geordnet.* Edited by Anna Freud, Edward Bibring, Willi Hoffer, Ernst Kris, and Otto Isakower. Vols. 1–17. London: Imago Publishing Co., 1940–1952. Vol. 18. Frankfurt: S. Fischer, 1968.

———. *The Standard Edition of the Complete Psychological Works of Sigmund Freud.* 24 vols. Translated from the German under the General Editorship of James Strachey. London: Hogarth Press, 1953–1974.

———. *Psychoanalysis and Faith: The Letters of Sigmund Freud and Oskar Pfister.* Edited by Heinrich Meng and Ernst L. Freud. Translated by Eric Mosbacher. New York: Basic Books, 1963.

———. *A Psycho-Analytic Dialogue: The Letters of Sigmund Freud and Karl Abraham* 1907–1926. Edited by Hilda C. Abraham and Ernst L. Freud. Translated by Bernard Marsh and Hilda C. Abraham. New York: Basic Books, 1965.

———. *Letters of Sigmund Freud* 1873–1939. Edited by Ernst L. Freud. Translated by Tania Stern and James Stern. London: Hogarth Press, 1970.

———. *The Letters of Sigmund Freud and Arnold Zweig.* Edited by Ernst L. Freud. Translated by Elaine and William Robson-Scott. New York: New York University Press, 1970.

———. *Sigmund Freud and Lou Andreas-Salomé: Letters.* Edited by Ernst Pfeiffer. Translated by Elaine and William Robson-Scott. London: Hogarth Press, 1970.

———. *The Freud/Jung Letters: The Correspondence between Sigmund Freud and C. G. Jung.* Edited by William McGuire. Translated by Ralph Manheim and R. F. C. Hull. Princeton, N.J.: Princeton University Press, 1974.

————. *L'Homme aux rats: Journal d'une analyse.* Translated by Elza Riberio Hawalka. Paris: Presses Universitaires de France, 1974.

————. *The Complete Letters of Sigmund Freud to Wilhelm Fliess* 1887–1904. Translated and edited by Jeffrey Moussaiff Masson. Cambridge, Mass.: Harvard University Press, 1985.

————. *A Phylogenetic Fantasy: An Overview of the Transference Neuroses.* Edited by Ilse Grubich-Simitis. Translated by Axel Hoffer and Peter T. Hoffer. Cambridge, Mass.: Harvard University Press, 1987.

————. *The Letters of Sigmund Freud to Eduard Silberstein* 1871–1881. Edited by Walter Boehlich. Translated by Arnold J. Pomerans. Cambridge, Mass.: Harvard University Press, 1990.

————. *The Complete Correspondence of Sigmund Freud and Ernest Jones* 1908–1939. Edited by R. Andrew Paskauskas. Cambridge, Mass.: Harvard University Press, 1993.

————. *The Correspondence of Sigmund Freud and Sándor Ferenczi.* Vol. 1, 1908–1914. Edited by Eva Brabant, Ernst Falzeder, and Patrizia Giampieri-Deutsch. Translated by Peter T. Hoffer. Vol. 2, 1914–1919. Edited by Ernst Falzeder and Eva Brabant, with the collaboration of Patrizia Giampieri-Deutsch. Translated by Peter T. Hoffer. Cambridge, Mass.: Harvard University Press, 1994–1996.

Friedan, Betty. *The Feminine Mystique.* New York: Norton, 1963.

Friedman, Richard C. *Male Homosexuality: A Contemporary Psychoanalytic Perspective.* New Haven: Yale University Press, 1988.

Fuss, Diana. *Essentially Speaking: Feminism, Nature, and Difference.* New York: Routledge, 1989.

Gallop, Jane. *The Daughter's Seduction: Feminism and Psychoanalysis.* London: Macmillan, 1982.

Garber, Marjorie. *Vested Interests: Cross-Dressing and Cultural Anxiety.* New York: Routledge, 1992.

Garfinkel, Harold. *Studies in Ethnomethodology.* Englewood Cliffs, N.J.: Prentice-Hall, 1967.

Garner, Shirley N., Claire Kahane, and Madelon Sprengnether, eds. *The (M)other Tongue: Essays in Feminist Psychoanalytic Interpretation.* Ithaca, N.Y.: Cornell University Press, 1985.

Garrison, Dee. "Karen Horney and Feminism." *Signs* 6 (1981): 672–691.

Gay, Peter. *Freud: A Life for Our Time.* New York: Norton, 1988.

Gedo, John E., and Arnold Goldberg. *Models of the Mind: A Psychoanalytic Theory.* Chicago: University of Chicago Press, 1973.

Geertz, Clifford. *The Interpretation of Culture: Selected Essays.* New York: Basic Books, 1973.

————. *Local Knowledge: Further Essays in Interpretative Anthrology.* New York: Basic Books, 1983.

————. *Works and Lives: The Anthropologist as Author.* Stanford, Calif.: Stanford University Press, 1988.

Ghiselin, Michael T. *The Triumph of the Darwinian Method.* Berkeley: University of California Press, 1969.

————. *The Economy of Nature and the Evolution of Sex.* Berkeley: University of California Press, 1974.

Gillespie, William H. "Ernest Jones: The Bonny Fighter." *IJP* 60 (1979): 273–279.

Gilligan, Carol. "In a Different Voice: Women's Conceptions of Self and Morality." *Harvard Educational Review* 47 (1977): 481–517.

———. *In a Different Voice: Psychological Theory and Women's Development*. Cambridge, Mass: Harvard University Press, 1982.

———. "The Conquistador and the Dark Continent: Reflections on the Psychology of Love." *Daedalus* 113 (1984): 75–95.

———. "Remapping the Moral Domain: New Images of the Self in Relationship." In *Reconstructing Individualism: Autonomy, Individuality, and the Self in Western Thought*, edited by Thomas C. Heller, Morton Sosna, and David E. Wellbery. Stanford, Calif.: Stanford University Press, 1986.

Gilligan, Carol, and Mary Field Belenky. "A Naturalistic Study of Abortion Decisions." In *Clinical-Developmental Psychology*, edited by Robert L. Selman and Regina Yando. New Directions for Child Development, no. 7. San Francisco: Jossey-Bass, 1980.

Gilligan, Carol, Nona P. Lyons, and Trudy J. Hanmer, eds. *Making Connections: The Relational Worlds of Adolescent Girls at Emma Willard School*. Cambridge, Mass: Harvard University Press, 1990.

Gilligan, Carol, and John Michael Murphy. "Development from Adolescence to Adulthood: The Philosopher and the Dilemma of the Fact." In *Intellectual Development Beyond Childhood*, edited by Deanna Kuhn. New Directions for Child Development, no. 5. San Francisco: Jossey-Bass, 1979.

Gilligan, Carol, Janie Victoria Ward, and Jill McLean Taylor, eds. *Mapping the Moral Domain: A Contribution of Women's Thinking to Psychological Theory and Education*. Cambridge, Mass.: Harvard University Press, 1988.

Glick, Thomas F., ed. *The Comparative Reception of Darwinism*. Chicago: University of Chicago Press, 1974.

Glover, Edward. Review of *The Psychoanalysis of Children*, by Melanie Klein. *IJP* 14 (1933): 119–129.

———. "Examination of the Klein System of Child Psychology." *The Psychoanalytic Study of the Child* 1 (1945): 75–118.

———. "The Position of Psycho-Analysis in Britain." *British Medical Bulletin* 6 (1949): 27–31. (Also published in Edward Glover. *On the Early Development of Mind*, 352–363. London: Imago Publishing Co., 1956.)

———. "Psychoanalysis in England." In *Psychoanalytic Pioneers*, edited by Franz Alexander, Samuel Eisenstein, and Martin Grotjahn. New York: Basic Books, 1966.

Goldenberg, Naomi R. *Returning Words to Flesh: Feminism, Psychoanalysis, and the Resurrection of the Body*. Boston: Beacon Press, 1990.

Goldner, Virginia. "Toward a Critical Relational Theory of Gender." *Psychoanalytic Dialogues* 1 (1991): 249–272.

Gould, Stephen Jay. *Ever Since Darwin: Reflections in Natural History*. New York: Norton, 1977.

———. *Ontogeny and Phylogeny*. Cambridge, Mass.: Harvard University Press, 1977.

———. *The Mismeasure of Man*. New York: Norton, 1981.

Graubard, Stephen R. Preface to "The Woman in America." *Daedalus* 93 (1964): 579–581.

Green, Richard. *The "Sissy Boy Syndrome" and the Development of Homosexuality*. New Haven: Yale University Press, 1987.

Green, Richard, Lawrence E. Newman, and Robert J. Stoller. "Treatment of Boyhood 'Transsexualism': An Interim Report of Four Years' Experience." *Archives of General Psychiatry* 26 (1972): 213–217.

Green, Richard, and Robert J. Stoller. "Two Monozygotic (Identical) Twin Pairs Discordant for Gender Identity." *Archives of Sexual Behavior* 1 (1971): 321–327.

Greenacre, Phyllis. "Special Problems of Early Female Sexual Development." *The Psychoanalytic Study of the Child* 5 (1950): 122–138.

———. "Early Physical Determinants in the Development of the Sense of Identity." *JAPA* 6 (1958): 612–627.

Greenberg, Jay R., and Stephen A. Mitchell. *Object Relations in Psychoanalytic Theory*. Cambridge, Mass.: Harvard University Press, 1983.

Greene, John C. *The Death of Adam: Evolution and Its Impact on Western Thought*. Ames: Iowa State University Press, 1959.

———. *Science, Ideology, and World View: Essays in the History of Evolutionary Ideas*. Berkeley: University of California Press, 1981.

Greenson, Ralph R. "On Homosexuality and Gender Identity." *IJP* 45 (1964): 217–219.

———. "A Transvestite Boy and a Hypothesis." *IJP* 47 (1966): 396.

———. *The Technique and Practice of Psychoanalysis*. Vol. 1. New York: International Universities Press, 1967.

———. "Dis-identifying from Mother: Its Special Importance for the Boy." *IJP* 49 (1968): 370–373.

———. "Transference: Freud or Klein." *IJP* 55 (1974): 37–48.

Greer, Germaine. *The Female Eunuch*. London: Paladin Grafton Books, 1970.

Grene, Marjorie, and Everett Mendelsohn, eds. *Topics in the Philosophy of Biology*. Boston Studies in the Philosophy of Science, no. 27. Dordrecht, Holland: D. Reidl Publishing Company, 1976.

Griffin, B. C., and N. Mullins. "Coherent Social Groups in Scientific Change." *Science* 177 (1972): 959–964.

Groddeck, Georg W. *The Book of the It*. Translated by V. M. E. Collins. London: Vision Press, 1949.

Gross, Alan G. *The Rhetoric of Science*. Cambridge, Mass.: Harvard University Press, 1990.

Grosskurth, Phyllis. *Melanie Klein: Her World and Her Work*. New York: Knopf, 1986.

———. *The Secret Ring: Freud's Inner Circle and the Politics of Psychoanalysis*. Reading, Mass.: Addison-Wesley, 1991.

Grossman, William I. "Freud and Horney: A Study of Psychoanalytic Models via the Analysis of a Controversy." In *Psychoanalysis, the Science of Mental Conflict: Essays in Honor of Charles Brenner*, edited by Arnold D. Richards and Martin S. Willick. Hillsdale, N.J.: Analytic Press, 1986.

Grossman, William I., and Walter A. Stewart. "Penis Envy: From Childhood Wish to Developmental Metaphor." *JAPA* 24 (Supplement) (1976): 193–212.

Grosz, Elizabeth. *Volatile Bodies: Toward a Corporeal Feminism*. Bloomington: Indiana University Press, 1994.

Grotstein, James. "The Significance of Kleinian Contributions to Psychoanalysis I. Kleinian Instinct Theory." *International Journal of Psychoanalytic Psychotherapy* 8 (1980–1981): 375–392.

———. "The Significance of Kleinian Contributions to Psychoanalysis II. Freudian and Kleinian Conceptions of Early Mental Development." *International Journal of Psychoanalytic Psychotherapy.* 8 (1980–1981): 393–428.

———. "The Significance of Kleinian Contributions to Psychoanalysis III. The Kleinian Theory of Ego Psychology and Object Relations." *International Journal of Psychoanalytic Psychotherapy* 9 (1982–1983): 487–510.

———. "The Significance of Kleinian Contributions to Psychoanalysis IV. Critiques of Klein." *International Journal of Psychoanalytic Psychotherapy* 9 (1982–1983): 511–535.

———. Review of *Reshaping the Psychoanalytic Domain: The Work of Melanie Klein, W. R. D. Fairbairn, and D. W. Winnicott,* by Judith M. Hughes. *The Psychoanalytic Quarterly* 60 (1991): 136–140.

Grotstein, James, and Donald B. Rinsley, eds. *Fairbairn and the Origins of Object Relations.* New York: Guilford, 1994.

Guntrip, Harry. *Personality Structure and Human Interaction: The Developing Synthesis of Psychodynamic Theory.* London: Hogarth Press, 1961.

———. Schizoid Phenomena, Object-Relations and the Self. London: Hogarth Press; New York: International Universities Press, 1968.

———. *Psychoanalytic Theory, Therapy, and the Self.* New York: Basic Books, 1971. Reprint, London: H. Karnac, Maresfield Reprints, 1977.

Hacking, Ian. *Rewriting the Soul: Multiple Personality and the Sciences of Memory.* Princeton, N.J.: Princeton University Press, 1995.

Hale, Nathan G. Jr. *Freud in America.* Vol. 1, *Freud and the Americans: The Beginnings of Psychoanalysis in the United States, 1876–1917.* Vol. 2, *The Rise and Crisis of Psychoanalysis in the United States: Freud and the Americans, 1917–1985.* New York: Oxford University Press, 1971–1995.

———, ed. *James Jackson Putnam and Psychoanalysis: Letters between Putnam and Sigmund Freud, Ernest Jones, William James, Sándor Ferenczi, and Morton Prince, 1877–1917.* Cambridge, Mass.: Harvard University Press, 1971.

Haraway, Donna J. *Simians, Cyborgs, and Women: The Reinvention of Nature.* New York: Routledge, 1991.

Harris, Adrienne. "Gender as Contradiction: A Discussion of Freud's 'Psychogenesis of a Case of Homosexuality in a Woman.'" *Psychoanalytic Dialogues* 1 (1991): 197–224.

Hartmann, Heinz. *Essays on Ego Psychology: Selected Problems in Psychoanalytic Theory.* New York: International Universities Press, 1964.

Hausman, Bernice L. *Changing Sex: Transsexualism, Technology, and the Idea of Gender.* Durham, N.C.: Duke University Press, 1995.

Heath, Stephen. "Joan Riviere and the Masquerade." In *Formations of Fantasy,* edited by Victor Burgin, James Donald, and Cora Kaplan. London: Methuen, 1986.

Heilbrun, Carolyn G. *Writing a Woman's Life.* New York: Ballantine, 1988.

Herdt, Gilbert, and Robert J. Stoller. *Intimate Communications: Erotics and the Study of Culture.* New York: Columbia University Press, 1990.

Hirsch, Marianne. *The Mother/Daughter Plot: Narrative, Psychoanalysis, Feminism.* Bloomington: Indiana University Press, 1989.

Horney, Karen. Review of *Zur Psychologie der weiblichen Sexualfunktionen,* by Helene Deutsch, *IJP* 7 (1926): 92–100.

———. "Der Männlichkeitskomplex der Frau." *Archiv für Frauenkunde* 13 (1927): 152–153.

———. "Culture and Neurosis." *American Sociological Review* 1 (1936): 221–235.

———. "The Problem of the Negative Therapeutic Reaction." *The Psychoanalytic Quarterly* 5 (1936): 29–45.

———. *The Neurotic Personality of Our Time.* New York: Norton, 1937.

———. *New Ways in Psychoanalysis.* New York: Norton, 1939.

———. *Self-Analysis.* New York: Norton, 1942.

———. *Our Inner Conflicts.* New York: Norton, 1945.

———. *Neurosis and Human Growth: The Struggle Toward Self-Realization.* New York: Norton, 1950.

———. *Feminine Psychology.* New York: Norton, 1967.

———. *The Adolescent Diaries of Karen Horney.* New York: Basic Books, 1980.

———. *Final Lectures.* Edited by Douglas H. Ingram. New York: Norton, 1987.

Hrdy, Sarah Blaffer. *The Woman That Never Evolved.* Cambridge, Mass.: Harvard University Press, 1981.

Hubbard, Ruth, Mary Sue Henifin, and Barbara Fried, eds. *Women Look at Biology Looking at Women: A Collection of Feminist Critiques.* Cambridge, Mass.: Schenkman, 1979.

Hughes, H. Stuart. *The Sea Change: The Migration of Social Thought* 1930–1965. New York: Harper and Row, 1975.

———. *Gentleman Rebel: The Memoirs of H. Stuart Hughes.* New York: Ticknor and Fields, 1990.

Hughes, Judith M. *Emotion and High Politics: Personal Relations at the Summit in Late Nineteenth-Century Britain and Germany.* Berkeley: University of California Press, 1983.

———. *Reshaping the Psychoanalytic Domain: The Work of Melanie Klein, W. R. D. Fairbairn, and D. W. Winnicott.* Berkeley University of California Press, 1989.

———. "Psychoanalysis as a General Psychology, Revisited." *Free Associations* No. 23 (1991): 357–370.

———. *From Freud's Consulting Room: The Unconscious in a Scientific Age.* Cambridge, Mass.: Harvard University Press, 1994.

———. "Another 'Impossible' Profession?" *The Psychohistory Review* 25 (1997): 119–126.

Hull, David L. *Philosophy of Biological Science.* Englewood Cliffs, N.J.: Prentice-Hall, 1974.

———. *Science as a Process: An Evolutionary Account of the Social and Conceptual Development of Science.* Chicago: University of Chicago Press, 1988.

Hunter, Dianne. "Hysteria, Psychoanalysis, and Feminism: The Case of Anna O." *Feminist Studies* 9 (1983): 465–488.

Irigaray, Luce. *Speculum of the Other Woman.* Translated by Gillian C. Gill. Ithaca, N.Y.: Cornell University Press, 1985.

———. *This Sex Which Is Not One.* Translated by Catherine Porter. Ithaca, N.Y.: Cornell University Press, 1985.

Israëls, Han. *Schreber: Father and Son.* Translated by H. S. Lake. Madison, Conn.: International Universities Press, 1989.

Jacobson, Edith. *The Self and the Object World.* New York: International Universities Press, 1964.

Janeway, Elizabeth. *Man's World, Woman's Place: A Study in Social Mythology.* New York: Morrow, 1971.

Joffe, Walter. "A Critical Review of the Status of the Envy Concept." *IJP* 50 (1969): 533–545.

Johnson, Miriam M. *Strong Mothers, Weak Wives: The Search for Gender Equality.* Berkeley:University of California Press, 1988.

Johnston, William M. *The Austrian Mind: An Intellectual and Social History* 1848–1938. Berkeley: University of California Press, 1972.

Jones, Ernest. "The Origin and Structure of the Super-Ego." *IJP* 7 (1926): 303–311.

———. Introductory Memoir to *Selected Papers of Karl Abraham.* Translated by Douglas Bryan and Alix Strachey. London: Hogarth Press, 1927. Reprint, London: H. Karnac, Maresfield Reprints, 1979.

———. "The Future of Psycho-Analysis." *IJP* 17 (1936): 269–277.

———. Review of *The Neurotic Personality of Our Time,* by Karen Horney. *IJP* 21 (1940): 240–241.

———. "A Valedictory Address." IJP 27 (1946): 7–12.

———. *Papers on Psycho-Analysis.* 5th ed. London: Baillière, Tindall and Cox, 1948. Reprint, London: H. Karnac, Maresfield Reprints, 1977.

———. *The Life and Work of Sigmund Freud.* Vol. 1, *The Formative Years and the Great Discoveries* 1856–1900. Vol. 2, *Years of Maturity* 1901–1919. Vol. 3, *The Last Phase* 1919–1939. New York: Basic Books, 1953–1957.

———. *Free Associations: Memories of a Psycho-Analyst.* New York: Basic Books 1959.

Jones, Katherine. "A Sketch of E. J.'s Personality." *IJP* 60 (1979): 271–273.

Kaye, Kenneth. *The Mental and Social Life of Babies: How Parents Create Persons.* Chicago: University of Chicago Press, 1982.

Keller, Evelyn Fox. *Reflections on Gender and Science.* New Haven: Yale University Press, 1985.

Kelly, Alfred. *The Descent of Darwin: The Popularization of Darwinism in Germany,* 1860–1914. Chapel Hill: University of North Carolina Press, 1981.

Kerber, Linda K., Catherine G. Greeno and Eleanor E. Maccoby, Zella Luria, Carol B. Stack, and Carol Gilligan, "On *In a Different Voice:* An Interdisciplinary Forum," *Signs* 11 (1986): 304–333.

Kern, Stephen. *Anatomy and Destiny: A Cultural History of the Human Body.* Indianapolis: Bobbs-Merrill, 1975.

Kernberg, Otto, F. "A Contribution to the Ego-Psychological Critique of the Kleinian School." *IJP* 50 (1969): 317–333.

———. *Object Relations Theory and Clinical Psychoanalysis.* New York: Jason Aronson, 1976.

———. *Internal World and External Reality: Object Relations Theory Applied.* New York: Jason Aronson, 1980.

———. "Identification and Its Vicissitudes as Observed in Psychosis." *IJP* 67 (1986): 147–159.

Kerr, John. *A Most Dangerous Method: The Story of Jung, Freud, and Sabina Spielrein.* New York: Knopf, 1993.

Kessler, Suzanne J. "The Medical Construction of Gender: Case Management of Intersexed Infants." *Signs* 16 (1990): 3–26.

Kessler, Suzanne J., and Wendy McKenna. *Gender: An Ethnomethological Approach.* Chicago: University of Chicago Press, 1978.

Kestenberg, Judith S. "On the Development of Maternal Feelings in Early Childhood." *The Psychoanalytic Study of the Child* 11 (1956): 257–291.

————. "Vicissitudes of Female Sexuality." *JAPA* 4 (1956): 453–476.

————. "Outside and Inside, Male and Female." *JAPA* 16 (1968): 457–519.

————. "Regression and Reintegration in Pregnancy." *JAPA* 24 (Supplement) (1976): 213–250.

————. "The Inner-Genital Phase—Prephallic and Preoedipal." In *Early Female Development,* edited by Dale Mendell. New York: Spectrum, 1982.

Khan, M. Masud R. "Mrs Alix Strachey." *IJP* 54 (1973): 370.

————. *Privacy of the Self: Papers on Psychoanalytic Theory and Technique.* London: Hogarth Press; New York: International Universities Press, 1974.

————. *Alienation in Perversions.* London: Hogarth, 1979.

————. *Hidden Selves: Between Theory and Practice in Psychoanalysis.* London: Hogarth Press, 1983.

King, Pearl H. M. "The Contributions of Ernest Jones to the British Psycho-Analytical Society." *IJP* 60 (1979): 280–284.

————. "The Education of a Psycho-Analyst." Scientific Bulletin, The British Psycho-Analytical Society (February 1981): 1–20.

————. "Identity Crises: Splits or Compromises—Adaptive or Maladaptive." In *The Identity of the Psychoanalyst,* edited by Edward D. Joseph and Daniel Widlöcher. International Psycho-Analytical Association Monographs, no. 2. New York: International Universities Press, 1983.

————. "The Life and Work of Melanie Klein in the British Psycho-Analytical Society." *IJP* 64 (1983): 251–260.

King, Pearl H. M., and Riccardo Steiner, eds. *The Freud-Klein Controversies* 1941–45. London: Routledge, 1991.

Kitcher, Philip. *Vaulting Ambition: Sociobiology and the Quest for Human Nature.* Cambridge, Mass.: MIT Press, 1985.

Kleeman, James A. "Freud's Views on Early Female Sexuality in the Light of Direct Child Observation." *JAPA* 24 (Supplement) (1976): 3–27.

Klein, Melanie. *The Writings of Melanie Klein.* Vol. 1, *Love, Guilt and Reparation and Other Works* 1921–1945. Vol. 2, *The Psycho-Analysis of Children.* Vol. 3, *Envy and Gratitude and Other Works* 1946–1963. Vol. 4, *Narrative of a Child Analysis: The Conduct of the Psychoanalysis of Children as Seen in the Treatment of a Ten-year-old Boy.* Under the general editorship of Roger Money-Kyrle, in collaboration with Betty Joseph, Edna O'Shaughnessy, and Hanna Segal. London: Hogarth Press, 1975.

Klein, Melanie, Paula Heimann, Susan Isaacs, and Joan Riviere. *Developments in Psycho-Analysis.* London: Hogarth Press, 1952.

Klein, Melanie, Paula Heimann, and R. E. Money-Kyrle, eds. *New Directions in Psycho-Analysis: The Significance of Infant Conflict in the Pattern of Adult Behaviour.* London:

Tavistock Publications, 1955. Reprint, London: H. Karnac, Maresfield Reprints, 1977.

Klein, Melanie, Joan Riviere, M. N. Searl, Ella F. Sharpe, Edward Glover, and Ernest Jones. "Symposium on Child-Analysis." *IJP* 8 (1927): 331–391.

Kofman, Sarah. *The Enigma of Women: Woman in Freud's Writings.* Translated by Catherine Porter. Ithaca, N.Y.: Cornell University Press, 1985.

Kohlberg, Lawrence, and Carol Gilligan. "The Adolescent as Philosopher: The Discovery of the Self in a Postconventional World." *Daedalus* 100 (1971): 1051–1086.

Kohn, David, ed. *The Darwinian Heritage.* Princeton, N.J.: Princeton University Press, 1985.

Kohon, Gregorio, ed. *The British School of Psychoanalysis: The Independent Tradition.* London: Free Association Books, 1986.

Kris, Anton O. "Freud's Treatment of a Narcissistic Patient." *IJP* 75 (1994): 649–664.

Kuhn, Thomas S. *The Structure of Scientific Revolutions.* 2d ed. Chicago: University of Chicago Press, 1970.

———. *The Essential Tension: Selected Studies in Scientific Tradition and Change.* Chicago: University of Chicago Press, 1977.

Kurzweil, Edith. *Freudians and Feminists.* Boulder, Colo.: Westview Press, 1995.

Kushner, Howard I. "Taking Erikson's Identity Seriously: Psychoanalyzing the Psychohistorian." *The Psychohistory Review* 22 (1993): 7–34.

Lakatos, Imre, and Alan Musgrave, eds. *Criticism and the Growth of Knowledge.* Cambridge: Cambridge University Press, 1970.

Lampl de Groot, Jeanne. *Man and Mind: Collected Papers.* New York: International Universities Press, 1985.

Laplanche, Jean. *New Foundations for Psychoanalysis.* Translated by David Macey. Oxford: Basil Blackwell, 1989.

Laplanche, Jean, and J.-B. Pontalis. "Fantasy and the Origins of Sexuality." *IJP* 49 (1968): 1–18.

———. *The Language of Psycho-Analysis.* Translated by Donald Nicholson-Smith. London: Hogarth Press, 1980.

Laqueur, Thomas. *Making Sex: Body and Gender from the Greeks to Freud.* Cambridge, Mass.: Harvard University Press, 1990.

Larrabee, Mary Jeanne, ed. *An Ethic of Care: Feminist and Interdisciplinary Perspectives.* New York: Routledge, 1993.

Lerman, Hannah. *A Mote in Freud's Eye: From Psychoanalysis to the Psychology of Women.* New York: Springer, 1986.

Lerner, Harriet E. "Parental Mislabeling of Female Genitals as a Determinant of Penis Envy and Learning Inhibitions in Women." *JAPA* 24 (Supplement) (1976): 269–283.

Lewes, Kenneth. *The Psychoanalytic Theory of Male Homosexuality.* New York: Simon and Schuster, 1988.

Leys, Ruth. "The Real Miss Beauchamp: Gender and the Subject of Imitation." In *Feminists Theorize the Political,* edited by Judith Butler and Joan W. Scott. New York: Routledge, 1992.

Limentani, Adam. "The Significance of Transsexualism in Relation to Some Basic Psychoanalytic Concepts." *IJP* 6 (1979): 139–153.

Lindon, John A. "Melanie Klein's Theory and Technique: Her Life and Work." In *Tactics and Techniques in Psychoanalytic Therapy*, edited by Peter L. Giovacchini. New York: Science House; London: Hogarth Press, 1972.

Litwin, Dorothy. "Autonomy: A Conflict in Women." In *Psychoanalysis and Women: Contemporary Reappraisals*, edited by Judith L. Alpert. Hillsdale, N.J.: Analytic Press, 1986.

Loeb, Loretta, and Morton Shane. "The Resolution of a Transsexual Wish in a Five-Year-Old Boy." *JAPA* 30 (1982): 419–434.

Loewald, Hans. *Papers on Psychoanalysis*. New Haven: Yale University Press, 1980.

Lorber, Judith, Rose Laub Coser, Alice S. Rossi, and Nancy Chodorow. "On *The Reproduction of Mothering*: A Methodological Debate." *Signs* 6 (1981): 482–514.

Lothane, Zvi. *In Defense of Schreber: Soul Murder and Psychiatry*. Hillsdale, N.J.: Analytic Press, 1992.

MacKay, Nigel. "Melanie Klein's Metapsychology: Phenomenological and Mechanistic Perspective." *IJP* 62 (1981): 187–198.

Mahler, Margaret, Fred Pine, and Anni Bergman. *The Psychological Birth of the Human Infant: Symbiosis and Individuation*. New York: Basic Books, 1975.

Mahony, Patrick J. *Freud as a Writer*. Expanded edition. New Haven: Yale University Press, 1987.

———. *On Defining Freud's Discourse*. New Haven: Yale University Press, 1989.

———. *Freud's Dora: A Psychoanalytic, Historical, and Textual Study*. New Haven: Yale University Press, 1996.

Marcus, Steven. *Freud and the Culture of Psychoanalysis: Studies in the Transition from Victorian Humanism to Modernity*. New York: Norton, 1984.

Marx, Karl. "Theses on Fuerbach" (1888). In *Karl Marx and Frederick Engels: Selected Works*. Moscow: Progress Publishers, 1968.

Marx, Karl, and Frederick Engels. *Manifesto of the Communist Party* (1848). In *Karl Marx and Frederick Engels: Selected Works*. Moscow: Progress Publishers, 1968.

Mayer, Elizabeth Lloyd. "'Everybody Must Be Just Like Me': Observations on Female Castration Anxiety." *IJP* 66 (1985): 331–347.

———. "The Phallic Castration Complex and Primary Femininity: Paired Developmental Lines Toward Female Gender Identity." *JAPA* 43 (1995): 17–38.

Mayr, Ernst. *The Growth of Biological Thought: Diversity, Evolution, and Inheritance*. Cambridge, Mass.: Harvard University Press, 1982.

McDougall, Joyce. *Plea for a Measure of Abnormality*. New York: International Universities Press, 1978.

———. *Theaters of the Mind: Illusion and Truth on the Psychoanalytic Stage*. New York: Basic Books, 1985.

———. "Identifications, Neoneeds and Neosexualities." *IJP* 67 (1986): 19–31.

———. "The Dead Father: On Early Psychic Trauma and Its Relation to Disturbance in Sexual Identity and in Creative Activity." *IJP* 70 (1989): 205–219.

———. *Theatres of the Body: A Psychoanalytic Approach to Psychosomatic Illness*. London: Free Association Books. 1989.

———. "Sexual Identity, Trauma, and Creativity." *Psychoanalytic Inquiry* 11 (1991): 559–581.

Meisel, Perry, and Kendrick, Walter, eds. *Bloomsbury/Freud: The Letters of James and Alix Strachey* 1924–1925. New York: Basic Books, 1985.

Meltzer, Donald. *The Kleinian Development: Part I, Freud's Clinical Development (Method-Data-Therapy).* Perthshire: Clunie Press, 1978.

———. *The Kleinian Development: Part II, Richard Week-by-Week.* Perthshire: Clunie Press, 1978.

———. "The Kleinian Expansion of Freud's Metapsychology." *IJP* 62 (1981): 177–185.

Meltzer, Françoise, ed. *The Trial(s) of Psychoanalysis.* Chicago: University of Chicago Press, 1988.

Mendez, Anita M., and Harold J. Fine, with comments by Harry Guntrip, "A Short History of the British School of Object Relations and Ego Psychology." *Bulletin of the Menninger Clinic* 40 (1976): 357–382.

Merck, Mandy. "The Train of Thought in Freud's 'Case of Homosexuality in a Women.'" *m/f* 11/12 (1986): 35–46.

Miller, Jean Baker. *Toward a New Psychology of Women.* Boston: Beacon Press, 1976.

Miller, Nancy K., ed. *The Poetics of Gender.* New York: Columbia University Press, 1986.

Millett, Kate. *Sexual Politics.* New York: Doubleday, 1970.

Milner, Marion. *The Suppressed Madness of Sane Men: Forty-Four Years of Exploring Psychoanalysis.* London: Tavistock, 1987.

Mitchell, Juliet. *Psychoanalysis and Feminism: Freud, Reich, Laing and Women.* New York: Pantheon, 1974.

———. Review of The Transsexual Experiment, Vol. 2 of *Sex and Gender,* by Robert Stoller. *IJP* 57 (1976): 357–360.

———. Introduction 1 to *Feminine Sexuality: Jacques Lacan and the école freudienne,* edited by Juliet Mitchell and Jacqueline Rose. New York: Norton, 1982.

———. *Women: The Longest Revolution.* New York: Pantheon, 1984.

Mitchell, Stephen A. "The Origin and Nature of the 'Object' in the Theories of Klein and Fairbairn." *Contemporary Psychoanalysis 17* (1981): 374–398.

Money, John. "Hermaphroditism, Gender and Precocity in Hyperadrenocortism: Psychologic Findings." *Bulletin of Johns Hopkins Hospital* 96 (1955): 253–264.

Money, John, Joan G. Hampson, and John L. Hampson. "Hermaphroditism: Recommendations Concerning Assignment of Sex, Change of Sex, and Psychologic Management." *Bulletin of Johns Hopkins Hospital* 97 (1955): 284–300.

Money, John, Joan G. Hampson, and John L. Hampson. "An Examination of Some Basic Sexual Concepts: The Evidence of Human Hermaphroditism." *Bulletin of Johns Hopkins Hospital* 97 (1955): 301–319.

Money, John, Joan G. Hampson, and John L. Hampson. "Imprinting and the Establishment of Gender Role." *American Medical Association: Archives of Neurology and Psychiatry* 77 (1957): 333–336.

Money-Kyrle, Roger E. "Melanie Klein and Kleinian Psychoanalytic Theory." In *American Handbook of Psychiatry,* edited by Silvano Arieti, vol. 3. New York: Basic Books, 1966.

Moulton, Ruth. "Early Papers on Women: Horney to Thompson." *The American Journal of Psychoanalysis* 35 (1975): 207–223.

Müller, Josine. "A Contribution to the Problem of Libidinal Development in the Genital Phase in Girls." *IJP* 13 (1932): 362–368.

Müller-Braunschweig, Carl. "Genesis of the Feminine Superego." *IJP* 7 (1926): 359–362.

Nash, Christopher, ed. *Narrative in Culture: The Uses of Storytelling in the Sciences, Philosophy, and Literature.* London: Routledge, 1990.

Newman, Lawrence E., and Robert J. Stoller. "The Oedipal Situation in Male Transsexualism." *The British Journal of Medical Psychology* 44 (1971): 295–303.

Nicholson, Linda J., ed. *Feminism/Postmodernism.* New York: Routledge, 1990.

Niederland, William G. *The Schreber Case: Psychoanalytic Profile of a Paranoid Personality.* New York: Quadrangle/New York Times, 1974.

Ogden, Thomas H. *The Matrix of the Mind: Object Relations and the Psychoanalytic Dialogue.* Northvale, N.J.: Jason Aronson, 1986.

———. "The Transitional Oedipal Relationship in Female Development." *IJP* 68 (1987): 485–498.

Ophuijsen, J. H. W. "Contributions to the Masculinity Complex in Women." *IJP* 5 (1924): 39–49.

Oppenheimer, Agnès. "The Wish for a Sex Change: A Challenge to Psychoanalysis?" *IJP* 72 (1991): 221–231.

Ortner, Sherry B. *Making Gender: The Politics and Erotics of Culture.* Boston: Beacon Press, 1996.

Ospovat, Dov. *The Development of Darwin's Theory: Natural History, Natural Theology, and Natural Selection, 1838–1859.* Cambridge: Cambridge University Press, 1981.

Padel, John. "Positions, Stages, Attitudes, or Modes of Being?" *Bulletin of the European Psycho-Analytic Federation* 12 (1978): 26–31.

Paris, Bernard J. *Karen Horney: A Psychoanalyst's Search for Self-Understanding.* New Haven: Yale University Press, 1994.

Payne, Sylvia. "The Concept of Femininity." *The British Journal of Medical Psychology* 15 (1935): 18–33.

Person, Ethel S., and Lionel Oversey. "Psychoanalytic Theories of Gender Identity." *Journal of the American Academy of Psychoanalysis* 11 (1983): 203–226.

Petot, Jean-Michel. *Melanie Klein.* Vol. 1, *First Discoveries and First System 1919–1932.* Vol. 2, *The Ego and the Good Object 1932–1960.* Translated by Christine Trollope. Madison, Conn.: International Universities Press, 1990–1991.

Pines, Dinora. *A Woman's Unconscious Use of Her Body: A Psychoanalytical Perspective.* London: Virago, 1993.

Popper, Karl R. "Philosophy of Science: A Personal Report." In *British Philosophy in the Mid-Century,* edited by C. Mace. London: Allen and Unwin, 1957.

———. *Conjectures and Refutations: The Growth of Scientific Knowledge.* 2d ed. London: Routledge and Kegan Paul, 1965.

Quinn, Susan. *A Mind of Her Own: The Life of Karen Horney.* New York: Summit Books, 1987.

Radó, Sándor. "Fear of Castration in Women." *The Psychoanalytic Quarterly* 2 (1933): 425–475.

Rich, Adrienne. *Of Women Born: Motherhood as Experience and Institution.* New York: Norton, 1976.

———. "Compulsive Heterosexuality and Lesbian Existence." *Signs* 5 (1980): 631–660.

Richards, Robert J. *Darwin and the Emergence of Evolutionary Theories of Mind and Behavior.* Chicago: University of Chicago Press, 1987.

Ridley, Matt. *The Red Queen: Sex and the Evolution of Human Nature.* New York: Viking, 1994.

Ringer, Fritz K. *The Decline of the German Mandarins: The German Academic Community, 1890–1933.* Cambridge, Mass.: Harvard University Press, 1969.

Rinsley, Donald B. "Object Relations Theory and Psychotherapy with Particular Reference to the Self-Disordered Patient." In *Technical Factors in the Treatment of the Severely Disturbed Patient,* edited by Peter L. Giovacchini and L. Bryce Boyer. New York: Jason Aronson, 1982.

Ritvo, Lucille B. *Darwin's Influence on Freud: A Tale of Two Sciences.* New Haven: Yale University Press, 1990.

Ritvo, Samuel. "Adolescent to Woman." *JAPA* 24 (Supplement) (1976): 127–137.

Riviere, Joan. *The Inner World and Joan Riviere: Collected Papers 1920–1958.* Edited by Athol Hughes. London: Karnac, 1991.

Roazen, Paul. *Freud and His Followers.* New York: Knopf, 1975.

———. *Erik H. Erikson: The Power and Limits of a Vision.* New York: Free Press, 1976.

———. *Helene Deutsch: A Psychoanalyst's Life.* Garden City, N.Y.: Doubleday, 1985. Reprint, New Brunswick, N.J.: Transaction, 1992.

———. "Freud's Patients: First Person Accounts." In *Freud and the History of Psychoanalysis,* edited by Toby Gelfand and John Kerr. Hillsdale, N.J.: Analytic Press, 1992.

———. "Erik Erikson as a Teacher." *The Psychohistory Review* 22 (1993): 101–117.

Robinson, Paul. "Freud and the Feminists." *Raritan* 6 (1987): 43–61.

Rosaldo, Michelle Zimbalist, and Louise Lamphere, eds. *Women, Culture, and Society.* Stanford, Calif.: Stanford University Press, 1974.

Rose, Jacqueline. Introduction 2 to *Feminine Sexuality: Jacques Lacan and the école freudienne,* edited by Juliet Mitchell and Jacqueline Rose. New York: Norton, 1982.

———. *Sexuality in the Field of Vision.* London: Verso, 1986.

———. *Why War? Psychoanalysis, Politics and the Return of Melanie Klein.* Oxford: Blackwell, 1993.

Rubens, Richard L. "The Meaning of Structure in Fairbairn." *The International Review of Psycho-Analysis* 11 (1984): 429–440.

Rubin, Gayle. "The Traffic in Women: Notes on the 'Political Economy' of Sex." In *Toward an Anthropology of Women,* edited by Rayna Reiter. New York: Monthly Review Press, 1975.

———. "Thinking Sex: Notes for a Radical Theory of the Politics of Sexuality." In *Pleasure and Danger: Exploring Female Sexuality,* edited by Carole S. Vance. Boston: Routledge and Kegan Paul, 1984.

Rubins, Jack L. *Karen Horney: Gentle Rebel of Psychoanalysis.* New York: Dial Press, 1978.

Ruddick, Sara. *Maternal Thinking: Toward a Politics of Peace.* Boston: Beacon Press, 1989.

Ruse, Michael. *The Philosophy of Biology.* London: Hutchinson and Co., 1973.

————. "Charles Darwin and Artificial Selection." *Journal of the History of Ideas* 36 (1975): 339–350.

————. *The Darwinian Revolution.* Chicago: University of Chicago Press, 1979.

Russett, Cynthia Eagle. *Sexual Science: The Victorian Construction of Womanhood.* Cambridge, Mass.: Harvard University Press, 1989.

Rycroft, Charles. *A Critical Dictionary of Psychoanalysis.* New York: Basic Books, 1968.

Sandler, Joseph, and Christopher Dare. "The Psychoanalytic Concept of Orality." *Journal of Psychosomatic Research* 14 (1970): 211–222.

Sandler, Joseph, Alex Holder, and Dale Meers. "The Ego Ideal and the Ideal Self." *The Psychoanalytic Study of the Child* 18 (1963): 139–158.

Sandler, Joseph, and Humberto Nagera. "Aspects of the Metapsychology of Fantasy." *The Psychoanalytic Study of the Child* 18 (1963): 159–194.

Sandler, Joseph, and Bernard Rosenblatt. "The Concept of the Representational World." *The Psychoanalytic Study of the Child* 17 (1962): 128–145.

Sandler, Joseph, and Anne-Marie Sandler. "On the Development of Object Relationships and Affects." *IJP* 59 (1978): 285–296.

Sayers, Janet. *Sexual Contradictions: Psychology, Psychoanalysis, and Feminism.* London: Tavistock Publications, 1986.

————. *Mothers of Psychoanalysis: Helene Deutsch, Karen Horney, Anna Freud, Melanie Klein.* New York: Norton, 1991.

Scarry, Elaine. *The Body in Pain: The Making and Unmaking of the World.* New York: Oxford University Press, 1985.

Schafer, Roy. *Aspects of Internalization.* New York: International Universities Press, 1968.

————. "Internalization: Process or Fantasy?" *The Psychoanalytic Study of the Child* 27 (1972): 411–436.

————. *A New Language for Psychoanalysis.* New Haven: Yale University Press, 1976.

————. *Retelling a Life: Narration and Dialogue in Psychoanalysis.* New York: Basic Books, 1992.

Schatzman, Morton. *Soul Murder: Persecution in the Family.* New York: Random House, 1973.

Schmideberg. Melitta. "A Contribution to the History of the Psycho-Analytic Movement in Britain." *British Journal of Psychiatry* 118 (1971): 61–68.

Schor, Naomi, and Elizabeth Weed, eds. *The Essential Difference.* Bloomington: Indiana University Press, 1994.

Schreber, Daniel Paul. *Memoirs of My Nervous Illness.* Edited and translated by Ida Macalpine and Richard A. Hunter. Cambridge, Mass.: Harvard University Press, 1988.

Schuker, Eleanor, and Nadine A. Levinson. *Female Psychology: An Annotated Psychoanalytic Bibliography.* Hillsdale, N.J.: Analytic Press, 1991.

Schur, Max. *Freud: Living and Dying.* New York: International Universities Press, 1972.

Schur, Max, and Lucille B. Ritvo. "The Concept of Development and Evolution in Psychoanalysis." In *Development and Evolution of Behavior: Essays in Memory of T. C. Schneirla,* edited by Lester R. Aronson and Ethel Tobach. San Francisco: W. H. Freeman and Co., 1970.

Schwabe, Arthur D., David H. Solomon, Robert J. Stoller, and John Burnham. "Pubertal

Feminization in a Genetic Male with Testicular Atrophy and Normal Urinary Gonadotropin." *Journal of Clinical Endocrinology and Metabolism* 22 (1962): 839–845.

Schwartz, David. "Questioning the Social Construction of Gender and Sexual Orientation." *Gender and Psychoanalysis* 1 (1966): 249–260.

Scott, Joan Wallach. *Gender and the Politics of History.* New York: Columbia University Press, 1988.

Searl, Nina. "A Note on the Relation between Physical and Psychical Differences in Boys and Girls." *IJP* 19 (1938): 50–62.

Segal, Hanna. *Introduction to the Work of Melanie Klein.* Enl. ed. London: Hogarth Press, 1978.

———. *Melanie Klein.* New York: Viking Press, 1980.

———. *The Work of Hanna Segal: A Kleinian Approach to Clinical Practice.* New York: Jason Aronson, 1981.

Segal, Naomi. "Freud and the Question of Women." In *Freud in Exile: Psychoanalysis and Its Vicissitudes,* edited by Edward Timms and Naomi Segal. New Haven: Yale University Press, 1988.

Shane, Morton and Estelle. "Obituary: Robert Stoller" *IJP* 73 (1992), 773–774.

Shapin, Steven. "History of Science and Its Sociological Reconstructions." *History of Science* 2 (1982): 157–211.

Shengold, Leonard. *Soul Murder: The Effects of Childhood Abuse and Deprivation.* New Haven: Yale University Press, 1989.

Showalter, Elaine. "Critical Cross-Dressing: Male Feminists and the Woman of the Year." *Raritan* 3 (1983): 130–149.

———. *The Female Malady: Women, Madness, and English Culture, 1830–1980.* New York: Pantheon, 1985.

Silverman, Kaja. *The Accoustic Mirror: The Female Voice in Psychoanalysis and Cinema.* Bloomington: Indiana University Press, 1988.

Silverstein, Barry. "Oedipal Politics and Scientific Creativity—Freud's 1915 Phylogenetic Fantasy." *Psychoanalytic Review* 76 (1989): 403–424.

Slipp, Samuel. *The Freudian Mystique: Freud, Women, and Feminism.* New York: New York University Press, 1993.

Smith, Barbara Herrstein. "Narrative Versions, Narrative Theories." *Critical Inquiry* 7 (1980): 213–236.

Smith, Joseph H., ed. *Psychoanalysis, Feminism, and the Future of Gender.* Psychiatry and the Humanities, vol. 14. Baltimore: Johns Hopkins University Press, 1994.

Smith-Rosenberg, Carroll. *Disorderly Conduct: Visions of Gender in Victorian America.* New York: Knopf, 1985.

Snitow, Ann, Christine Stansell, and Sharon Thompson, eds. *Powers of Desire: The Politics of Sexuality.* London: Virago, 1984.

Sober, Elliott. *The Nature of Selection: Evolutionary Theory in Philosophical Focus.* Cambridge, Mass: MIT Press, 1984.

Spelman, Elizabeth V. *Inessential Women: Problems of Exclusion in Feminist Thought.* Boston: Beacon Press, 1988.

Spence, Donald P. *The Rhetorical Voice of Psychoanalysis: Displacement of Evidence by Theory.* Cambridge, Mass.: Harvard University Press, 1994.

Spillius, Elizabeth Bott. "Some Developments from the Work of Melanie Klein." *IJP* 64 (1983): 321–332.

Spillius, Elizabeth Bott, ed. *Melanie Klein Today: Developments in Theory and Practice.* Vol. 1, *Mainly Theory.* Vol. 2, *Mainly Practice.* London: Routledge, 1988.

Sprengnether, Madelon. *The Spectral Mother: Freud, Feminism, and Psychoanalysis.* Ithaca, N.Y.: Cornell University Press, 1990.

Stein, Ruth. "Analysis of a Case of Transsexualism." *Psychoanalytic Dialogues* 5 (1995): 257–289.

Steiner, Riccardo. "Some Thoughts about Tradition and Change Arising from an Examination of the British Psycho-Analytical Society's Controversial Discussions (1943–1944)." *The International Review of Psycho-Analysis* 12 (1985): 27–71.

———. " 'To Explain Our Point of View to English Readers in English Words.' " *The International Review of Psycho-Analysis* 18 (1991): 351–392.

Sterba, Richard F. *Reminiscences of a Viennese Psychoanalyst.* Detroit: Wayne State University Press, 1982.

Stern, Daniel N. *The First Relationship: Mother and Infant.* Cambridge, Mass.: Harvard University Press, 1977.

———. *The Interpersonal World of the Infant: A View from Psychoanalysis and Developmental Psychology.* New York: Basic Books, 1985.

Stimmel, Barbara. "From 'Nothing' to 'Something' to 'Everything': Bisexuality and Metaphors of Mind." *JAPA* 44 (Supplement) (1997): 191–214.

Stimpson, Catherine R., and Ethel Person Spector, eds. *Women: Sex and Sexuality.* Chicago: University of Chicago Press, 1980.

Stockard, Charles R. *The Physical Basis of Personality.* New York: Norton, 1931.

Stoller, Robert J. "A Contribution to the Study of Gender Identity." *IJP* 45 (1964): 220–226.

———. "Gender Role Change in Intersexed Patients." *Journal of the American Medical Association* 188 (1964): 684–685.

———. "The Sense of Maleness." *The Psychoanalytic Quarterly* 34 (1965): 207–218.

———. "The Mother's Contribution of Infantile Transvestic Behavior." *IJP* 47 (1966): 384–395.

———. "A Further Contribution to the Study of Gender Identity." *IJP* 49 (1968): 364–369.

———. "The Sense of Femaleness." *The Psychoanalytic Quarterly* 37 (1968): 42–55.

———. *Sex and Gender.* Vol. 1, *The Development of Masculinity and Femininity.* New York: Science House, 1968. Reprint, London: Karnac, Maresfield Library, 1984.

———. "The 'Bedrock' of Masculinity and Femininity: Bisexuality." *Archives of General Psychiatry* 26 (1972): 207–212.

———. "Fact and Fancies: An Examination of Freud's Concept of Bisexuality" (1973). In *Women and Analysis: Dialogues on Psychoanalytic Views of Femininity,* edited by Jean Strouse. New York: Grossman, 1974.

———. *Splitting: A Case of Female Masculinity.* London: Hogarth Press, 1974. Reprint, New Haven: Yale University Press, 1997.

———. "Symbiosis Anxiety and the Development of Masculinity." *Archives of General Psychiatry* 30 (1974): 164–172.

———. *Perversion: The Erotic Form of Hatred.* New York: Pantheon, 1975. Reprint, London: Karnac, Maresfield Library, 1986.

———. *Sex and Gender*. Vol. 2, *The Transsexual Experiment*. London: Hogarth Press, 1975.

———. "Primary Femininity." *JAPA* 24 (Supplement) (1976): 59–78.

———. *Sexual Excitement: Dynamics of Erotic Life*. New York: Pantheon, 1979. Reprint, London: Karnac, Maresfield Library, 1986.

———. "Femininity in Females." In *Women in Context: Development and Stresses,* edited by Matina Horner and Martha Kirkpatrick. New York: Plenum, 1980.

———. "Femininity." In *Women's Sexual Development: Explorations of Inner Space,* edited by Martha Kirkpatrick. New York: Plenum, 1980.

———. *Observing the Erotic Imagination*. New Haven: Yale University Press, 1985.

———. *Presentations of Gender*. New Haven: Yale University Press, 1985.

———. *Pain and Passion: A Psychoanalyst Explores the World of S&M*. New York: Plenum, 1991.

———. *Porn: Myths for the Twentieth Century*. New Haven: Yale University Press, 1991.

———. Correspondence between Robert J. Stoller and Nancy Chodorow. Robert J. Stoller Papers. Department of Special Collections-University Research Library, UCLA.

Stoller, Robert J., Harold Garfinkel, and Alexander Rosen. "Passing and Maintenance of Sexual Identification in an Intersexed Patient." *Archives of General Psychiatry* 2 (1960): 379–384.

Stoller, Robert J., and I. S. Levine. *Coming Attractions: The Making of an X-Rated Video*. New Haven: Yale University Press, 1993.

Stoller, Robert J., and Alexander C. Rosen. "The Intersexed Patient." *California Medicine* 91 (1959): 261–265.

Strachey, Alix. "A Note on the Use of the Word 'Internal,'" *IJP* 22 (1941): 37–43.

Strouse, Jean. *Alice James: A Biography*. Boston: Houghton Mifflin, 1980.

———, ed. *Women and Analysis: Dialogues on Psychoanalytic Views of Femininity*. New York: Grossman, 1974.

Stubrin, Jaime P. *Sexualities and Homosexualities*. London: Karnac, 1994.

Suleiman, Susan Rubin, ed. *The Female Body in Western Culture: Contemporary Perspectives*. Cambridge, Mass.: Harvard University Press, 1985.

Suppe, Frederick, ed. *The Structure of Scientific Theories*. 2d ed. Urbana: University of Illinois Press, 1977.

Sutherland, John D. "Object-Relations Theory and the Conceptual Model of Psychoanalysis." *The British Journal of Medical Psychology* 36 (1963): 109–124.

———. "The British Object Relations Theorists: Balint, Winnicott, Fairbairn, Guntrip." *JAPA* 28 (1980): 829–860.

———. *Fairbairn's Journey into the Interior*. London: Free Associations Books, 1989.

Symonds, Alexandra. "Gender Issues and Karen Horney." *The American Journal of Psychoanalysis*. 51 (1991): 301–312.

Tavris, Carol. *The Mismeasure of Woman*. New York: Simon and Schuster, 1992.

Taylor, Jill McLean, Carol Gilligan, and Amy M. Sullivan. *Between Voice and Silence: Women and Girls, Race and Relationship*. Cambridge, Mass.: Harvard University Press, 1995.

Thompson, Nellie L. "Helene Deutsch: A Life in Theory." *The Psychoanalytic Quarterly* 56 (1987): 317–353.

Toews, John S. "Male and Female Perspectives on a Psychoanalytic Myth." In *Gender and*

Religion: On the Complexity of Symbols, edited by Caroline Walker Bynum, Stevan Harrell, and Paula Richman. Boston: Beacon Press, 1986.

Toulmin, Stephen. *Human Understanding.* Vol. 1, *General Introduction and Part I.* Princeton N.J.: Princeton University Press, 1972.

Tronto, Joan C. "Beyond Gender Difference to a Theory of Care." *Signs* 12 (1987): 644–663.

Tyson, Phyllis. "A Developmental Line of Gender Identity, Gender Role, and Choice of Love Object." *JAPA* 30 (1982): 61–86.

———. "Bedrock and Beyond: An Examination of the Clinical Utility of Contemporary Theories of Female Psychology." *JAPA* 42 (1994): 447–467.

Webster, Brenda S. "Helene Deutsch: A New Look." *Signs* 10 (1985): 553–571.

Weingart, Peter. "Biology as Social Theory: The Bifurcation of Social Biology and Sociology in Germany, circa 1900." In *Modern Impulses in the Human Sciences* 1870–1930, edited by Dorothy Ross. Baltimore: Johns Hopkins University Press, 1994.

Weininger, O. *The Clinical Psychology of Melanie Klein.* Springfield, Ill.: Charles C. Thomas Publisher, 1984.

Westkott, Marcia. "Mothers and Daughters in the World of the Father." *Frontiers* 3 (1978): 16–22.

———. *The Feminist Legacy of Karen Horney.* New Haven: Yale University Press, 1986.

———. "On the New Psychology of Women: A Cautionary View." *Feminist Issues* 10 (1990): 3–18.

Wilkinson, Sallye M. "The Female Genital Dress-Rehearsal: A Prospective Process at the Oedipal Threshold." *IJP* 74 (1993): 313–330.

Winnicott, D. W. *Collected Papers: Through Paediatrics to Psycho-Analysis.* London: Tavistock Publications, 1958.

———. *The Maturational Processes and the Facilitating Environment: Studies in the Theory of Emotional Development.* London: Hogarth Press, 1965.

Wisdom, J. O. "Fairbairn's Contribution on Object Relationship, Splitting, and Ego Structure." *The British Journal of Medical Psychology* 36 (1963): 145–159.

———. "Freud and Melanie Klein: Psychology, Ontology, and Weltanschauung." In *Psychoanalysis and Philosophy,* edited by Charles Hanley and Morris Lazerowitz. New York: International Universities Press, 1970.

———. *Freud, Women, and Society.* New Brunswick, N.J.: Transaction, 1992.

Wollheim, Richard. *Sigmund Freud.* New York: Viking Press, 1971. Reprint, Cambridge: Cambridge University Press, 1990.

———. *The Mind and Its Depths.* Cambridge, Mass.: Harvard University Press, 1993.

———, ed. *Freud: A Collection of Critical Essays.* Garden City, N.Y.: Doubleday, 1974.

Wollheim, Richard, and James Hopkins, eds. *Philosophical Essays on Freud.* Cambridge: Cambridge University Press, 1982.

Wright, Elizabeth, ed. *Feminism and Psychoanalysis: A Critical Dictionary.* Oxford: Blackwell, 1992.

Wyre, Harriet Kimble. "Bodily States of Mind: Dialectics of Psyche and Soma in Psychoanalysis." *Gender and Psychoanalysis* 1 (1996): 283–296.

Yorke, Clifford. "Some Suggestions for a Critique of Kleinian Psychology." *The Psychoanalytic Study of the Child* 26 (1971): 129–155.

Young, Marion. "Is Male Gender Identity the Cause of Male Domination?" In *Mothering: Essays in Feminist Theory,* edited by Joyce Trebilcot. Totawa, N.J.: Rowman and Allanheld, 1983.

Young, Robert M. *Darwin's Metaphor: Nature's Place in Victorian Culture.* Cambridge: Cambridge University Press, 1985.

Young-Bruehl, Elisabeth. *Anna Freud: A Biography.* New York: Summit Books, 1988.

————. "Reading Freud on Female Development." *Psychoanalytic Inquiry* 11 (1991): 427–440.

————."Gender and Psychoanalysis: An Introductory Essay." *Gender and Psychoanalysis* 1 (1996): 7–18.

————, ed. *Freud on Women: A Reader.* New York: Norton, 1990.

Zanardi, Claudia, ed. *Essential Papers on the Psychology of Women.* New York: New York University Press, 1990.

Zetzel, Elizabeth R. "Ernest Jones: His Contribution to Psycho-Analytic Theory." *IJP* 39 (1958): 311–318.

Zilboorg, Gregory. "Masculine and Feminine: Some Biological and Cultural Aspects." *Psychiatry* 7 (1944): 257–296.

Index